THE STORY
OF THE
TORAH

The Story of The Torah

The First Volume of 'Is the Bible a Dangerous Book?'

By
Beryl Lavender

Xulon Press

Xulon Press
2301 Lucien Way #415
Maitland, FL 32751
407.339.4217
www.xulonpress.com

© 2017 by Beryl Lavender

All rights reserved solely by the author. The author guarantees all contents are original and do not infringe upon the legal rights of any other person or work. No part of this book may be reproduced in any form without the permission of the author. The views expressed in this book are not necessarily those of the publisher.

Scripture quotations taken from the Holy Bible, New International Version (NIV). Copyright © 1995 by Zondervan Publishing. Used by permission. All rights reserved.

Scripture quotations taken from the King James Version (KJV) – *public domain*.

Printed in the United States of America.

ISBN-13: 9781545605042

For God, whose help I sought, and for Cathy and Vaughan, Guy and Karen, Penny and Craig and Michael, Matthew, Amy and James.

Table of Contents

PREFACE xv
INTRODUCTION xxi

Part One

A Brief History 1
Catastrophic Beginnings 3
Parallels with Our Own Time 5
Why the Jews? 9
God 10
Horns on the Head of Moses 11
The World's Oldest Bible 14
Paraphrases and Translations 15
Which Bible? 17
Going steadily back to the Beginning 18
The World's first Printed Book 20
The Geneva Bible 21
The Great Bible 21
The Bishops' Bible 22
Tyndale and the Matthew Bible 23
Wycliffe uses the Bible as a Weapon against Corruption 23
Douay-Rheims Translation and the Complutensian Polyglot 25
The Masoretic Text 27

The Latin Vulgate 32
Origen's Hexapla 33
The Septuagint 34
The Samaritan Pentateuch 35
The Great Schism 36
The Importance of the Copies 37
A Miraculous Invention and a Miraculous Find 39
The Dead Sea Scrolls 42
Why the Scrolls are so Important 45
Why Moses Couldn't Have Written The Whole Of The Torah 46
Julius Wellhausen and the Documentary Critics 47
How the Torah came into Existence 48
Archaeological Support for the Torah 49
The Amarna Letters 50
The Ras Shamra Tablets 51
The Ebla Tablets 52
The Nuzi Tablets 52
The Very First Ballads and Writings 53

Part Two

Genes and Genesis 55
Introduction 57
Genesis 1 – 2: The Two Creation Stories 58
Theistic Evolution 65
The Holy Trinity 66
An Englishman divides the Latin Bible into Chapters .... And Finds
    Magna Carta in the Bible 69
Everything was good – Then enter the Serpent 71

The Mystery of the Trees.	75
Destruction of At-one-ment	76
Chapters 4 – 5: Cain and Abel – Am I my Brother's Keeper?	77
Chapters 6 – 9: Noah and the Flood	79
Noah gets drunk!	81
Chapter 10: The Table of Nations	82
Chapter 11: Genes and the Tower of Babel	84
Abraham, Founder of the Israelites	86
Chapter 12: An Early Prophecy of the Messiah	87
Chapter 13: Sodom	88
Chapter 14: Melchizedek	91
Chapter 15: Covenant and Promise	93
Chapter 16: Hagar and Ishmael	94
Chapter 17: Circumcision and Abram becomes Abraham	95
Chapter 18: Mysterious Visitors	96
Chapter 19: Destruction of Sodom	96
Chapter 20: Not Again!	98
Chapters 21 and 22 – The Birth and Near Sacrifice of Isaac	99
Chapters 23 – 25: Deaths of Sarah and Abraham; Isaac marries Rebekah; Esau and Jacob	101
Chapters 26 - 28: Jacob deceives Esau and flees for his life	104
A Hard Pillow	106
Chapters 29 - 31: Deceiver Deceived	108
Chapters 32 - 33: Jacob becomes Israel	111
Chapters 34 – 38: Dinah and the Twelve Sons of Israel	116
Joseph and the Flamboyant Coat	117
A Feisty Ancestress of Jesus	119
Good-looking Joseph	121

Chapters 42: Israel's Sons in Egypt and the End 122
End of the Beginning. 123

Part Three

Entrance to Exodus 129
Introduction. 131
Chapter 1: Israel in Egypt 132
Chapters 2 – 3: Drown all the Boy Babies 135
Manslaughter and Escape to Midian 136
The Burning Bush and the Name of God 137
Chapter 4: Another Serpent 140
Moses Returns to Egypt 141
Chapters 5 - 6: Three Days or Forever? 145
Chapters 7 – 11: The Plagues 147
The Ipuwer Papyrus. 148
Chapter 12: The Passover 151
Chapters 13 – 14: Miraculous Crossing of the Red Sea 154
Chapters 15 -16: The Sinai Desert, Manna and Quail. 156
Chapters 17 – 18: The Problem of the Amalekites 160
Moses reunited with his Family and Jethro contributes to
    the Ten Commandments 162
Chapters 19 – 24: The Ten Commandments 164
Chapters 25 – 30: The Ark, The Mercy Seat, Blood-painted
    Toes and Sacrifice 168
Special Clothing for the Priests and Painted Toes. 170
Yom Kippur. 172
Chapters 31 - 34: Rebellion and The Broken Tablets 173
The Golden Calf 174

Chapter 35 – 40 Final Instructions 178
Exit from Exodus 179

Part Four

Living Leviticus 183
Introduction 185
Chapters 1 – 4: Sacrifices 186
Chapter 5: Whistle-blowing, Clean, Unclean and
    Taking Oaths 187
Chapters 6 - 9: Dealing with Sin in the millennium
    before Christ 190
Chapter 10: Sudden Disaster 191
Chapters 11 – 15: How to be Holy and How to be Safe 192
Leprosy and Other Diseases 195
Chapter 16: The Engraved Cherubim. 195
Chapters 17 – 18: The Sexual Taboos. 197
Chapter 19: The Second Greatest Commandment. 200
Chapters 20 - 23: The Punishments and the Perfect Priest 202
Chapter 24 – 27: Coming to the End 204
Leaving Leviticus 205

Part Five

Safety in Numbers 207
Introduction 209
Chapters 1 – 2: Too Many Israelites 210
Chapters 3 - 5: The Mysterious Bitter Water Test. 213
Chapter 6: Total Commitment and the Great Blessing. 220

Chapters 7 – 11: The Tabernacle Dedicated and on their
   Way at Last 222
Poisonous Quail 223
Chapter 12: Aaron and Miriam's Disloyalty 224
Chapters 13 - 15: The Fatal Sin of the Spies 225
Chapter 16: The Korah Rebellion 230
Chapters 17 – 19: Aaron's staff blooms and the Red
   Heifer Sacrifice 232
Chapter 20: Moses not allowed to lead the Israelites
   into Canaan; Deaths of Miriam and Aaron 234
Chapter 21: The Brazen Snake 236
Chapters 22 – 24 Balaam and his Donkey 238
Chapter 25: Worshiping Baal and Sexual Orgies 245
Chapter 26 – 27: Another Census and Zelophehad's
   daughters 246
Chapters 28 – 30: Oath-taking 248
Chapter 31 – Battle against the Midianites 248
Chapters 32 – 33: The Journey 249
Chapters 34 – 36: Final Instructions 250
Conclusion: The Son Rises Higher 251

Part Six

Due to Deuteronomy 253
Introduction 255
Chapter 1: No Progress 255
Chapter 2 - 3: The Lands they could not possess – and
   Og's Bed! 257
Chapter 4: Tampering with the Law 258

Chapter 5: The Second Sermon	260
Chapters 6 – 9: The Central Belief of Judaeo-Christianity	260
Wild Animals	263
Springs Flowing in the Valleys	264
Hear, O Israel	265
Chapters 10 – 14: Circumcise your Hearts!	265
The Third Sermon	266
Chapters 15 – 18: The Implementation of the Rule of Law for the First Time in History	268
The Rule of Law	271
Chapters 19 – 22: The Law of Retaliation; How to Get out of Conscription; Care of Animals; Difficult Laws about Women	273
How Did They Ever Raise an Army?	274
Dealing with Teenagers	277
Chapters 23 – 25: More laws about Relationships	279
Chapters 26 – 28 Was the Altar to be built on Mount Ebal or on Mount Gerizim?	282
The Samaritan Pentateuch again	284
Chapters 29 – 34: The Final Chapters of both Deuteronomy and the Torah	288
Accept the Word	289
Conclusion	297
Bibliography	303

PREFACE

In November 2013 security police in North Korea publicly executed eighty people, some of them merely for possessing Bibles.¹ In Uzbekistan owners of religious material including Bibles can be imprisoned 'for keeping and storing extremist materials.'² In fifty countries including China, Saudi Arabia, Iran and Somalia one can be arrested if one is seen carrying a Bible.³ This is not something new. The first attempts to suppress the Bible are recorded in the Bible itself. Jehoiakim, king of Judah, cut up and burned a scroll that prophesied dire consequences for disobeying the law.⁴ Antiochus Epiphanes, king of the Seleucid Empire, decreed that 'all scrolls of the law that were found be torn up and burnt.'⁵

The first attack on the Bible in Christian times was by the Roman emperor, Claudius, who a mere twenty years after Christ's execution in a far-flung corner of his empire, expelled Jews and Christians from

---

¹ JoongAng Ilbo (The Central Times) Seoul 3 November 2013

² www.state.gov/documents/organization/256535 2016

³ The 2017 World Watch List by Open Doors U S A; it lists 50 countries in which Christians are being persecuted and where those found in possession of a Bible are punished

⁴ Jeremiah 36:23

⁵ The Apocrypha, 1 Maccabees 1: 56-57

Rome and banned their writings 'because Jews were continually creating disturbances at the instigation of Chrestus'[6] For the next three hundred years persecutions continued on and off culminating in the great persecution under Diocletian (244-311 A.D.) who ordered that all Christians, their churches and their books be burned. He was succeeded by Constantine who stopped the persecutions whereupon the Roman Catholic Church grew into a vast institution and in the way of all institutions, became corrupt. The popes of the late Middle Ages, Innocent III, Leo X, Clement VII and Paul III, ordered that vernacular copies of the Bible be burnt because modern European languages were too 'vulgar' for writing about God[7]. The real reason was that most people could not understand the Latin Bible, and the church was determined to keep things that way. Translations and translators were burned, among them some of Britain's finest thinkers who had defiantly produced English Bibles.

The question is, why? Why do tyrants, despots and corrupt institutions hate the Bible? Part of the answer lies in something the Uzbekistan authorities realized. The Bible *is* 'extremist material.' It inaugurated and insists on the Rule of Law, a concept that makes its first ever appearance on earth in the Bronze Age section of the Bible. Stephen Langton, 13th Century Archbishop of Canterbury and one of the compilers of Magna Carta, read in the Biblical book of Deuteronomy that nobody was above the law and that even kings

---

[6] Suetonius, *The Twelve Caesars,* Translated by Graves R, Revised Edition, Penguin Books, London, 2007

[7] Schaff P *History of the Christian Church* 3rd Edition, Vol VI, Hendrickson, Massachusetts, 1960

(which today would mean any rulers or governments) had to study and obey it.[8] We know that Langton was familiar with Deuteronomy and was determined to include its ideas in Magna Carta because before he became Archbishop of Canterbury, he preached a series of sermons in Paris showing how Christian European monarchs were falling far short of how Deuteronomy decreed they should govern. Langton made sure that the Deuteronomic stipulations were included in Magna Carta. It is one of the reasons the charter is so revered by those who fight for human rights. King John, understandably, tore up the first draft claiming he had signed it under duress, but Langton bided his time and in the end persuaded John's successor, Henry III, to sign a final version, ensuring that the Rule of Law would underpin the British, and subsequently the American and Commonwealth, political, judicial and legal systems forever. And it was not any old law either. It is a manifestation of the Moral Law.

It demands social justice for widows, orphans, servants, foreigners, the land and animals. One does not pretend that western monarchs and governments have always upheld the laws of Deuteronomy or the relevant chapters of Magna Carta, but both these documents have ceaselessly been the means by which citizens have pulled their leaders back to what is just and right. In the later books of the Bible Christ insisted that his followers care for the entire world and especially for the poor, the disabled and those

---

[8] Griffith-Jones, Robin and Hill, Mark: *Magna Carta, Religion and the Rule of Law,* Cambridge University Press, 2015, Introduction: 'Archbishop Stephen Langton hoped with Magna Carta to realise an Old Testament Covenantal kingship in England' and '...how important to Langton were the story and covenant of Deuteronomy.'

whom they regarded as their enemies. So it is easy to see why dictators, one-party states, and those who thrive on hate, regard the Bible as extremist material. However, it does not explain why there is currently so much opposition to the Bible in the west where governments practise a reasonably high degree of justice and socialism and mostly adhere to the concept that everybody is equal in the eyes of the law.

What anti-Bible campaigners in the west abhor is, I think, that the Bible is a book about God, and attributes the moral law and the need to practise social justice to God. Secularists, naturalists and atheists do not accept that God exists and they denigrate the Bible, especially its Bronze Age Torah section, as a hotchpotch of myths and fables, many of which they claim were plagiarised from earlier faiths. Mostly based on out-of-context reading, they accuse the Torah of promoting misogyny, racism, homophobia and genocide, and find it incomprehensible that millions of people, worldwide, still believe in God, and that thousands are being persecuted, tortured and killed rather than reject either God or the Bible.

So the last question is why the Bible continues to have a hold on public consciousness. Partly, I think, it's because there is a growing uneasiness about the religion-free society in which everybody loves everybody else, everybody does his own thing, and just about everything is permitted provided it does not impinge on the rights of others. It has not turned out to be the longed for Utopia. Secular Britain is turning into a nightmare. Communities are disintegrating; families are breaking up; neighbourhoods are unsafe; violence is increasing; children are rudderless and confused; the elderly are neglected and disparaged; depression and mental illness are on the rise; hospitals and prisons are overflowing; rudeness, unkindness, addictions and suicides are increasing; globalisation and robotics have made the rich mega-wealthy, exhausted and impoverished the middle classes and made the poor destitute; non-biblical religious factions that proselytise with violence and do not accept the right of other religions to exist have increasingly filled the vacuum left by receding Judaism and Christianity. The future that was supposed to be so bright when the west got rid of Judaeo-Christianity now appears bleak and fearful.

Applied science that many believed would solve all problems, now seems to be adding to them. Artificial intelligence, clones and drones are raising fearful spectres. Unbridled scientific applications and products are contributing to pollution, global warming, droughts, destructive storms, floods, melting polar caps, and contaminated and rising oceans. At the last estimate (March 2017) it is going to cost £160 billion safely to dispose of Britain's decaying and eroding nuclear power facilities. The miracle anti-biotics of the second half of the twentieth century are proving true to their name and spawning drug-resistant microbes that threaten all multi-cellular life.

In spite of all the above and of being attacked by new diseases, infestations, famine and disaster, humanity is growing too fast for the planet to sustain either it or any other form of life. As the numbers go up the gap between the haves and the have-nots is widening. Millions are feeling betrayed, ignored and abused, and are rejecting politically-correct media and establishment-politicians in favour of social media, mavericks and alternative solutions. There's more than a murmur of civic unrest and rebellion in the air. At this dangerous moment, some, particularly among the young, have stopped, and thought, and wondered. Could answers be found in that much maligned book that tyrants, dictators, the rich and the powerful don't want us to read? Should one reach for a dust-covered bible?

The trouble is that as soon as one takes one from the shelf, blows off the dust and opens the cover, one discovers that it is a very difficult collection of writings. With endless lists of begats, battles, repetitions, contradictions, myths, fables, poetry and parables, parts of the Bible are boring and parts of it incomprehensible. How does one get to grips with its sixty six books, some of them three thousand five hundred years old, and how does one discover whether they contain anything relevant for the twenty first century?

Is the Bible a Dangerous Book? is a series of commentaries that I'm writing in everyday English in an attempt to answer some of those questions and to try to make more accessible this extraordinary, life-changing book. The first in the series, *The Story of the Torah*, begins with a history of the Bible showing how it began, how it survived, how it was translated and how archaeology has either supported or challenged it. It goes on to identify problems in, and give explanations where possible of the first five books, Genesis, Exodus, Leviticus, Numbers and Deuteronomy, collectively called the Torah by the Jews, who wrote them. Finally it draws attention to those verses that show that life is a quest on which anyone can embark with confidence and hope.

INTRODUCTION

No commentary on the Bible can be unbiased. To be human is to have a worldview and a worldview means bias. As a Christian who worships God through the sacraments, liturgy, music and aesthetics of the Church of England, I have a particular view of the Bible. But at least it also means that I accept what the Bible says, that God has a special love for Jews, for people of all faiths and none, for outcasts, for the deprived, for the poor, for the homeless, for the disabled, and for the marginalised, and that he prefers the questions of an honest atheist, whom he is prepared to go out of his way to encounter, to the pious platitudes of hypocrites.

The Bible is the product of human minds and hands and these sometimes get in the way of its mysterious revelations about God and His love for the world. But those revelations, which come from the pages like a still, small voice, the Bible's own description of the voice of God (1 Kings 19:12) can be heard at its beginning and followed to the very end.

The purpose of this commentary is, as I said in the preface, to try to make the Bible more accessible and to show that it is possible to read it with an honest and questioning mind and to arrive at its essential truth without having to dump one's intelligence. I hope that it will help a reader to discover why powerful and unscrupulous governments and tyrants hate the Bible so much, and why those who think they can design a better society than the God-ordained one, dislike it. I hope that a reader will discover how much the Bible inspires and enables self-discipline, courage, empathy, patience, commitment, selflessness and generosity. And finally I hope that a reader will discover why, from the moment Gutenberg invented the printing press in 1453 and produced the first ever mechanically printed book, a Bible, it has remained, in spite of all attempts to suppress it, not only the world's all-time number-one best seller, but also its most challenging, provocative and dangerous read.

Part One
A Brief History

Who wrote it and how it got to us

Catastrophic Beginnings

Although there is no consensus about exactly when it was written, most authorities agree that the Torah is the work of a group of Bronze Age migrants called the Hebrews who some 3,500 years ago, plodded along the river valleys and desert wastes of the Middle East. Their endless, weary and fraught migration, which was often dogged by thirst and hunger, coincided with a desperate time in human history, the sudden and total collapse of the Bronze Age civilisations of the Middle East, humanity's first urban cultures. Historians refer to the collapse as the Catastrophe and many of them regard it as worse than the disintegration of the Roman Empire that plunged Europe into the millennium-long Dark Ages. Just as modern Europe ultimately rose from the debris of fallen Rome, so did Ancient Greece arise from the ashes of the Bronze Age. Something else survived both disasters, something intangible, mysterious, spiritual and indefinably resilient.

It began its existence in revelations and insights that the leader of the Hebrew migrants claimed had come from God. As they huddled around the camp fires in the desert night they discussed the revelations and wondered about the nature of God. Either the leader himself or literate members of his tribe (the Hebrew migrants came from the country in which writing was invented) began to write down the revelations on ephemeral tablets of clay and transient rolls of papyrus, adjuring their brethren to keep on re-telling and transcribing them, generation by generation. Humble and insignificant, this was the beginning of the Torah, an extraordinary piece of writing, produced by man but claiming to be the Word of God. (Some authorities deny that the Hebrews could write this early in their history and are of the opinion that it is to the oral tradition only that we owe the Torah. However, as these notes will show, the latest archaeological discoveries reveal that the Hebrews could write much earlier in their history than was formerly thought.)

The countries through which those ancient migrants travelled and in which they sometimes set up camp, or for periods of time erected more substantial dwellings, were Iraq, Syria, Egypt, Jordan, Lebanon, Turkey, and Israel, countries across which the first ever humans traipsed when they migrated from their birthplace in Africa and trekked across the Middle East to every continent on earth. It has rightly been called the Middle East, that bit of earth. Middle is the operative word. Those desert wastes, mountains and fertile river valleys link three continents. All the great trade routes of antiquity passed through the Middle East: The Silk Road, The Spice Road and The Incense Road. The inevitable clash of disparate customs, ideas and beliefs is probably why the area was and still is being brutalised by war, genocide and enforced migrations. It has given birth to both the worst and best in human thinking and behaviour. Some of the finest Greek thinkers including Thales, Anaximander and Anaximenes came from the Mediterranean coast of the Ancient Levant and from its hinterland came some of the greatest heroes of antiquity, Abraham, Hector, Moses, David and Jesus. The Bible, its great literary masterpiece, shows that good and evil are entwined in the make-up of every human psyche and that for any individual, no matter how lost or fallen, there is a way out.

Echoes of many of the Middle Eastern cultures that either disappeared or underwent destructive change during the Bronze Age Collapse can be detected in the pages of the Torah, proving what the Torah itself claims, that the Ancient Hebrews spent varying amounts of time inter-mixing with and absorbing much from other Bronze Age cultures. These Hebrews or Ancient Israelites are increasingly being identified with the Habiru, or Abiru, one of the tribes of Semitic nomads mentioned in ancient texts as infiltrators of the Bronze Age cultures of the Levant and in some instances contributing to their downfall. Among them were the Canaanite Hyksos who invaded Egypt and ruled it for more than a century.

Parallels with Our Own Time

When one studies this ancient period in human history one cannot help noticing the extent to which the world of the Torah was beset by conditions similar to those of the twenty first century. There was war in the Middle East, migration, new diseases and climate-change. Of course there were differences. The people of those days did not possess the advanced scientific applications that both benefit and bedevil today's world. And over-population was not an issue. But there was much that was similar.

History and archaeology are agreed that it was a change in climate that if it did not precipitate then it certainly contributed to the sudden collapse of the Middle Eastern Bronze Age civilisations. At some point in the second millennium B.C. the weather began to change and it had a devastating effect on the Fertile Crescent, that arc of productivity that stretched from the Persian Gulf along the valleys of the Tigris and Euphrates Rivers through parts of Syria and Turkey and then down to the Mediterranean coast and the Nile Valley. It is generally agreed that this is where civilization began, first at the two ends of the crescent, near the river mouths of Egypt and Mesopotamia, and then along the entire arc. It is difficult to determine why just as what we call civilisation got really going, the weather suddenly changed and together with some other factors caused those first urban attempts to implode in a chaos of mayhem and disaster.[9] Current thinking is that the climate change was probably caused by at least two mega volcanoes, several high-Richter-scale earthquakes and what is increasingly looking like a comet or asteroid plunging through the atmosphere and bursting immediately above the Dead Sea.

The first and worst of the volcanic eruptions was the one that almost annihilated the Eastern Mediterranean Island of Thera or Santorini and probably gave rise to the Atlantis myth. It caused cataclysmic tsunamis and tephra (volcanic ash) that wreaked havoc on the lands of the Eastern Mediterranean. Carried around the earth by prevailing winds, the tephra caused a global dip in weather with incessant fog, longer, colder winters, heavier frosts, un-melted ice and snow and short ineffective summers. Current thinking is that Thera ejected four times more matter into the atmosphere than Krakatoa did in 1883. The effect on Thera's immediate surroundings, which included the lands of the Bible, was catastrophic, tsunamis

---

[9] Cline E H *1177 B.C. The Year Civilisation Collapsed,* Princeton University Press, Princeton, 2014.

and floods in the short term and droughts and plagues in the long. Throughout the period the entire area experienced increasing desertification, and rivers became polluted and began to dry up, the Nile at the time of the first Biblical writings.

Almost unbelievably, archaeologists working on a dig in Jordan have exposed what they believe are signs that shortly before Thera blew up, a comet or asteroid exploded in the air above the northern section of the Dead Sea causing the apocalyptic destruction of a group of powerful Bronze Age cities on the Kikkar (Circular plain) of Jordan. They have tentatively identified the largest of the cities destroyed in the blast as Sodom.[10] In other areas cities and towns seem to have been destroyed by earthquakes.

But if nature was partly responsible for the destruction of the first human civilisations, it was ably assisted by humans themselves. There was the systematic deforestation of the great cedar forests cladding Cyprus, Lebanon and the mountainsides of modern day Turkey. Trees were chopped down with ruthless efficiency for ships, houses, floors, roofs, furniture and most of all as fuel for bronze-producing smelters. As the trees disappeared, leaving unprotected top soils, winter storms caused devastating floods and silted up river mouths. Estuary trading ports like Troy, Priene, Patara and Ephesus found themselves increasingly distanced from the sea, which was their lifeblood. Exposed to new diseases carried by insects, particularly mosquitoes breeding in the newly created swamps, the last inhabitants packed their belongings and fled.

---

[10] Scott, Latayne C and Collins, S *Discovering the City of Sodom,* Howard Books, Simon & Shuster, New York, 2013

Then too there was the fact that Semitic tribes were not the only ones making things difficult for Bronze Age civilizations. Far greater damage was caused by the 'sea people' (probably from southern Europe and including the Greeks) who invaded the Middle East. It was the Greeks who united to attack and destroy Troy, the Bronze Age city that guarded the Dardanelles and effectively barred others, unless they paid huge taxes, from the coast of the Black Sea (the Euxine) with its rich deposits of tin, one of the metals from which bronze was alloyed. The Greeks who besieged Troy almost certainly wanted the tin more than they wanted Helen, or so our delightful Turkish guide told us when my daughter, Cathy, and I visited the ruins of Troy recently.

Another cause of the Bronze Age Catastrophe was the technological revolution in which iron began to supplant bronze. Bronze is a better metal but iron was much more freely available and easier to work. It led to bigger armies better armed. The sword made its appearance, and armour. Light-weight chariots drawn by a single horse and fitted with iron axels, wheels and scythes increasingly entered the fray.

Because the Bronze Age cultures were sophisticated and specialised, supporting too many bureaucrats and aristocrats who lacked initiative, were overly dependent on others and were no longer able to survive on their own, their more primitive enemies all but wiped them out. Cities were totally destroyed (Knossos, Troy, Miletus, Ebla, Ugarit, Hattusas, Mycenae, Ramesess and Bethel among others) some never again to be occupied, some to remain uninhabited for a thousand years. Communities were uprooted, enslaved or escaped into exile. Trade routes collapsed. The new skill of writing (as important for the dissemination of knowledge in the late Bronze

Age as the invention of the printing press in the fifteenth century and the internet in our own time) went into sharp decline.

Among the few Bronze Age revelations, songs and histories that did manage to survive were those that the Hebrew migrants were creating and protecting. These were the sources of the first five books of the Bible, the heritage of a people caught up in the collapse of towns and countries, sometimes as oppressors, mostly as oppressed, always on the margins, a people who found themselves asking the same questions that people ask today: How and why did it all begin? Why do people exist? What is the meaning of it all?

Why the Jews?

One has to wonder why it was the Ancient Israelites rather than any other Bronze Age people who not only asked these questions but also claim to have found answers which they fanatically protected during their years of migrant wandering. In the past two centuries archaeology has been revealing that beneath the ruins of many Bronze Age cities are writings that ask similar questions but in no cases are the answers remotely comparable to the quiet, rational ones in the Torah. Strangely, it was possibly their nomadic existence that helped the Ancient Israelites to preserve their writings. While cities and towns were destroyed in the Bronze Age collapse, together with everything in them, refugees, migrants and country dwellers were among those who survived.

Like the Greeks, the Ancient Israelites became stronger and more resilient during the Bronze Age Catastrophe, and they then went on, uniquely and astoundingly, to survive even worse catastrophes in the next three and a half thousand years. This is in spite of the fact that for most of their history they have been the victims, the reviled, the banished, the persecuted and without a homeland. Yet, while many of their Bronze Age contemporaries have to all intents and purposes disappeared from the pages of history, the Jews are still with us, a small but powerful race. So the book to which they clung, and on which they base their religion, law and culture, could be significant.

What is certain is that little else in philosophy or science even begins to suggest an answer to the hopeless nihilism of the current atheist belief that humans accidentally came into being on a small planet in a universe that sprang into existence by chance. According to this view, the only purpose of life is to get out of it what one can and to put one's own wants above all others. Against this, the Torah, central book of Judaism, claims that God brought both the universe and each person into being with a specific purpose, and for humanity the essential purpose was to love God and one another.

GOD

God? An invisible presence that may be responsible for everything? One has to wonder how the human mind came up with that idea. The Israelites were not first to grapple with it. That the visible universe was the product of an invisible spiritual force arose in human consciousness long before the Bible. It shows up in ancient rock and cave art some of which goes back 40 000 years. Graves of Neanderthals currently dated to about 50 000 B.C. contain remains of gifts and animals suggesting belief in the supernatural and even in an afterlife. Perhaps it is a fall-back position for primitive minds grappling with natural phenomena and the implacable blows of fate and time.

But then one then has to wonder why such sophisticated minds as those of Socrates, Plato, Aristotle, Newton, Kepler and modern scientists like Max Planck (one of the founders of Quantum Mechanics) and Francis Collins (who headed the Human Genome Project) are theists. What drives such minds towards God and an awareness of the spiritual? (Both Planck and Collins have written books about their belief – the titles are in the Bibliography at the end.) If such awareness arose in man's consciousness millennia ago, since long before the Bible was written, could it be that spirituality is almost hard-wired into human consciousness?

Horns on the Head of Moses

It took thousands of years for the artistic scratchings of humanity's cave-dwelling ancestors to develop into writing, and at least another two to three millennia before language and writing grew into the powerful machines that modern writers enjoy. English, if you include its technical vocabularies, has more than a million words. That wasn't so for Bronze Age languages all of which had minuscule vocabularies. Ancient Hebrew had fewer than 10 000 words. This is probably why some ideas in the Torah have been ineptly expressed and often in figurative language no longer understood. There's the set of horns on the head of Moses for instance that one reads about in the Latin Bible of the Middle Ages. It's the reason so much medieval art and even Michelangelo's Moses (easy to google this up if you want to see it) show Moses with two horns on his head. The original Hebrew writers were unable to express the concept of light radiating from the face of Moses after his encounter with God and said his face was as if horns were coming from it, meaning that light was radiating from it like the spokes of a wheel, or horns from a head. They didn't have words for rays, radiate or luminous, so they used horns. Jerome, who translated the old manuscripts into what became known as the Latin Vulgate, misunderstood and said horns were coming from the head of Moses. The King James translators got it right: They said, 'And when Aaron and all the children of Israel saw Moses, behold, the skin of his face shone; and they were afraid to come nigh him, and till Moses had done speaking with them he put a vail on his face.' Ex 34: 30-33. (This is a proof by the way that the King James translators did not just translate the Latin Vulgate – an accusation often made. They used other sources as well.) The bit about the veil is interesting, a significant detail that gives one faith in the description, the sort of thing that only an actual witness or a participant in the incident would remember: Moses was so enveloped in light that he had to cover his head with a scarf so that his people could stop being afraid of him.

So, inconsistencies, anachronisms and errors in the Torah are often the fault of limited original languages and translations. Obviously not all of them. There are other problems in the Bible's first five books that have nothing to do with translations but which still have to be discounted or accommodated. Agnostics and secularists will pounce on this. Who decides, and how, what the controversial bits mean, they'll say. It is for a reader to decide, but only a reader who reads each book in its entirety. One should read a biblical book as one reads any book, when the opportunity arises, in the train, before one goes to bed, until it is finished. Reading small bits out of context can lead to confusion and misunderstanding. As Shakespeare put it in *The Merchant of Venice,* 'The devil can cite scripture for his purpose', a reference to the devil's quoting bits from the Torah when he tempted Jesus (the incident recounted in Matthew 4: 3-9.) Reading books like Numbers and Deuteronomy in their entirety solves even the problem of God's seeming to have ordered the Israelites to commit genocide when he commanded them to wipe out the Amorites, man, woman and child.

There remains the question of why it was the Israelites that were given the Torah. Why not some other people then on earth? Nobody can answer that question satisfactorily but it was probably because an ancient Hebrew, whose name may have been Abraham, was the first human to go deeply and repeatedly into his mind seeking an answer to the mystery of being. Deep within himself, in the spiritual realm, that other dimension, that other universe, that heaven, which is around us and within us and to which God promised any person could gain access, he encountered God. It was an encounter that changed his life. He told his family and others about the revelation he had received, and persuaded them to leave their country with its man-made gods and to go to where they could worship the one and only God in freedom and peace. So began the long journey towards the Promised Land, a journey that any person can undertake. It seems that God rewarded Abraham's faith by granting his people intelligence and wisdom so that a core of them would always remain in relationship with him and make him known to the rest of the world. More than that, one of Abraham's descendants would single-handedly and in an astounding way make God's kingdom known and accessible to all mankind.

It cannot be a coincidence that Abraham came from exactly where writing was invented, and very shortly after it first began to be used to express ideas rather than as a system for keeping records. Clearly, it was when humans reached the capacity to understand ultimate truth that God revealed it to them, and at the same time bestowed on them a tool by means of which that truth could be recorded and disseminated. That is why Abraham was able to take the first Torah sayings and writings about creation with him when he left Ur in south west Mesopotamia (Iraq). It isn't a coincidence that the Torah is one of the world's first pieces of serious writing. It isn't a coincidence that writing was invented in the land of Abraham's ancestors and just before the time in which he lived. It isn't a coincidence that the one thing that separates man from the rest of the animal world is language, of which writing is the physical record.

The World's Oldest Bible

In attempting to discover how the Bronze Age Torah made it into the twenty first century, one has to realize that today's end of the story concerns the whole Bible, not just the Torah, because the Bible has been a complete book for almost two thousand years. One of the British Library's most treasured possessions is a hand-written copy of the Bible called the Codex Sinaiticus. It is the world's oldest Bible and is more than one thousand six hundred years old. Jews began to canonise their scriptures into the definitive Masoretic Text when that copy of the Bible in the British Library had already been in physical existence for almost three hundred years. I took two of my grandchildren to see it a few months ago, those clear, dark letters on those ancient sheets of vellum. In koiné (common or kitchen) Greek, it is centuries older than the Masoretic Text or the Quran. The Old Testament in the Codex Sinaiticus is a version of the Septuagint, the Greek translation of the Jewish scriptures that was produced in Alexandria in northern Egypt between the third and fourth centuries B.C. Jesus and his disciples were familiar with the Septuagint and Jesus often quoted from it. The Codex Sinaiticus was found in St Catherine's Monastery near the southern tip of the Sinai Peninsula in the nineteenth century, hence its name. A codex is an ancient book written on pages rather than on a scroll.

Paraphrases and Translations

Because the Bible is so old and has been subject to so many translations, any discerning reader would want to know how reliable the current versions are. The paraphrases that are so beloved are all new interpretations, and that applies to the 'Poverty and Justice Bible' (Contemporary English Version), the 'Good News Bible', 'The Living Bible', 'The Message' and many others. They wouldn't exist if their writers did not think that they could translate and interpret original material in a way that could be better understood. The result is that the versions differ from one another. In some the sixth commandment is 'Thou shalt not kill' and in others it is 'Thou shalt not commit murder.' Some translations leave out altogether the second commandment about not making graven images.

The problem is compounded when one remembers that Jesus said that not one jot or tittle of the Torah would be changed until everything was accomplished (Matt 5: 17-21.) 'Do not think that I have come to abolish the Law or the Prophets; I have not come to abolish them but to fulfil them. I tell you the truth, until heaven and earth disappear not the smallest letter, not the least stroke of a pen will by any means disappear from the Law until everything is accomplished.' (The Torah is often called the Law because it is the part of the Bible that contains almost the whole of the Jewish Law.)

Christians know that the prophecy that Jesus made above was partly fulfilled in the crucifixion and the resurrection. That was when, in two earth-shattering upheavals, Jesus fulfilled and accomplished the reconciliation between God and man. Several modern translators of the Bible give one of the last statements that Jesus made from the cross as 'It is accomplished' rather than the more familiar 'It is finished.' (An instance of how understanding of the words is evolving.)

Ironically, immediately after saying that he had not come to abolish the law and the prophets but to fulfil them, Jesus changed several of them! Careful reading shows that what he was doing was not abolishing them but driving them to new heights. Understanding the original law makes it easier to follow what Jesus was doing. About 'Thou shalt not murder,' for instance, he says that anyone who is angry with another person is in danger of judgement, and that anyone who calls another person a fool is in danger of hell fire! (His denouncing name-callers should give pause to those who brand others as bigots, idiots, gays, homophobes, racists, thieves, criminals, middle-class bourgeoisie or corrupt capitalists.) Jesus goes on to consider other of the laws in the same way, showing that it is what causes one to sin that one should eradicate before it ever becomes a sin.

WHICH BIBLE?

If one does decide to read the Torah, hopefully as a start to reading the rest of the Bible, which Bible should one use? The problem with that best known and most beloved of all Bibles, the famous King James, is that it is in Elizabethan English, not always easy to understand. It is probably better to start with a modern version. There are several around. In addition to the paraphrases there are more literal translations for those who feel that authors of paraphrases may have influenced the text with a prejudiced view or a denominational perspective. Even the literal translations are all different, because the Bible is not a dead book. It is alive and ever developing as it meets the demands of successive generations with their new problems and new perceptions. Significantly, the original words do not change. It is how they are interpreted that does.

There are some superb translations around today. The five study bibles that are almost universally acknowledged among scholars and bible readers alike to be the best are: The **New International Version (NIV)** begun in 1956 as a 'faithful translation of the scriptures.' It is not only international but also inter-denominational and as its name suggests was translated from ancient texts by biblical pundits from all over the world; then there is the scholarly **English Standard Version Study Bible**, which is a revision of the 1971 edition of the Revised Standard Version, and is also inter-denominational and international; third is the **New King James Study Bible,** a completely new translation but one that the translators were determined would 'retain the purity and stylistic beauty of the original King James'; the fourth is the **Harper Study Bible,** this one based on the American Standard Version and with strong links to the King James. It is also international and inter-denominational; finally there is the **New Jerusalem Study Bible,** a version favoured by the Catholic Church and with the Book of Jonah translated by J R R Tolkien, author of 'The Hobbit' and 'Lord of the Rings.' Two popular new study Bibles are the **New Living Translation Study Bible** and the **Life Application Study Bible.**

The fact remains that all the above Bibles, and in fact any Bibles not in Ancient Hebrew, Aramaic or Biblical Greek, are translations. How can one be sure that the translators got it right? And what about the so-called original materials? How reliable are they? Where are the oldest extant copies now?

Going steadily back to the Beginning

The only way to sort it all out is to go steadily back in time. In the English speaking world when one moves back from today's versions one encounters the King James Bible which until the middle of the last century was the authorised version in most English-speaking countries. Although it bears his name and he authorised the translation, James I (Elizabeth I's successor) did not himself translate the Bible into English. Very soon after his coronation, he was asked to consider a new translation of the Bible. The king liked the idea. He had already decided that there were too many translations around, and he intensely disliked the most popular one, the Geneva Bible, not because of the translation itself but because all its appended notes made it very clear that the Bible challenged tyranny and the divine right of kings. James was having none of that. Probably hoping that his subjects would not spot what the Bible itself was actually saying, he announced that he wanted a straight translation with no notes. From Oxford, Cambridge and Westminster he summoned 54 scholars who among them spoke Hebrew, Greek, Latin, Syriac and a number of modern European languages. Some of the translators died but in the end 47 worked on the translation.

One of the foremost of these, in fact he oversaw much of the translation, was Lancelot Andrewes, Dean of Westminster. Poetry lovers may not realize it but Andrewes wrote the first five lines of the T S Eliot poem 'The Journey of the Magi.' (You have to spot the apostrophes to become aware that the first five lines of the poem are a quotation.)[11] Andrewes wrote the words in a nativity sermon.

> 'A cold coming we had of it
> Just the worst time of the year
> For a journey, and such a long journey:
> The ways deep and the weather sharp,
> The very dead of winter.'

---

[11] Andrewes, Lancelot, *Nintety Six Sermons by the Right Honourable and Reverend Father in God, Lancelot Andrewes, Sometime Lord Bishop of Winchester, Vol 1,* Wipf and Stock Publishers, Eugene, Oregon, 2011

Just as Eliot owed the inspiration for his well-loved poem to Andrewes, so do lovers of the King James Bible owe much to the then Dean of Westminster. Not only was he a master of ancient tongues but from the quotation above it is clear that he had a way with an English word that was imaginative, bold and free.

He and his colleagues translated most of the Old Testament from Hebrew and Aramaic texts, making particular use of the Hebrew Rabbinic Bible of Daniel Bomberg (1524) but the King James translators adjusted this to conform to the demands of the Protestants. The fact remains, however, that the compilers of the King James Bible relied greatly on Hebrew manuscripts, and made use of Jewish commentaries to decipher obscure passages in the Jewish Texts. They used all available resources and the King James Bible, product of the finest British minds of the seventeenth century, deserves its reputation as the greatest translation of the ancient scriptures into a modern European language.

The World's first Printed Book

Something that can never be over-looked in bringing an English Bible to the people of England occurred not in this country but in Germany. It was there, in 1439, that Johannes Gutenberg invented movable type, built the first printing press and shortly afterwards produced the world's first printed book, the Bible. There are two copies of the Gutenberg Bible in the British Library. They are copies of the Latin Vulgate, but ironically their publication began to topple the impenetrable wall of Latin that had been protecting the tyranny of the Pope and the church for centuries, because vernacular bibles were going to make most use of the printing press, and were going to show people what the Bible really said. The most popular English Bibles that benefitted from Gutenberg's invention in the decades before the King James Bible were the Geneva Bible, the Great Bible, the Bishops' Bible and the Matthew Bible.

The Geneva Bible

Circulating in England some 35 years before the King James was the Geneva Bible, originally printed in Geneva in 1560 and in England in 1576. It was largely the work of English Protestants who fled from England to Switzerland when Henry and Catherine of Aragon's daughter, Bloody Mary (half-Spanish and totally Catholic) became queen (before Elizabeth) and began executing Protestants as fast as she could find them. The Geneva Bible seems to be the one that was used by both Shakespeare and John Bunyan. It is sometimes derogatively called the 'Breeches Bible' because Genesis 3:7 was translated as: 'And the eyes of them both were opened, and they knew that they were naked; and they sewed fig leaves together and made themselves breeches.' The King James said they made themselves aprons. I don't know which is funnier.

The Great Bible

The Great Bible of 1539 was the first authorised translation of the Bible into English. It was authorised by Henry VIII who had just broken away from the Catholic Church and wanted to have done with all things Roman, Catholic and Latin. It was largely the work of Myles Coverdale who had been associated with an earlier translation and was appointed by Cromwell, Henry's secretary and vicar general, to provide a large English volume to be set up in churches to be read aloud to congregations. Although because of its huge size it was called the Great Bible, it was also known as the Cromwell Bible, the Whitchurch Bible (name of the man who printed it) and the Chained Bible, because it was kept chained in parish churches so that it couldn't be stolen! Sadly, after only a few years Henry ordered that the Bibles be removed from churches. He did not want his subjects able to read in their own language that kings had to obey the law. Better for them to have Latin Bibles that they could not understand!

The Bishops' Bible

The Bishops' Bible was the High Church response to the Geneva Bible which, since it was produced in Switzerland, was very influenced by Calvin. Matthew Parker who was Archbishop of Canterbury from 1559 to 1575, did not like Calvin's ideas which rejected Episcopalian church government (by bishops) preferring a Presbyterian system (government by elected elders.) So he instructed the bishops to produce a version of their own. It was never a popular Bible – the writing was too pompous and turgid. Readers preferred the Geneva and Tyndale Bibles.

Tyndale and the Matthew Bible

The real credit for the Geneva Bible's being regarded as a better translation than the Great Bible, and the reason it was the one used by Shakespeare and later by Bunyan, must go to William Tyndale because the Geneva translators used about 80 per cent of the wonderful translation that Tyndale had made some 40 years earlier, in the 1530s. In forceful and beautiful English, Tyndale's Bible had a powerful influence on even the King James Bible. Sadly, he had not absolutely finished his translation when he was executed (strangled to death and then burnt) but it was completed by Myles Coverdale and John Rogers. Rogers was also executed, but Coverdale managed to survive and supervised the translation of the Great Bible. Tyndale's Bible was not known as such when it began to circulate in England. It was incorporated in the Matthew Bible so that the authorities would not realize that most of the translation was in fact Tyndale's. The crime for which he was executed was heresy for daring to supplant the venerable Latin of the Vulgate with a common English version. But it was not common; it was a translation of rare and singular beauty.

Wycliffe uses the Bible as a Weapon against Corruption

It was while he was at Oxford that Tyndale, who was fluent in English, French, German, Latin, Greek and Hebrew and received his Master of Arts Degree when he was twenty one, came across an English Bible that had been translated at Oxford from the Latin

Vulgate 124 years before he arrived at the university. (The Latin Vulgate was the only Bible used by the Christian Church in Europe during the Middle Ages.) The English Bible that Tyndale encountered was a secret copy of a translation of this Latin Bible by John Wycliffe (1320-1384) to whom goes the honour for masterminding the first translation of the entire Bible into English. (It is commonly accepted today that Wycliffe did not do the entire translation himself but was assisted by colleagues, notably his friend, Nicholas of Hereford.) Like Tyndale, Wycliffe was a notable Oxford scholar and committed to the reform of some of the worst excesses of the church, particularly the selling of indulgences (selling forgiveness for future sins.)

The church in the declining years of the Middle Ages was hugely corrupt. It pursued its greedy, bloated, obscene lifestyle at the expense of ordinary people whom it misled, exploited and abused with heavy taxes and threats of eternal damnation. Wycliffe realized that it was the Latin Bible that enabled the church to keep control of the masses. When the church claimed to be doing God's will no parishioners could dispute its actions because most of them, and a good number of clergy, could not understand Latin. The solution was to give the people an English Bible so that they could see for themselves what Christ said and how he expected his people to live. So Wycliffe asked those of his colleagues who were the finest Latin scholars at Oxford to help him to translate the Vulgate into English. They did so, and the book was published in 1382, exactly a thousand years after St Jerome published the original Vulgate.

The church reacted quickly. It summoned Wycliffe to a trial in London and he was convicted of heresy. Parliament prevented the church from excommunicating him or sentencing him to death, but

Wycliffe died two years later in 1384, apparently from a stroke. Forty years later his bones were dug up and burned, to deprive him, so said the church, of eternal life! Wycliffe's determination to make the Bible available in English and his criticism of the worst excesses of the church did not die with him. Many scholars, as well as clergy and laity, secretly read and circulated his Bible. Derogatively known as the Lollards, they kept alive the need for reform with the result that when the Reformation spread through Europe it found fertile ground in England, particularly at Cambridge and Oxford. The existence of the Wycliffe translation made it easier for scholars to produce the next generation of vernacular bibles, almost all of them associated with the Reformation.

Douay-Rheims Translation and the Complutensian Polyglot

There was, however, one notable English translation that was not part of the Protestant movement. This was the Douay-Rheims Bible published in France by Catholics some fifty years after Tyndale's Bible in an effort to offset rising Protestantism and uphold the Catholic tradition. The Challoner revision of the Douay-Rheims Bible remained a favourite among Catholics in both Britain and the United States until the nineteenth century and is still popular in some quarters.

Another great Bible from the Continent was the Complutensian Polyglot. It was not a translation but it brought together three ancient versions, Jewish, Greek and Latin. It was the work of a remarkable Spaniard, Cardinal Francisco Jiménez de Cisneros (1436-1517) who was born 60 years before William Tyndale. About 600 of De Cisneros's six-volume polyglots were printed, and of those 123 are known to have survived. Each page has three columns, Hebrew on the outside, the Latin Vulgate in the middle, and the Greek Septuagint on the inside. At the bottom of each page of the Torah is an Aramaic text with its own Latin Translation. So the Complutensian has a total of five versions of the Torah.

According to the preface to the Complutensian Polyglot, the Latin Vulgate was placed between the Greek (representing the Eastern Orthodox Church) and the Hebrew (representing the Jews) to symbolise the thieves on either side of Christ at the Crucifixion. That idea should give one pause, and it is a known fact that the translators of the Complutensian Polyglot, if they found disagreement between the Greek and Latin texts, chose the Latin and fiddled the Greek and Hebrew to conform. It came to light because a brilliant Spanish scholar of the time, Antonio de Nebrija, while working on the Complutensian Polyglot, found errors in the Vulgate when consulting original Hebrew, Aramaic and Greek texts. He urged Cardinal De Cisneros to go back to the Greek when there was disagreement between the Latin and Greek, and, where the Latin and Greek disagreed with the Hebrew, to go back to the Hebrew. The Catholic cardinal refused. In the end Nebrija resigned his role because he did not want to be associated with an unreliable text.

The Complutensian Polyglot remains valuable, especially if one bears Nebrija's reservations in mind and remembers that in some controversial translations involving Jewish, Greek, Catholic and Protestant versions of the Bible, one needs to be on one's guard, and to realize that they all had reasons for tampering with the text (the Jews some 800 years before the Polyglot.) Bible readers do not have to be put off by this tampering; it is easy to find all the versions on line and compare them. Polyglot texts (several others were produced over the next few years) are important in a search for the origins of the Bible. By comparing the idiom of the languages and finding agreements among them, linguists have gained much understanding of what the original languages probably said.

The Masoretic Text

Between the seventh and tenth centuries A.D. Jews in Palestine made an authoritative list of the Jewish Scriptures. The canon (list) that they chose became the Tanakh of the Jews and the Old Testament of most Protestant Bibles. To understand why the Jews began to authorise their writings at that time one has to go back to what happened in the Middle East after the fall of Rome: The rise and spread of Christianity and later of Islam. After the Romans sacked Jerusalem and destroyed the Temple in 70 A.D. surviving Jews and early Christians fled from Judaea and sought homes elsewhere, Jews in Egypt, Europe and the Persian territories to the east, and Christians mostly in Egypt, modern Turkey, Syria, Iraq and in Europe. A remnant of Jews and Christians remained in Judaea, and gradually people from surrounding countries saw that Galilee and Judaea had become relatively peaceful again and they made their way back into the area.

In 132 A.D. having ordered the building of a somewhat famous wall on the western edge of his empire, Roman Emperor Hadrian turned his attention to the eastern edge. He combined Galilee and

Judaea into a new Roman colony called Syria Palaestina and renamed Jerusalem Aelia Capitolina. The area settled down into one of its few periods of relative peace and calm, and the decades went by, with Palestine remaining a Roman-occupied territory. A new emperor, Constantine, declared himself a Christian. He was no more principled than any of his predecessors or successors (in fact he was ruthless and evil)[12] but at least he was wise enough not to make the empire Christian. However he stopped the persecutions and as a result Christianity began to spread more rapidly. In 326 A.D Constantine's mother, Helena, a sincere Christian, visited Palestine and from then on, because it had been the homeland of Jesus, Palestine became a Christian country. Shrines and churches were built, and monks and religious scholars began to take up their abode there. The years drifted by, three hundred of them, and in all that time Palestine remained a Christian country (in its last years as part of the Byzantine Empire) until it was conquered by the Muslims in 636 A.D.

The following year the Muslims laid siege to Jerusalem, occupied it, and from then on except for a brief spell under the Crusaders, Palestine and Jerusalem were to remain in Muslim hands until 1948. The Muslims built the Dome of the Rock on the site of the Jewish temple. There were still Jewish remnants living in Palestine but these shrank steadily until by the end of the Muslim occupation there were scarcely any Jews left in their original homeland. Shortly after Jerusalem came under Islamic control, Jewish scribes and scholars living in Jerusalem, decided that it was necessary to compile a

---

[12] Potter, David, *Constantine the Emperor,* Oxford University Press, 2013

definitive set of Jewish scriptures because there were too many different texts being used in synagogues all over Europe and the Middle East, and there was much resentment at the way Christians had appropriated the texts for themselves. Liaising with scribes in Tiberias (on the western shore of Lake Galilee) and Babylon and calling themselves Masoretes (possibly meaning traditionalists) the scribes collected as many texts as they could find and began to compile a canon of Jewish scripture known to this day as the Masoretic Text. Produced between the seventh and eleventh centuries A.D., it is a major source of today's Old Testament.

It was not always easy for the Masoretes to compile a definitive text because the original Hebrew scrolls and manuscripts had only consonants, no vowels. This led to pronunciation difficulties and arguments not only about how best to say the words but also about what they meant. The Torah Scroll was never allowed to have vowels added; nothing could be added to or taken away from it. The problem for the Masoretes was that there were several versions of the Torah around and no-one could say which was the most authentic. They would clearly have made some arbitrary choices. In addition to choosing particular scrolls and transcribing them as accurately as possible, the Masoretes provided notes about the vowel sounds, stresses, interpretations and conflicting sources. They called this additional material the Masorah, which may also have given rise to the word Masorete; it probably means religious tradition.

Most Protestant Bibles use the Masoretic Text as the most reliable of all the ancient sources, and Protestant translators are somewhat disparaging of the Septuagint but the Septuagint, used by Eastern Orthodox churches, is almost a thousand years older than the Masoretic Text, and the Latin Vulgate is centuries older than the Masoretic. So it is not surprising that some authorities have reservations about the Masoretic Text today. By the time it was compiled, Christianity was the dominant religion of both Europe and the Byzantine Empire (the Greek-speaking continuation of the Roman Empire) centred on Constantinople (Istanbul) in Turkey and including Egypt and the Holy Land. The Masoretes had no reason to feel sympathy for Christians or other Gentiles (non-Jews). They had seen their people enslaved and massacred by successive waves of conquest, and had seen their homeland become to all intents and purposes first a Roman country, then a Christian one and finally a Muslim one. They resented the way in which Christians helped themselves to the Jewish scriptures, and they particularly abhorred the way in which Christians propagated their faith by claiming that the Jewish Messianic prophecies were fulfilled in Jesus. They had also been contending with anti-Semitism for centuries. So the Masoretes were in no mood to choose texts that supported Christian teaching. They had an agenda, and one has to be aware of that. In addition to the above, many Jews after the fall of Jerusalem moved away from the Roman Empire, where Greek was spoken and travelled eastwards into the Persian Empire. These Mizrahi Jews, as they were called, and who settled in Syria, Lebanon, Persia, Iraq and Afghanistan began increasingly to rely on Hebrew and Aramaic and less on Greek.

It was with all this historical baggage that the Masoretes began to choose and edit ancient texts to produce their definitive Masoretic Text. And it is this text that half a millennium later was chosen by Protestant translators as the source of the Old Testament found in most bibles today. Presumably the Protestants did this because they were opposed to anything Roman and wanted nothing to do with the Latin Bible, and were equally opposed to Eastern Orthodox Christianity and their Old Testament, the Septuagint. They were determined to go back to the Hebrew writings, seemingly unaware that the Masoretic text was a much later version of the ancient scriptures than the Old Testaments in either the Latin or Greek Bibles then in use.

Although the thirty nine books of the Old Testament are arranged differently in the three texts, they all contain all the books. It makes little difference which of the orders one follows. In the Jewish Tanakh the beautiful story of Ruth is among the writings. Christians have it among the histories, obviously to push the point that Ruth is an ancestress of David and therefore of Christ. Chronicles, which is in many ways a repetition and enlargement of the books of Kings, is among the writings in the Jewish Tanakh but straight after the two books it repeats in Christian Bibles. About the Torah there is no question; it contains the first five books in all three versions, and in the same order: Genesis, Exodus, Leviticus, Numbers and Deuteronomy. In the following sections of the Bible one finds Daniel among the prophets in Christian Bibles and among the writings in the Tanakh. This difference is more significant because by placing it among the writings the Jews downplay its importance as prophecy while Christians regard it as one of the great books of Messianic prophecy. Both the Septuagint and the Jewish writer, Josephus (37 – 100 A.D.) list Daniel among the prophets, and their writings pre-date the Masoretic Text by centuries.

The Latin Vulgate

Three hundred years *before* the Masoretes produced their acclaimed text, the Catholic Church produced a Bible that became the only one used in the west for the next thousand years. This was the Latin Vulgate, largely the work of St Jerome, Eusebius Hieronymus, pseudonym Sophronius, (342-420 A.D.) Jerome was commissioned by Pope Damasus I to produce a Latin translation of initially only the Gospels but in the end of the whole Bible. He set about the task and left a record of the texts that he used: a Hebrew text; Theodotion's Greek translation of Daniel; the Septuagint for part of Esther; the Hexapla Septuagint; a secondary Aramaic version; revision of an old Latin version; and old Greek versions that were not the Septuagint.

Jerome did not produce the entire Vulgate himself. He deputised others to do some of the sections. He was forced to leave Rome in 385 A.D. (after a trumped up charge by Roman clergy that he was having an illicit relationship with a widow called Paula.) He went to live in Bethlehem, where he discovered a surviving manuscript of Origen's Hexapla. Although he is credited with producing the first Latin Old Testament directly from Hebrew, he clearly used a substantial amount of Greek material, including the Septuagint. However, he preferred Hebrew manuscripts and used them when he could. In the end he did a complete revision of his first Old Testament translation and called it *Iuxta Hebraeos* (close to the Hebrews.) He was the first person to call the books that were inserted between the Old and New Testaments the Apocrypha. The Apocrypha books are in the Septuagint and the Vulgate but are not included in Protestant Bibles.

Jerome's Bible supplanted all the earlier Latin texts and became the Bible commonly used, the *Versio Vulgata*.

Jerome wrote a large number of prologues in which he made clear that he preferred the *Hebraic veritas* (Hebrew Truth) to the Septuagint because, said Jerome, the Hebrew texts more clearly prefigured Christ than did the Septuagint. Strangely, today the position is reversed. Most Biblical scholars, particularly the secular ones, prefer the Hebrew Masoretic Text to the Septuagint because the Masoretic Text, they say, gives fewer prefigures of Christ and thus, they illogically and irrationally assume, it is closer to the truth. The Masoretes understandably chose texts that were more anti-Jesus.

Origen's Hexapla

About a hundred years before the Vulgate an early version of a polyglot was produced by Origen of Alexandria. One of the first Christian theologians, Origen was born to Christian parents in Alexandria in 182 A.D. A great scholar and textual critic of the ancient scriptures, he supervised the writing of the Hexapla, six different versions of the Old Testament arranged in columns. The six versions are: Hebrew, Hebrew in Greek characters, a revision of the Septuagint, a revision of the Septuagint by Theodotion, a Greek version by Aquila of Sinope and a Greek version by Symmachus. Origen was one of the first writers to come to the conclusion that hundreds, if not thousands of statements in the Old Testament give images and details that prefigure Jesus of Nazareth as the Christ. His revision of the Septuagint is believed to be the Old Testament version that exists today in the Codex Sinaiticus in the British Library.

The Septuagint

That brings one at last to the Septuagint. It was the first translation of the Hebrew Scriptures into another language, and was done by Jews themselves almost 300 years before the birth of Christ. It came about when Alexander the Great (356-323B.C.) conquered Egypt and placed it under Macedonian rule. He re-named the Egyptian city that he found on the Mediterranean coast west of the Nile Delta after himself and within a short time Greek became its spoken language. The city grew in importance as both a trading city (its famous lighthouse built between 280 and 247 B.C. was one of the 'Seven Wonders of the Ancient World') and a cultural centre (its library was the largest and most important in the ancient world.) There was a sizeable Jewish population in the city even before Alexander conquered it.

People began to flock to this new international hub. In a wealthy city with an influential library, the Jewish writings were bound to attract attention because other than Greece and Egypt few countries at that time had a literary tradition of much significance. (What writings there were were buried beneath Bronze Age cities and temples destroyed during the Catastrophe) So when scholars in Alexandria discovered in the third century B.C. that the Jews had a body of religious, legal, historic, poetic and epic literature that could match that of Greece it did not go unnoticed. Also, within two generations of Alexander's conquest almost all the Jews in Alexandria were speaking Greek and hardly any were able to converse in Hebrew or Aramaic. There was a danger that the Jews in Alexandria would lose their heritage which was wrapped up in their writings. They needed a translation.

According to tradition 72 scribes – six from each tribe – undertook the translation. The first real evidence for the existence of the Septuagint is in the writing of Aristobulus, a Jew, who lived at the beginning of the second century B.C.[13] Aristobulus says that the Septuagint was completed during the reign of Ptolemy Philadelphus (309 – 246 B.C.) and that Demetrius Phalereus (who was in charge of the great Alexandrian Library) had been involved in the translation which was undertaken by Jewish scribes. Demetrius died early in the reign of Ptolemy Philadelphus so most of the translation probably occurred during the reign of Ptolemy Soter (367 – 283 B.C.)

From all the above, it will be apparent that the Old Testament exists in three major versions today: the Greek Septuagint, produced by Jewish scribes almost three hundred years before the birth of Christ, the version in Eastern Orthodox Bibles; the Masoretic Text, produced a thousand years later from ancient Jewish texts and the version in the Jewish Tanakh and most Protestant Bibles; and the Latin Vulgate, the version in Catholic Bibles. The Torah itself has a fourth source, the Samaritan Pentateuch.

THE SAMARITAN PENTATEUCH

The Samaritan Pentateuch is a text of the Torah (the Samaritans did not consider any of the other writings sacred or worthy of

---

[13] *Septuagint* translated by L C L Brenton (1807-1862) in his *Introduction: An Historical Account of the Septuagint Version,* Brenton says (Kindle edition, location 102) 'The earliest writer who gives an account of the Septuagint version is Aristobulus...'.

canonisation) that developed in the northern part of the Holy Land probably from the time when the kingdom split into two.[14] In many ways it is closer to the Septuagint than to the Masoretic Text, although most of the differences between the Samaritan Pentateuch and the Masoretic Torah concern spelling and grammar and are largely insignificant. But there is one that is important, the insistence of the Samaritan Pentateuch that Mount Gerizim is the place chosen by God for Joshua's altar. Both the Masoretic Text and the Septuagint say Joshua was told to build the altar on Mount Ebal. The Dead Sea Scrolls support the Samaritan Pentateuch naming Mount Gerizim as the place where the altar was to be built, and was.

THE GREAT SCHISM

In the same way that a split between Catholicism and Protestantism resulted in two different versions of the Bible, the Latin and the vernaculars, so was the survival of the Septuagint caused by a split among biblical peoples. This break, known as the Great Schism, occurred when the Byzantine Church of the East broke away from the Roman Church in the West in 1054 A.D. Originally

---

[14] Barton, William E, *The Samaritan Pentateuch*, Bibliotheca Sacra, Oberlin, Ohio, 1908
Anderson, R.T. and Giles T, *The Samaritan Pentateuch,* Society of Biblical Literature, Atlanta, 2012, pages 2 – 3: 'The discovery of the SP by Europe in the seventeenth century has led to a religious controversy that would last nearly two hundred years. This controversy cast the SP into a support role propping up either the LXX or the Masoretic Text reading.'

there were five national divisions of Christianity, equally important, Jerusalem, Rome, Byzantium (Istanbul), Antioch and Alexandria. But Rome began to insist that it was the most important. It was partly this and partly because the Greek churches and the other eastern churches preferred Greek to Latin, and also because of some quite insignificant doctrinal differences, that the eastern church finally broke completely away from the Roman Catholic Church in 1054. This break had important repercussions for the Bible, because the Eastern Orthodox churches used the Greek version of the Old Testament, the Septuagint, while the western churches used Latin versions. This has brought unexpected benefits to the twenty first century, because the schism occurred a thousand years ago leaving us with two versions to compare.

The Importance of the Copies

Until the discovery of the Dead Sea Scrolls, the oldest extant fragment of the Septuagint was the Nash Papyrus, a few first century fragments of the Torah and second century fragments of Leviticus and Deuteronomy. The fourth century Codex Vaticanus and Codex Sinaiticus are both almost complete manuscripts of the Septuagint, as is the fifth century Codex Alexandrinus. These are the oldest surviving manuscripts of the Old Testament in any language, pre-dating the Masoretic Text by at least 500 years.

All scholars are agreed that the New Testament stands head and shoulders above any ancient writing (including the entire literary and scientific production of Greece and Rome) when it comes to the number of near-original manuscripts and the short time lapse between the actual pieces of original writing (autographa) and the oldest extant bits that have survived. The Old Testament is not so fortunate. A long period of time elapsed between even the latest dates for the autographa and the oldest extant copies. So everything depends on the copies. The Bible is not unique in this. Nothing would be known about the writing of Greece and Rome but for the work of copyists. Great libraries and museums employ huge resources to preserve authentic documents but no chances are taken: Documents are copied onto new surfaces, and today, digitalised. Even in this digital age, preservation of original material is an enormous problem. New technology makes reading and listening to earlier technology difficult if not impossible. Unless it is transcribed onto newer, and newer, and newer technology, our photographs and computer diaries, our videos and tapes, our primary sources, will disappear forever.

So it is to the copyists, scribes and linguists that every century owes much, not only as keepers of its own records, but as conveyors of the past. Almost as much is owed to writers or historians who quote from contemporary or earlier documents. Ironically, the proof of the authenticity of the biblical documents is partly dependent on how much they are quoted by early writers and partly on the fact that from almost the beginning they have been in the possession of diverse groups opposed to one another. With the hindsight of history it is fairly easy to recognise and understand the editing and translations of those who throughout the millennia have tried to shape the documents to convey their own worldview.

A Miraculous Invention and a Miraculous Find

Remarkably, the writings would not even exist but for a miraculous invention; and could not be powerfully authenticated but for a miraculous find. The invention was that of writing itself and when and where that occurred. The find was that of the Dead Sea Scrolls. Most people know that writing was invented in Sumer in about 3200 B.C. What most people do not know is that Sumer, in modern day Iraq, is precisely where, according to the Bible and archaeological evidence, the Israelites came from, probably about a millennium after writing was invented and when it first began to be used to express ideas and stories rather than simply as a means of keeping business and financial records. A Semitic tribe, the first Israelites perhaps under the leadership of someone called Abraham, began their story in Ur in the Chaldeans (subsequently identified as Ur in Sumer.) From there they migrated northwards to a place called Haran, in modern day Syria, close to the border with Turkey, and finally into Canaan (Palestine and Israel) after a long sojourn in Egypt. In Egypt, almost unbelievably, a second form of writing, hieroglyphics, was invented shortly after its appearance in Sumer. Some think that traders, nomads and migrants, who may have included the Habiru, conveyed the new skill of writing to Egypt from Sumer. Neither Mesopotamian cuneiform nor Egyptian hieroglyphics had an alphabet. That was the contribution of Semites living in or near Egypt, possibly in Byblos, the ancient Phoenician port of Gebal. Most authorities credit the invention of the alphabet to the Phoenicians.

What is obvious from the above is that the ancient Israelites lived in the three places in the world, and at the same time, in which both forms of writing and the first alphabet were invented (this last in their own type of language, Semitic.) That the Israelites would have latched onto these new discoveries with delight, and used them to record their story and their understanding of God, seems equally obvious to me. Exiled, enslaved, persecuted, hated and reviled throughout their history, they have proved to have not only an uncanny resilience to extermination and an unbelievable ability to survive as a nation, but also to possess among the finest minds on earth; they have contributed more to human understanding than any other race. (No, sadly, I'm not a Jew.)

The Jews number about 0.2 per cent of the world's population, but they have won 22 per cent of all the Nobel Prizes, and 36 per cent of those awarded in the United States. Among women it's higher: 36 per cent of all those awarded and 50 per cent of those awarded to United States women. (There are lists of Nobel laureates on-line) Einstein was a Jew. Considering their ability to survive and thrive, no matter how many times they were forced out of their homeland, and their own writers insist that this usually happened because they drifted away from God and stopped obeying His commands, and accepting, from the Nobel Prize record, that they appear to be blessed with exceptional intellectual ability, it should not be surprising to discover that the ancient Israelites lived in the three countries in which writing was invented and developed, Mesopotamia, Egypt and Canaan. They may not have invented it, but they would have been very quick to use it. So one should not discount the possibility that their first writings could go back to the dawn of their history.

Many scholars dispute this and feel that the Israelites did not learn to write until they were exiled to Babylon about five hundred years before the birth of Christ. Largely they base this assumption on the fact that for a long time no pieces of Ancient Israelite writing were unearthed by archaeologists, but now some older fragments are coming to light. The reason not much ancient Israelite writing has been found could be related to the Israelites' system of employing scribes ceaselessly to make new copies of old writings. Once inscribed on a new tablet or piece of papyrus or parchment they do not seem to have cared much about what happened to the old copy and often purposefully destroyed it. Another reason for the dearth of examples of ancient Israelite writing is that they were nomadic for centuries and therefore erected no permanent buildings on the walls of which examples of their writing could have been found.

However, in 2008 a 3000-year-old pottery shard with an inscription in proto-Canaanite was discovered 18 miles west of Jerusalem. It was dated to the 10th Century B.C. and was identified as Hebrew, making it the oldest extant bit of Hebrew writing ever found. There is also the 1979-80 find in a cave near Jerusalem of two amulets from the late seventh century B.C. each containing a rolled up piece of silver inscribed with the priestly blessing from Numbers 6: 24-26 in ancient Hebrew characters: 'The Lord bless thee and keep thee; the Lord make His face shine upon thee, and be gracious unto thee; the Lord lift up his countenance upon thee, and give thee peace.' These amulets were produced at least a hundred years before the Jews were enslaved in Babylon, proving not only that there were Ancient Israelites who could already write but also that this blessing, from the Book of Numbers, was in existence before the Babylonian Diaspora which is when many critics claim the Israelites first learned to write.

If the first miracle associated with the Bible was the invention of writing in the biblical world in about 3000 B.C. then the second was the discovery of the Dead Sea Scrolls in 1947, the year before the Israelites returned to their homeland for the first time in 2000 years. Before the discovery of the scrolls, the oldest extant bit of the Old Testament was the Nash Papyrus, which is actually not a single papyrus, but four small bits of a sheet of papyrus, so it's not from a scroll. It contains the Ten Commandments, from both Exodus and Deuteronomy, and the start of the Shema Yisrael from Deuteronomy 6: 4-5 'Hear, O Israel: The Lord our God, the Lord is one. You shall love the Lord your God with all your heart and with all your soul and with all your might.' The writing is Hebrew but it is closer to the Septuagint than to the Masoretic Text, suggesting that in the centuries before Jesus there was a Hebrew text in Alexandria that was different from the one chosen by the Masoretes.

THE DEAD SEA SCROLLS

But now, the Dead Sea Scrolls! Their discovery constitutes the second miracle, the one that has contributed to the knowledge of, and can give one faith in, the religious documents that comprise the Old Testament. Unlike most other significant archaeological discoveries which have come about as the result of looking and digging in places suggested by ancient writings and/or from a knowledge of history, geography and geology, the Dead Sea Scrolls were discovered completely by chance. Nobody knew about them and nobody was looking for them. Before one considers how they were found, the time of their finding is significant.

The Jews have left or been thrown out of the Holy Land and then returned to it on four occasions, and on each occasion either the leaving or the return or both have been marked with a gift of holy scripture.

- When they established themselves in Canaan, perhaps after some time in Egypt, a leader possibly called Moses is credited with writing down most of the Torah.
- When Israel split into two, Israel in the north and Judaea in the south, Israel was defeated by the Assyrians. A remnant of survivors reached Judaea in the south, taking with them their sacred documents, bringing the northern and southern versions together.
- The Jews in the south were overrun by Babylon and taken into slavery. When the Persians conquered Babylon they allowed the Jews to return to Judaea where they produced a new set of writings showing how they were renewing their belief in God, rebuilding Jerusalem and the temple and recording new revelations, laws and interpretations, a new understanding of God, new prayers and prophecies.
- After the Romans put down the Jewish uprising of 70 A.D. they sacked Jerusalem, destroyed the Temple and in 135 A.D. wreaked a final and hideous destruction of Judaea. The

survivors fled into banishment. Their descendants endured 2000 years of exile before being allowed to return to the new state of Israel in 1948. Just months before the proclamation of Israel, some Bedouin shepherd boys looking for strayed goats near Qumran on the north western shore of the Dead Sea found a cave with some large earthenware jars that disappointingly contained only old scrolls wrapped in linen. They sold the scrolls for £5. What the boys had found were the first of the Dead Sea Scrolls, regarded as almost priceless today.

Using carbon dating, ink analysis and palaeography (study of old handwriting) experts have determined that the scrolls were put into the caves at the time of Christ, or shortly after. The writings seem to have belonged to a monastic community and although there is some controversy about this, most authorities believe that the community was part of a Jewish sect called the Essenes.[15] It is thought that they probably hid the scrolls in the caves when the Romans put down the rebellions and threw the survivors out of the Holy Land. Most of the scrolls are vellum parchments, but there are some papyrus scrolls and some bronze sheets. The languages are Hebrew, Aramaic, Greek and Nabataean. Most of the scrolls seem to have been produced in the last two centuries B.C. and the first fifty years A.D.[16]

---

[15] Vermes, Geza, *The Dead Sea Scrolls, A Selection of Original Manuscripts Translated and Edited by Geza Vermes,* The Folio Society, London, 2000, p 26

[16] Ibid p 25

Why the Scrolls are so Important

The reason the Dead Sea Scrolls are so important is that among them are far and away the oldest extant bits of the Old Testament. Many of them were in actual physical existence when Jesus was alive. Although some of the scrolls are nearly identical to the Masoretic Test, others are closer to the Septuagint, and some are different from both the Masoretic and the Septuagint and even from the Samaritan Pentateuch, showing that there were more Hebrew texts around than was previously thought. It is remarkable that mankind has discovered by pure chance an ancient set of scrolls that attest to the accuracy and reliability of the Old Testament, and shed new light on those very few areas where there is disagreement among the versions. They show that two thousand years of copying have made hardly any difference to the documents. What differences there are are usually matters of spelling or grammar. What is significant is that these scrolls are associated with two momentous movements of the Jewish people, their banishment from Israel by the Romans from 70 A.D. to 135 A.D. which is when the scrolls were probably deposited in the caves to keep them safe, and their being found just months before the Jews returned to Israel in 1948.

Although the scrolls reveal only very few differences among the major texts, they have shed light on some crucial and controversial issues such as the extent to which the crucifixion of Christ is foretold in Jewish scripture. On this the Dead Sea Scrolls have something profound to say to the twenty first century, that yes, much that is foretold about the Messiah in ancient Jewish writing was fulfilled in the ministry, crucifixion and resurrection of Jesus of Nazareth. This will be discussed in detail in the notes on the New Testament.

WHY MOSES COULDN'T HAVE WRITTEN THE WHOLE OF THE TORAH

A final question needs to be asked. From where did the Israelites in the north and the Jews in the south get their writings? Tradition has it that Moses originally wrote the Torah but this has been questioned for centuries because, as any serious reader will discover, there are problems with ascribing every word of the first five books of the Bible to Moses. Moses couldn't have written the last chapter of Deuteronomy which tells how he died and includes a eulogy of him. There are two or even three versions of some stories and they do not always agree with one another. The books are written in the third person so they are not autobiographical. Some place names were not used until centuries after Moses lived. There are two versions of the Ten Commandments and contradictions among the minor laws. Sometimes something is ascribed to the Moabites but later the same thing is ascribed to the Midianites. The phrase 'to this day' is used as a comment, which would not have been the case in the description of a contemporaneous event.

From earliest times increasing numbers of careful readers began to observe and comment on these anomalies. One defence was that Joshua wrote the last chapter of Deuteronomy.

Julius Wellhausen and the Documentary Critics

Of all the critics, one of the most eminent was Julius Wellhausen,[17] a German scholar of the nineteenth century who divided the Torah into four oral sources:

- The J Source, for Yahweh or Jehovah, originating in Judea in about 900 B.C.
- The E Source, for El, begun in about 850 B.C. in the northern kingdom of Israel.
- The D Source, for Deuteronomy, believed to have been written in Jerusalem in the time of King Josiah in about 620 B.C.
- The P Source, thought to have been a priestly editor or scribe who lived in Babylon at the time of the exile (597 – 537 B.C.)

The Documentary Critics had an enormous following among biblical scholars until a few decades ago. It was almost academic suicide to question it. Largely because of archaeological discoveries and from a growing awareness that there was some anti-Semitism underlying it, much of the Wellhausen hypothesis has been discredited in recent years and current scholarship is reverting to the belief

---

[17] Wellhausen, Julius *Prolegomena to the History of Ancient Israel,* Translated by J Sutherland Black and Alan Menzies, published by Adam and Charles Black, Forgotten Books, 2008, Kindle Edition

that a powerful personage who lived somewhere between 1,400 B.C. and 1,200 B.C. and who may have been called Moses, did indeed contribute much of what is in the Pentateuch or Torah, but clearly not all of it.

How the Torah came into Existence

The consensus today is that enormous use was made by Moses, or somebody like him, of a very early oral tradition and also of some very ancient pieces of sacred writing in the possession of the early Israelites. The account of creation and the origin of man clearly arose while the Israelites were still in Mesopotamia; similar accounts have been found in archaeological digs in Mesopotamia (Iraq.) The beginning of the history of the Israelites and the first laws were probably transcribed from these ancient sources and written down immediately before and at the time that the Israelites settled in Canaan.

Almost immediately after the death of this Moses, the writings came into the possession of the new Israelite leadership under Joshua. Aided by priests and scribes the leaders of the next few hundred years added to, edited and even rewrote some portions of the writings. When Israel split into two, Israel in the north and Judah in the south, the two areas both had copies of the writings, and edited them in the context of their own positions. When the northern Israelites were almost wiped out by the Assyrians, some of the northern writings were almost certainly taken south by fugitives, and fused with the southern texts leading to repetitions and duplications. The writings assumed enormous importance when the Jews were deported to Babylon (the Diasporas of 597, 587 and 582

B.C.) With the temple destroyed, the sacred writings became central to worship. When the Jews returned to Jerusalem and the temple was rebuilt the writings were again edited and added to. About 300 years before the birth of Christ the ancient scriptures were translated into Greek by scholars in Alexandria, the LXX or Septuagint. At the time of the Maccabean Revolt (167 – 160 B.C.) new writings emerged and this is when most of the Apocrypha was written. The writings were translated into Latin, and became the Old Testament of the Vulgate, from 382 to 405 A.D. From the 7th to the 11th centuries A.D. Jewish scribes and scholars (the Masoretes) collated all the ancient Hebrew writings in their possession into a final Jewish canon, the Masoretic Text. During the Reformation, vernacular Bibles came into being with some of the greatest minds of the Middle Ages and the Renaissance going back to old manuscripts to produce Bibles in most European languages.

The translators and editors of both the NIV Study Bible and the ESV Study Bible think Moses is the principal author of the first five books – and there are a number of eminent scholars among them. They argue that intensive archaeological and literary research 'has tended to undercut many of the arguments used to challenge Mosaic authorship.'

Archaeological Support for the Torah

Archaeology and some plain common sense are indeed bringing serious arguments against the Wellhausen hypothesis. Of all the finds that support the Bible, the Amarna Letters, the Ebla and Ras

Shamra Tablets, the Nuzi Tablets and of course the Dead Sea Scrolls have delivered the most powerful blows against the anti-Mosaic hypothesis.

The Amarna Letters

These tablets, hundreds of them, were found in Egypt on the Hill of Amarna in 1877. They support the Bible in several ways. They are written in Akkadian, the oldest known form of Semitic writing, which developed in Mesopotamia alongside Sumerian, mankind's first writing. The oldest bit of Akkadian writing ever found is an inscription on a bowl found in Ur, the place from which Abraham came. It dates back to 2,800 B.C. Akkadian gradually displaced Sumerian, spread to Assyria, and became the lingua franca of the entire Fertile Crescent. It seems that wherever the early Israelites went, Akkadian writing went too. It is significant that these tablets found in Egypt are in cuneiform, not Hieroglyphics. They are mostly official reports from all over the Levant to the authorities in Egypt, and give a wonderful insight either into the Canaan into which the Israelites were migrating, or, if one gives the later date to Exodus, into the gradual conquest of Canaan from the perspective of the Israelites' enemies. One of the letters, from the King of Uru Salim, the original name of Jerusalem, pleads for help because of invasions by the Apiru, or Habiru who are described in writings from all over the Ancient Middle East, as descendants of slaves, outcasts, marauders, brigands, invaders and mercenaries, all of which would describe the Hebrews, or early Israelites, from the point of view of their enemies.

THE RAS SHAMRA TABLETS

In the first half of the last century, archaeologists unearthed ruins in Syria which they later identified as the ancient Phoenician city of Ugarit. In the ruins they found two libraries of documents, known as the Ras Shamra Tablets. They support the Bible in a number of ways:

- The language of the tablets is Ugaritic, closely allied to Ancient Hebrew. The tablets contain numerous Aramaisms that show that Aramaic came into Semitic languages long before the Babylonian exile, disproving the Wellhausen theory that it was during the exile in Babylon that the Israelites learned to speak Aramaic.
- The tablets refute another of the 'higher' critics' arguments, the fact that the Israelites had no alphabet at the time of Moses. Ugaritic is an alphabetised language with a letter sequence the same as modern Hebrew and it has enabled scholars to trace the evolution of Hebrew script with considerable accuracy from about 1500 B.C.
- About the psalms Julius Wellhausen, said that the question was not whether there were any post-exilic psalms but whether there were any which were pre-exilic.[18] He's wrong. A close affinity between the psalms and the Ugaritic epic

---

[18] Wellhausen, Julius, *Prolegomena to the History of Ancient Israel*, translated by J Sutherland Black and Alan Menzies, Republished by Forgotten Books, 2008.

poetry found on the Ras Shamra Tablets shows that the psalms could date as far back as the age of the patriarchs (long before Moses).[19]

The Ebla Tablets

Almost five thousand fragments, dug up from the palace archives of the ancient city of Ebla, also in Syria, provide a wealth of information about the lands in which the early Israelites found themselves. Several of the tablet stories parallel Bible stories, including the one about the release of a scapegoat. Numerous biblical names have been found in the Ebla texts: Abram, Eber, Ishmael, Esau, Saul, David, Israel and others. The texts do not describe the biblical characters but they do show that these names were common in those times.

The Nuzi Tablets

The Nuzi Tablets reveal customs practised in the Middle East that clearly affected the Hebrew population living among them, one of them being that a childless couple could adopt a slave as an heir, shedding light on Abraham's fear that a servant would inherit his estate because he was childless (Gen 15: 1-2.)

---

[19] Dahood, Mitchel *Psalms 1 1-50 A New Translation with Introduction and Commentary,* The Anchor Yale Bible, Doubleday, 1965, pages xv and xvi of the Introduction.

THE VERY FIRST BALLADS AND WRITINGS

If someone called Moses did write most of the first five books of the Bible, the question remains that the beginning of Genesis concerns events that happened aeons before he lived, and the end of Genesis concerns events that happened centuries before he lived. He was not an eyewitness of any of it. Where did he get his information? It is almost certain that there was a powerful oral tradition (probably including ballads that congregations could sing) because the Pentateuch itself tells us how Moses *told* the Israelites to *listen* and to *hear* what was being told to them. However, because of the Israelites' connection with the invention and development of writing, it is equally certain that there were some very early written tablets and papyri as well.

As to how these originally came to be told and later written, about that there can be only speculation. It would seem that from the moment that he created mankind, God used people to communicate truths about himself and his universe in ways that the recipients of the revelations did not and do not always themselves understand. Many are the examples of dreams, visions and inexplicable chance that have brought new discoveries and knowledge to humanity, even in science. There's Einstein's famous dream of cows against an electric fence that helped in his development of the Theory of Relativity, Pasteur's chance discovery that led to chicken cholera vaccine, Alexander Fleming's accidental discovery of penicillin, and even Newton's falling apple. God still speaks to humans in many and varied ways, as he has done since he gave them minds and consciousness. Hypotheses and theories are not scientific. They come from the mind of man. Proofs are scientific. In the same place in which one can encounter new ideas and new understanding, one can encounter God, and it is in the Bible that one can read how to seek him.

Nobody knows the identities of the original writers of the Torah. What is known is that they were Hebrews, or Ancient Israelites, and that they began their account nearly four thousand years ago when they set out from Mesopotamia, modern day Iraq, on a quest for a Promised Land. By the time they ended their decades of nomadic wandering and settled in Canaan, they had a powerful story. Coming as they did from three centres in which writing began and was alphabetised, they almost certainly had treasured tablets of script. Just as now, there were those among them who looked upon the world and saw and sensed the pattern of hours and seasons and time; the pattern of place; the design in the night sky and the dependability of the sun by day and the moon and stars by night. They detected and responded to the rhythm of the winds and the droughts and the rains, and the shape in the waves that beat upon the shore. They wondered about the beauty and ugliness in the fields and the joy and grief in the songs of the birds. They looked upon their fellow humans and questioned the reasons for goodness and evil, and birth and death. They experienced brutality and horror, and moments of respite and peace. Just as now, there were those who stopped and listened and heard amidst all the fret and fume the still small voice of the Holy Spirit of God say that, 'In the beginning God created the heavens and the earth.'

Part Two
GENES AND GENESIS

In the Beginning God

Introduction

One cannot be impervious to the first ten words of the Torah: 'In the Beginning God created the heaven and the earth.' But neither can one be open-minded about them. Who, what or where one is affects one's response. Theists and deists believe what the words say, that God brought the universe into being. Atheists, naturalists and secularists do not accept that God exists. If they do read the Bible it will most likely be the King James, held to be one of the great feats of English literature and, with the Latin Vulgate, source and inspiration of much of western civilisation's culture, music, architecture, and art. Jews revere the words; their ancestors wrote them and in the Torah is the formulation of their religion, culture, judicial system and national identity. To many Catholics, the church and sacraments are as important as the Bible, while to others it is the means of ensuring that the church remain true. Fundamentalist Protestants believe every word in the Torah while liberal Christians, conscious that Jesus taught with parables, comfortably regard much in the Old Testament as parable too. Adherents of other faiths read the Bible as literature and as a means to understanding western civilisation. Every reader approaches the Bible from a different perspective, and every approach is valid.

In addition to perceptual limitations, there are of course contextual considerations. Under what circumstances and by whom was a particular passage or story written? With what purpose was it written and when and where? Not only that but one also needs to be aware of the agenda of all the editors and redactors who have translated and interpreted the texts for millennia before passing them on to the twenty first century. Much of this was covered in Part One.

Genesis 1 – 2: The Two Creation Stories

One of the first things one notices at the start of Genesis is that there are two creation stories. They almost certainly originated in Mesopotamia (Iraq) in the very earliest years of the Israelites' existence. Ancient literary parallels to the Genesis accounts of creation have been found in Mesopotamia, particularly in the *Enuma Elish,* discovered by Austen Henry Layard in 1849 in the ruined library of Ashurbanipal at Nineveh (Mosul, Iraq, so much in the news at the moment) and bearing some resemblance to the creation stories in Genesis. The version of the *Enuma Elish* that Layard found is dated to about 700 B.C. but archaeologists think that the story itself goes back to long before the version Layard found. The dates currently favoured are 1800 to 1600 B.C. So it would seem that when the Israelites left Mesopotamia, this account of creation was already in existence. They clearly took their own version with them, and left behind a version that was more mythical and polytheistic.

I have Timothy J Stephany's translation of the *Enuma Elish* on my Kindle[20] and it shows that creation is not the main concern of the *Enuma Elish*. It is more concerned with the Mesopotamian pantheon and the rise to power of the god Marduk. Its limited section on the creation does, however, have similarities with the Genesis accounts and attests to the age of these creation ideas. It is ridiculous to argue about which version came first; they are almost certainly both adaptations of a still earlier source and not surprisingly therefore express similar beliefs about how the world was created.

An important difference between Genesis and the *Enuma Elish* is that the Israelites ascribe creation to one Supreme Being and not to a pantheon of somewhat brutal and squabbling deities. Another important difference between Genesis and not only the *Enuma Elish* but most other creation accounts, is that in Genesis God brings the universe into being with a Word. He does not resort to armpits, snakes, a varied collection of mythical creatures and plants, storms and all the other nightmare origins in the other creation stories. That brings one to the main purpose of Genesis.

Ironically, it was not to express arguments for the existence of God. Genesis is not a book of Jewish or Christian apologetics. The writer of Genesis takes God's existence for granted. His reason for writing the book is to show his fellows, all of them members of a small, displaced race called the Hebrews, that the one, true and supreme God had revealed himself to them and would protect and care for them if they acknowledged his existence, obeyed

---

[20] Stephany, Timothy J: *Enuma Elish: The Babylonian Creation Epic – includes Atrahasis, the First Great Flood myth.* Electronic Edition, 2014

his commandments and became the conduit for this knowledge to reach the rest of the world. Moses, if it was he and not some other early leader of the Ancient Israelites, knew that he had to write this revelation down as part of a complete and unified work that his Hebrew brethren would have access to for all time and would pass on not only to their own descendants, but to all people. It was a truth that had come from God to the patriarchs of his tribe hundreds of years before he lived but It was too important a revelation to be entrusted any longer to the vagaries of the oral tradition, some crumbling clay tablets and odd scrolls of parchment. It had to be written down as a single work which had to be entrusted to his successors and to future generations of scribes who would have to copy it onto new surfaces generation by generation to ensure its survival. As one reads the next books of the Torah one realizes that an important element of this purpose was to write down the system of law that God commanded them to keep. It is a written version of the moral law that many great minds have perceived to be a universal aspect of human conscience. It suggests that it must have been inscribed on the human mind by something greater and beyond humanity since it opposes some of the most basic human desires. Finally, although the original writer could not have understood the implications himself, some of the writings introduce the prophecies of the Messiah, the one that would save the world from the evil that enslaved it and that prevented humans from keeping the moral law that in their hearts they knew to be right.

    The Hebrew name for the first book of the Bible is *bereshith* which means 'In the beginning...' . The word 'Genesis' comes from the Septuagint, meaning both birth and origin. In the first creation story Genesis says, quite simply, that God created the heavens and the earth, the dry land and the seas, vegetation, day and night, sea creatures, land creatures and finally man, whom he created 'in his own image,' male and female. This, says Genesis, was all done in six days. Even the very first author of this creation story would have known that six days was nonsense; perhaps he simply felt he would divide creation into seven periods, six of activity and one of being, and describe them as days. Whatever else, it is certainly an attempt to express aeons of time, as the writer of the 90th psalm realized: 'For a thousand years in thy sight are but as yesterday.' God does not exist in linear time or space time. The past, present and future are all present for Him. That a Bronze Age writer could have grasped even the remotest concept of this and sought to express it by condensing the whole thing into a period of symbolic days is thought-provoking. That he should have introduced the idea of the Sabbath so early is also interesting. The knowledge that people, made in the image of God, will spend most of their time creating and working but will need a time of merely being, came from God himself.

Having begun by saying that everything that one could see, including the heavens above and the earth on which one stood, were created by God, the writer went on to explain it in more detail. The physical universe, he says, was created by an action from the spiritual: 'The Spirit of God' was hovering over the waters (formless, empty chaos). And God said, 'Let there be light, and there was light.' No other creation account from anywhere in the world expresses creation with such a depth of simplicity and with the comprehension that before anything else God spoke light into being from which came the universe and everything in it - the instant of the Big Bang.

God separated light from darkness, says the writer. Only today are scientists beginning to understand that that is precisely what the universe is, dark matter and light and that they are indeed separated. The fact that the writer of Genesis calls light 'day' and darkness 'night' is metaphoric language still effective today. Then comes the separation of earth from space. Perceived but not understood by this Bronze Age writer was that somehow earth with its atmosphere and oceans was held apart from formless space beyond it, 'an expanse between the waters to separate water from water.' Today it is called gravity. The writer of Genesis saw creation as an orderly process, and although he got the order glaringly wrong in some places, like his notion that plants preceded the sun, moon and stars (it is interesting however that until plants cleared the atmosphere and oxygenated it, the sun, moon and stars would not have been visible) he is right in believing that the great sea creatures and birds probably preceded mammals and man. In this Genesis account, God does not resort to any weird tactics of the sort used in many of the other creation stories. He simply brings life into existence in all its forms by ordaining it. Because God is timeless, no aspect of life, from the humblest uni-cellular creature that began it all, is meaningless or unimportant. All are part of the timeless whole.

In the second chapter, in the fourth verse, begins the second story, which is much more of a parable, and which describes creation in the wrong order. One has to remind oneself time and again that these were Bronze Age seers and thinkers, trying to work out the origins and meaning of life from a minuscule data base. The author of this second story knew that God created the universe but had no idea how he did it. He thought wrongly that there was no cultivated vegetation on earth because there was no rain and no man to work the ground. (In the first creation story, vegetation appeared before man.) In the seventh verse, one reads that God formed man from the dust of the earth and breathed life into him. This 'breathing of God's life into man' is surely the writer's attempt to describe the moment in which man became a spiritual being. In support of this, the LXX (Septuagint) says that when God breathed life into man, 'man became a living *soul*.' This is different from most Protestant Bibles that say that man became a living *being* or *creature*.

The writer goes on to say that God placed the spiritual man he had created in a garden 'eastward in Eden.' This seems to be a contradiction because man was being created to bring vegetation into being. It makes sense only if one distinguishes between natural vegetation, forests, plains, bush, etc. - and cultivated crops. The garden in Eden would have been natural vegetation, waiting for man to cultivate it. But that distinction is not made clear in the verses and one has to remember that this is a parable, not a description of reality. It is concerned with much deeper issues: The meaning and purpose of reality.

After man was established in the garden, God decided that his new creation, Adam, should not be alone, and so he created a woman from one of Adam's ribs. Adam said, 'This is now bone of my bones, and flesh of my flesh: she shall be called Woman, because she was taken out of Man.' Feminists don't like this. They feel it implies inferior status for women. The chapter ends with Adam and Eve walking around the garden naked and innocent.

The second creation story is clearly much more a parable than the first, and for that reason is more difficult to understand. It does suggest that a husband should care for his wife as if she were part of his own body. A woman, physically weaker than a man, can safely go into marriage with a man who treats her as he would that part of his anatomy that is closest to his heart and vital to its protection. It should be pointed out that there are scholars[21] who do not think that there are two creation stories, but that the second story is merely a broadening out of the sixth day in the first account.

Whether there are one or two, neither story is literally true. They are attempts by a Bronze Age people to account for the world and for life. But, as with any parables, there are remarkable truths hidden in the writings. That people so long ago could have thought that what separated man from the rest of the animal kingdom (the bringing into life of an ancestral Adam and Eve in other words) was perhaps the acquisition of self-consciousness or self-awareness, the realization of spirituality and mortality, the conviction that there was a being beyond space and time who could be responsible for the world and all its teeming life, the intuitive grasp of good and evil called the moral law, and the ability to use language, is little short of miraculous.

Some of this realization is expressed in the nineteenth verse of the second chapter which says that God brought all the animals and birds to Adam so that he could name them, surely a parable about God's granting to man the gift of language, one of his most awesome characteristics and that which distinguishes him from every other species on earth. The writer understood too that all life consists of

---

[21] Kitchen K.A. *Ancient Orient and Old Testament* p 117 '...a skeleton outline of all creation on one hand, (first story) and the concentration in detail on man and his immediate environment on the other (second story)...'

earth, what scientists in later centuries would realize were atoms of star dust: 'The Lord God formed the man from the dust of the ground' and 'and out of the ground the Lord God formed every beast of the field.'

THEISTIC EVOLUTION

That someone could have perceived even glimmers of this almost four thousand years before orbiting telescopes, electron microscopes, geological probes, maths, advanced physics, satellites and computers made current knowledge possible, is remarkable. It's a pity that there is still an argument between those who think Genesis is scientifically accurate and those who think that life evolved. Those who battle with the apparent contradictions should perhaps take a look at theistic evolution. One of its chief proponents is Arthur Peacocke[22] (1924-2006) British bio-chemist and Anglican Priest who identified himself as a panentheist. By this he meant that evolution was consistent with an all-knowing, all-powerful God and that the Holy Spirit of God interpenetrated every part of the universe while extending timelessly and spacelessly beyond it.

Another great scientist who became an Anglican priest is the Rev Dr John Polkinghorne, theoretical physicist who worked on elementary particles and played a role in the discovery of the quark, a fundamental constituent of matter. Polkinghorne says that working in both science and religion has given him binocular vision, and that

---

[22] Peacocke, Arthur *Evolution The Disguised Friend of Faith?* Templeton Foundation Press, U.S. 2004

God is the answer to Leibniz's great question, 'Why is there something rather than nothing?' Knowledge and understanding are still evolving. Newton didn't get it absolutely right. Einstein was appalled by the new truths of quantum physics. As Polkinghorne puts it[23] 'Those early scientists (Galileo and Newton) liked to say that God had written two books, the Book of Scripture and the Book of Nature. Both needed to be read, and when this was done aright there could be no contradiction, since the two had the same author.'

THE HOLY TRINITY

More astounding than the Genesis revelations about creation is what Genesis reveals about God. The word for God in the first sentence of Genesis is Elohim. In the beginning Elohim created the heavens and the earth. This is a plural form of 'El' a Semitic word for 'god.' The plural form Elohim occurs only in Hebrew and in no other Semitic language. It does not mean 'gods.' It means God, an extraordinary being in whom the entire universe has its being. The first followers of Christ found the concept of the Trinity not only in the word Elohim but also, and more importantly, in the first three verses of Genesis. This is in direct refutation of those who claim that the Holy Trinity was dreamed up by Christians some three hundred years after Christ's presence on earth.

The first word of Genesis, and therefore of the Bible, is Elohim, God, the first being of the Trinity, who created the heaven and the

---

[23] Polkinghorne, J: *Quantum Physics and Theology* Society for Promoting Christian Knowledge, London, 2007, p108

earth. The second being of the Trinity, the Holy Spirit, is in verse two, 'And the Spirit of God moved upon the face of the waters.' So in the first two verses of the Bible, are two members of the Trinity in spite of the fact that Jews have no concept of the Trinity whatsoever, and Muslims regard Christians as infidels and blasphemers for daring to say that God is three. The opening of Genesis becomes even more amazing. In the third verse it says: And God *said*, 'Let there be light' And there was light. The obvious question is: To whom was God speaking? Who is his co-creator? *Who made light?* After all, the writer of Genesis could have said: And God created light, and he saw that it was good. Why does it say that God told someone to bring light into being? To whom was he speaking? Both St John and St Paul saw instantly that this was Jesus Christ, hence the words about Jesus in the Gospel of John, in St Paul's letter to the Colossians, in the Nicene Creed and in the Anglican liturgy, 'by whom and through whom all things were made.' For readers not familiar with the structure of the Bible, Genesis pre-dates Christ by at least a thousand years. Christianity was still a thousand years into the future when the first three verses of Genesis describing the Holy Trinity came into being.

The idea of the Trinity comes up again towards the end of the first chapter. In Gen 1: 26 God says: 'Let *us* make man in *our* image, in *our* likeness.' To Christians this is equally exciting, and it was perceived by the earliest followers of Christ, these words that show that he was there, with the Father, part of the Father, when it all began. There are of course those who say this was simply the royal 'we' but ancient Hebrew did not have the concept of the royal 'we'. David, Solomon and the other kings of Israel used the first person singular pronoun 'I' when speaking about themselves. Only for God was the plural used by the writer or writers of the Torah. Elohim, Adonai and El Shaddai, all names for God, are plural forms. Critics who under no circumstances want this plurality to be associated with the Trinity, say the plural form was merely an emphatic form, or they ascribe its use to what they consider was the early polytheism that they say preceded the Israelites' monotheism. But, from the very beginning the notion of just one supreme God was absolutely central to Israelite belief. So why make the word plural? The easiest way to knock any polytheistic tendencies out of the Israelites would have been for the scribes to make God's name singular. This was never done. What instinct drove those early writers and the centuries of later copyists to keep the plural form that showed that God was a complex being?

There's something else about God's *speaking* creation into being. This is why John calls Jesus 'the word:' 'In the beginning was the Word, and the Word was with God, and the Word was God. He was with God in the beginning.' Word is a peculiar image no matter which way you look at it. Why word? Why doesn't John call Jesus power or redeemer or lamb or king or messiah? Why does he use the word 'word?' Surely it is because God *speaks to Christ* at the beginning of time and space. Not only is Christ the recipient of the word; in some mysterious way he *is* the word. And He is the reason that we in our turn have words and language: So that we can begin to understand God and creation and give expression to those beliefs. Karl Barth,[24]

---

[24] Barth, Karl: *The Epistle to the Romans,* Translated by C Hoskyns, Oxford University Press, 1968

the twentieth century Swiss theologian, provides a good explanation of this. He believed that God was so transcendent that it was impossible to perceive or understand him with human reason. If a word is the revelation of a concealed thought, Barth says, then Christ is the revelation of God, who is equally mysterious and concealed. Christ is the Word of God, the idea of God, made audible and visible. So if the Word of God in one way means the Bible, in a deeper and much more important way it means Jesus Christ.

It's astounding to find the Holy Trinity in the first three verses of the Bible. Everything about this is awe inspiring. It was written by Jews who had and have no concept of the Trinity. It was only in the fullness of time, when Christ appeared on earth to fulfil the law, and gifted the Holy Spirit to all those who sought him that those three verses made complete and utter sense. Jesus exists sublimely in the third verse of the Bible, not only as the servant of the word and member of the Threesome, the Trinity, but also as the Light of the World, 'And God said, 'Let there be light' and there was light.' (Gen 1:3) Christ is the creator of the light and energy that, as Einstein perceived, constitute, empower and illuminate everything.

An Englishman divides the Latin Bible into Chapters...

As one reads the first two chapters of Genesis it becomes obvious that the first chapter should end after the first three verses of the second chapter, and that the second chapter should begin at what is currently the 4th verse of the second chapter. It makes sense only when one remembers that the Bible was not originally written with chapters and verses. Chapters were inserted in the Latin Vulgate Bible in the Middle Ages to help people find particular texts, and the man who did it was an Englishman, a former Archbishop of Canterbury, Stephen Langton, in the early 1200s.

... And Finds Magna Carta in the Bible

Yes - he is the same man who won fame for his opposition to the tyranny of King John and for being involved in writing the first draft of the *Magna Carta.* Perhaps his reason for dividing the first two chapters of Genesis in the way that he did was to blend the two creation stories and not to emphasise the fact that there were two. The Wycliffe translators of a century later were the first to use Langton's chapter divisions. As for verses, those were not inserted until the mid1500s when a Jewish rabbi named Nathan, divided the Old Testament into verses. Some 20 years later, in 1555, a Parisian printer called Robert Estienne, also known as Stephanus, divided the New Testament into verses. For the Old Testament he used Nathan's divisions. Langton clearly had a brilliant mind, and would have been aware that there were two creation stories. Perhaps he tried to blend them or perhaps he believed that the second was a broadening out of what had happened on the sixth day. There's no way of knowing. What a reader today can be thankful for is that he made Magna Carta what it is and divided the Bible into chapters so early on that those divisions are universal today and apply to all the translations.

Everything was good – Then enter the Serpent

There is a prevailing truth in the opening chapters of Genesis that cannot leave one unaffected: Again and again the writer of Genesis says that when God brought the world and all its vibrant life into being, 'God saw that it was good.' The light was good, the seas and continents were good, vegetation was good, sun, moon and stars became visible and they were good, the living creatures were good. Finally came humanity, on the sixth day, 'And God saw all that He had made, and it was very good.' God was well pleased with what he had brought about.

But no sooner is man created in all goodness than he descends into all badness. The story of his fall is riddled with difficulties. Deep human issues and problems are encompassed in the seemingly simple myth of Adam, Eve, the forbidden fruit and the serpent. Where does evil come from? Why does an omnipotent, omniscient and loving God allow evil and suffering to prevail on earth? Is there a devil? If there is, does he limit God's power in any way? Hundreds of books have been written on these topics and not surprisingly none of them has delivered a definitive answer. None can. But the Bible probably gives one of the clearest expositions of the problem of evil and provides something that no other philosophy or religion even attempts, a solution to the problem.

Here are the first five words of the chapter in the King James Version: 'Now the serpent was more subtil.' And here they are in the NIV: 'Now the serpent was more crafty.' I prefer the King James translation; temptation does not always appear 'crafty' which has negative connotations, but it is always subtle. Why a serpent? Was there in human consciousness some strange residual fear of a reptilian breed that had dominated the earth millennia before and but for whose extinction mammals would not have gained the ascension?

The Genesis serpent was not originally a snake because it was only after it tempted Eve that God condemned it to slither forever on the ground. So originally it probably looked more like a giant lizard with a flaming orange tongue, like those mythical evil creatures that St Michael and St George are said to have fought. Whatever else, both the snake and the dragon represent the Devil in this ancient biblical account of man's rebellion and fall from grace. But nothing is simple. Dragons feature *positively* in many cultures: Welsh flag, Chinese culture and a serpent symbol is associated with medicine from the Greek god of healing, Asclepius, whose symbols were a rod and a snake. Because a snake was found wrapped around the infant Erichthonius, whom Athena adopted, snakes were holy to her (one adorns the shield of the Parthenon statue.) So the biblical association of evil with a snake is probably no more than using an animal that is silent, fast and deadly as a metaphor for evil.

For many Christians, hell and the devil are a problem. They shy away from those parts of the Bible that broach the subject. However, there is something about evil, or if one were to express it in a French possessive form, d'evil, that one needs to face, the fact that the devil is not a sinister being with cloven hooves, horns and a forked tail. Evil or the devil is beautiful and desirable, which is why the New Testament always portrays him as a deceiver. How often does one not yearn for things that one thinks are desirable? Jesus himself said that the *love* of money was the root of all evil. And the desire for fame and status? And the desire for power? And the longing for freedom? And lust for any person one is forbidden to pursue sexually, which Jesus points out in Matthew 5: 27–30 is anyone outside marriage? And the desire for revenge?

Mis-placed loves and desires, what the Torah calls 'idols', are the root cause of much evil. There's love of self, making one selfish, self-centred and proud; there's love of one's own beliefs, making one opinionated, narrow-minded, misogynist, homophobic, prejudiced, fanatical and even terrorist; there's love for one's race or country making one jingoistic, nationalist, racist and genocidal; there's love of a political ideology or party, a football club, sex, celebrity, religion, freedom, morality or piety. They can all cause blind, distorted, harmful behaviour. Too many Christians put love of their denomination, sect, ritual or tradition above Christ. They think theirs is the only right way and all others are wrong in spite of the fact that Christ told them categorically not to make such judgements. To believe that one walks the moral high ground while all others struggle on various slippery slopes of immorality is to be utterly deceived by the arch deceiver. That is not to say that one should close one's eyes to real evil: The murderous and genocidal acts of Daesh, Boko Haram and the armed forces who are attacking civilians in the Middle East are as blatantly evil as were the actions of the Nazis, the Inquisition or the conquistadores.

If one's misplaced love for anything causes one to think, say or do anything needlessly harmful to oneself or to any other human being one is succumbing to evil. The word 'needlessly' is necessary because there are clearly cases when, for instance, a doctor would have to cause a degree of pain and suffering to avert worse suffering or death. It still does not answer the question of where evil comes from. Is the devil merely a metaphor for the evil drives and desires that afflict all people? Jesus, who was wholly human as well as wholly God, would have known what it was to be tempted. In his case it was to use his godly gifts (to perform miracles) to achieve wealth, political power and world domination, the three temptations that he experienced in the desert, and a much easier route to follow than the painful way of the Cross.

There are those who think that all evil emanates from Adam and Eve, from humanity in other words. That's not what the Genesis story shows. It shows that Adam and Eve aligned themselves with an evil that already existed. The question remains: Who created the serpent? Did God, who created the universe, create evil as part of it? Among the answers that theists have suggested is that evil is as much part of creation as that defined by the physical laws, like dark matter for instance, without which the universe could not function as it does. Without evil would it be possible for humans to be good or would we be a bunch of robots? Another belief is that evil is not something in itself so much as the absence of something, in this case of goodness, in the same way that cold does not exist but is the absence of heat, dark is the absence of light and vacuum the absence of matter. The Old Testament prophets clearly felt that there was purpose in God's allowing evil to exist and that in time he would call an end and establish a New Jerusalem.

The Mystery of the Trees

The attempt in the third chapter of Genesis to grapple with the problem of evil is linked to the mystery of the two trees. The tree of life seems reasonably obvious; originally there was no death for spiritual man, until sin entered the picture. But the forbidden tree, the tree of the knowledge of good and evil? Why was it there in the first place? Why was there something that people had to obey? Was this an attempt to link the problem of evil with the gift of free will, showing that from the beginning humanity had a choice? Eat from the tree (there was plenty of other fruit around) or don't? Was it an attempt to show that humanity had to learn obedience to God, goodness, as opposed to obedience to evil? As soon as man disobeyed God, law became necessary, enforced discipline in other words. From having only one 'thou shalt not' as soon as he became arbiter of his own morals, man had five books of law, the whole of the Torah, thrust upon him. This is where it becomes easier for Christians. They have only two laws, and they're not even 'Thou shalt nots...' They're what they must do, not what they must not do. They have to love God, and they have to love their neighbour (that means everybody including enemies.) That's all there is to it. Back to that blasted tree. Is it inviting a reader to see that in divorcing himself from God's morality and becoming the independent arbiter of his own ethics, there is a danger of succumbing to relativism? Does the story also show the danger of hubris, pride, that makes humans want to be on the same level as God? Perhaps. The serpent did say to the woman, 'You will be like God, knowing evil from good.'

Destruction of At-one-ment

A problem that concerns some readers is why all-powerful, all-seeing God had to call out to ask Adam where he was. The first thing to remember is that the story of Adam and Eve is a parable to explain the creation of people as spiritual beings, and their succumbing to evil. The writer of the parable would have been aware of the omnipotence and omniscience of God and that God would have known where Adam and Eve were and what they had just done. But he wanted to show how succumbing to evil separates man from God. By calling for Adam, God forced Adam to reveal that he no longer felt at one with God and had gone into hiding. Adam's innocence was gone. He was ashamed of being human, which is what the naked metaphor means. He had to admit that he was hiding because he had disobeyed God and was embarrassed by what he had become. He began by blaming Eve. He had a long way to go. Everybody has a long way to go and everybody has to do it in the same way: To listen for God's voice calling one, to admit where one is and what one has done, and to ask for His help in dealing with the situation one has brought upon oneself. The wonder is that no matter how far one has fallen, the only price one has to pay is genuine acknowledgement and regret, and, where possible, reparation. Jesus does the rest.

Having chosen the path of rebellion and shame, Adam and Eve were expelled from the garden so that they could not eat from the Tree of Immortal Spiritual Life. And so it remained, until, in the fullness of time another quite insignificant tree was made into a cross, and mankind was once more invited to partake of the fruit of the Tree of Life.

Chapters 4 – 5:
Cain and Abel – Am I my Brother's Keeper?

On a first, quick reading, the most troubling question in the fourth chapter is: Why didn't God like Cain's offering? This must be particularly difficult for vegetarians. If one takes a second look at the story, however, one can see that something has been left out, something that is alluded to, in verse 6. God asked Cain why he was angry and told him that if he did not resist temptation, sin was crouching at his door. What had Cain done? One reads that he had taken some of the fruits of the soil as an offering to the Lord, only what he could spare (some of the fruits) and when he could (in the course of time) not the first fruit, not the best fruit. Then comes that word 'but' before one reads what Abel brought, and that was the best of his production, the fat portions of some of the firstborn, not just one lamb, but a few.

Considering that Cain murdered his brother, he was dealt with leniently by God. When he asked the immortal question, 'Am I my brother's keeper,' a question that was an implicit lie and an attempt to evade justice, God told him that the earth that had received the blood of his brother, cried out against him, and that it would no longer support him. Cain's question is the immortal rhetorical question: Every person on earth is indeed the keeper or protector of everyone else. But Cain broke that agreement and so he became 'a restless wanderer on the earth.' Not that he showed much remorse, more like loads of self-pity in the wake of his greed, grudging obedience, selfishness, jealousy, hatred and fratricide. But God let him go, albeit into exile, and changed his identity, 'marks' him, so that others could not recognize him and take revenge on him for the death of Abel. As always, retribution is God's business, not man's.

That the story of Adam as the first man is a parable or myth becomes clearer in this chapter, because there were other humans (Cain's wife) in addition to the 'Adam' family. Eve gave birth to a third son, Seth, and Seth later had a son, Enosh. At the end of the fourth chapter a little sentence is tagged on that has some significance: 'At that time men began to call on the name of the Lord.' It seems that Seth's line kept seeking God, calling on his name, whereas the descendants of Cain moved determinedly away from God. This clearly looks like an attempt to explain why some people, and it remains the same to this day, acknowledge the spiritual aspect of their beings while others emphatically, or by lazy default, deny it. Cain and Seth were each given six descendants, and their names were deliberately linked. Cain - Seth, Cain – Kenan, Enoch - Enoch, Irad - Jared, Mehujael - Mahalalel, Methushael - Methusela and Lamech - Lamech.

Some of Cain's progeny were involved in city-building, but others were tent-dwellers. The reader is given a picture here of the tent-dwelling Hebrew migrants moving among the Bronze Age urban cultures who thought they were safe inside their walled cities, busying themselves with their bronze metalwork, music, bigamy, corruption, vengeance, crime and violence. But those cultures were already beginning to crumble and it sounds as if the Hebrews were seeking reasons and finding them in the degenerate living in the cities. One can't leave Genesis five without thinking about the great ages that the writers say were reached by those early Hebrews. Some today think it is the result of accidental corruption by the many copyists and translators, others that numbers had different values from those traditionally ascribed to them, and there are even some who think that conditions were different in those days enabling people to live longer. It will have to remain a mystery.

In the eighteenth verse of chapter five one reads about Enoch, the father of Methuselah, and the great grandfather of Noah. Everybody else in this genealogy just lived and died. But 'Enoch walked with God, and then he was no more because God took him away.' However secular and immoral a people become, there are always a remnant, a few, who walk with God, and already there is an awareness that those who do, will not die but will walk with Him into eternity. Exactly how secular and immoral most of those ancient humans had become is frighteningly revealed in the story of the flood.

Chapters 6 – 9: Noah and the Flood

An enormous and devastating flood occurs in the myths and legends of almost every people on earth, so it is clear that there was either a single catastrophic flood in the distant past, or several. Scientists, philosophers and other scholars have come up with all sorts of theories to explain what might have happened, and why, but nobody knows for sure. All that they agree on is that there was some kind of flood. Mark Edward Lewis in his book about Chinese flood myths[25] says: 'Tales of a world-destroying flood are one of the most widespread and continuously evolving categories of stories in the world and probably the most exhaustively studied by scholars over the centuries.' Among the prevailing theories about the causes of such a flood are great rivers breaking their banks, the Mediterranean's breaking into the Black Sea, tsunamis caused by either volcanic eruptions or mega-meteor strikes, end of an ice age, sudden global warming, earth-crust displacement or plate tectonics.

The Bible suggests in Genesis 6 that the flood was caused by man's sinfulness. What isn't at all clear is what the following words mean: 'the sons of God saw that the daughters of men were beautiful, and they married any of them they chose.' Some think 'sons of God' were angels but perhaps it simply means that even those of Seth's line, who originally lived godly lives, began to intermarry with those who did not. Sinful living became the norm, leading, so say the biblical sages, to inevitable doom. There would have been total obliteration had God not found just one good man, Noah, and decided to save him, his family, and a representative group of animals.

Although the biblical version of the story is the most famous, there are early versions from Mesopotamia in which the hero is called Ziusudra, Atra-Hasis or Ut-napistim. A definitive translation and account of a Mesopotamian version appeared in 1999 in *Atra-Hasis: The Babylonian Story of the Flood* by W. G. Lambert

---

[25] Lewis, M.E. *The Flood Myths of Early China* (New York, State University Press, 2006)

and A. R. Millard.[26] Like Noah's, Atra-hasis's boat was huge, about two thirds the size of a football field. He had to take two of each kind of animal aboard. After a period of time, the boat grounded on a mountain-top and Atra-Hasis sent birds out to see if dry land had reappeared. Although names and details are different, the Mesopotamian version corroborates the main elements of the Bible story. What is intriguing is that either the boat-builder was a superb meteorologist or God had warned him. It takes time to build a boat that size. One can't start when the weather becomes sultry and the storm clouds gather. According to the Torah version of the story, God rewarded Noah with a covenant for his obedience. Never again, said God, would he curse the ground because of man 'even though every inclination of his heart is evil from childhood.' (So much for those who think people are born good!) To give visual emphasis to his promise, God placed a rainbow in the sky, the sign that although there might be rain, there would also be sunshine. God extended the promise that He made to Adam when man was given plants to eat. Now 'everything that lives and moves will be food for you. Just as I gave you green plants, I now give you everything.' So sad! The end of vegetarianism.

NOAH GETS DRUNK!

One of the wonderful things about the Old Testament patriarchs is that they were never portrayed as perfect or pious. What

---

[26] Lambert W.G and Millard A.R. *Atra-Hasis: The Babylonian Story of the Flood,* Eisenbrauns, Ann Arbor, Michigan, 1999.

distinguishes them is that when others worshipped idols and turned away from God, they determinedly remained close to Him. But, just like the rest of us, in some way or other they were all sinners. Some lied, some cheated and some were cowardly.

Noah planted a vineyard, drank the wine, stripped off his clothes and in a drunken stupor fell naked into his tent. Ham, the father of Canaan, went inside, looked on his father's nakedness, went out and told his brothers about it. Instead of quietly covering his father, he broadcast it. Shem and Japheth took a cloak, laid it across their shoulders and walked backwards into the tent to cover their father's nakedness with their faces turned away. When Noah came round and heard from his sons what had happened, he cursed Ham and Ham's son, Canaan, and blessed Shem and Japheth. His treatment of Canaan seems harsh. It is possible that this a parable to account for the difference between idol-worshipers (Canaanites) and God-worshipers (Semites) or perhaps it is a story to account for the discovery of wine and its inherent dangers.

Chapter 10: The Table of Nations

The Table of Nations is an attempt by ancient Hebrew writers to show how various nations began to populate the known earth – little more than the Middle East in biblical times – after a flood almost wiped out mankind. There is a tradition that Ham's descendants were great travellers and that some of them journeyed south into Africa while others went east into India and China. The Chinese believe that one of their first kings, Fu-Xi, and his sister-wife Nü Wa or Nu Gua (a female Noah?) survived a flood and re-populated the world. In one version Fu-Xi and Nü Wa made their appearance on the Mountain of Kunlun, surrounded by intertwined smoke or perhaps a rainbow, after the world had been covered with water, and there they sacrificed animals to God.[27] The Miao tribe of south west China have a tradition that goes back to before the first Christian missionaries, that God destroyed the whole world in a flood because of the wickedness of man, and that only one righteous man survived with his wife and three sons.

There is an ancient Celtic belief that the whole Celtic race is descended from Gomer (eldest son of Japheth) although Irish chronicles and genealogies suggest that they were descended from the Scythians as well. This is in some way substantiated by archaeological evidence from Russia and Eastern Europe showing that the Celts and Scythians share cultural and linguistic elements. The Romans called the Celto-Scythae, the 'Galli', or Gauls, some of whom migrated to Galatia, in central Turkey, after an unsuccessful attempt to invade Rome. The Jewish historian, Josephus, wrote that the Gauls or Galatians, were previously called Gomerites.

Professor Joseph T Chang of the Department of Statistics at Yale University, using a simplified computer model that admittedly ignored the complexities of geography and migration, claims that the model shows that humanity's most recent common ancestor would have lived less than 2000 years ago. (His article appeared in

---

[27] Lewis, Mark Edward, *The Flood Myths of Early China,* Suny Series in Chinese Philosophy and Culture, State University of New York, Press, 2006, p 123

a September 2004 issue of 'Nature' Magazine.) Other experts favour a date a thousand years earlier. Both findings suggest that every person in the world today is in fact a distant cousin of everyone else. And that puts the Genesis Table of Nations well within the bounds of possibility!

Chapter 11:
Genes and the Tower of Babel

Chapter Eleven has two major themes: The danger of pride, and the beginning of the story of the Israelites. The Tower of Babel explores the problem of pride that among other things persuades people that they do not need God. Things have not changed much; Bronze Age humans tried to build a tower that would reach Heaven and show God that they were as good as He was. Today there is a belief that science makes God unnecessary, that neither the universe nor life was created by God but by quarks and genes. We have not advanced much from our pagan ancestors who worshipped the sun, the moon, bulls and crocodiles; now we worship their elemental parts.

With genes as the author of life, one does not have the problem of trying to reconcile a world dominated by evil, suffering and death with a creator God who is supposed to be good, loving and in control. Genes are easier than Genesis. They're selfish bastards, the genes, and there's nothing one can do about it. The only reason to be good, kind and caring is that it ensures that the genes will survive, for a while at least, although actually they will die out in the end, so why bother? Life has no purpose, no meaning, no morality and no hope;

in fact humanity might as well commit mass suicide and have done with it. Christians believe that they have found an answer to this nightmarish nihilism, Jesus Christ. It is in Jesus that they discover a truth that sets them free from the hopelessness and despair that one reads in so many faces.

Before one leaves this story there is its moral or truth, that to design or make something to challenge God could have unforeseen consequences. The storyteller says that since it was intellectual snobbery and the mis-use of the gift of language that persuaded humans that there was nothing they could not do with their own intellects, God, knowing how dangerous this was for them, confused them by making them speak different languages. Hence babel or babble. It is in the New Testament that one reaches the real end to this story. When the disciples received the Holy Spirit of God on the first Day of Pentecost, they rushed out onto the streets of Jerusalem to tell the Jews assembled for the Feast of Shavuot what Jesus Christ had done for mankind. The disciples would have been able to speak the three languages that religious Jews from Galilee (which is where they all came from) could speak – Hebrew, Greek and Aramaic – and that would have enabled them to address most of the Jewish pilgrims. Possibly one or two of them could speak other languages as well. What is significant is that different languages that had held people apart from the days of the Tower of Babel became on the Day of Pentecost the servants of the Word.

Abraham, Founder of the Israelites

Until now Genesis has been concerned with the origin of the world and of mankind in general. Now begins the story of the Israelites, starting with *Abram*. (That's how his name was spelt at the start.) Two nations, Jews and Arabs, and three religions, Judaism, Christianity and Islam, claim Abram as their patriarch. Who was he? When did he live? Where did he come from? Is he an historical or a mythical figure?

Whoever he was, he probably represents a movement or migration between three thousand five hundred and four thousand years ago of a group of semi-nomadic Hebrews from Southern Mesopotamia (Iraq) to Haran in northern Mesopotamia (on the border of Syria and Turkey.) The story begins in the 26th verse of the 11th chapter of Genesis where we encounter Terah who lived in Ur of the Chaldeans and who had three sons, Abram, Nahor and Haran. There seems to have been much in-breeding because Abram was married to his half-sister, Sarai, and Nahor was married to his niece, Milcah. So it is not surprising to read that Sarai was barren.

When Abram's brother, Haran, died, their father, Terah decided to leave Ur, taking the rest of the family with him. There were probably other reasons as well; Ur was subject to repeated attacks from the Elamites and it is also thought that there had been a succession of droughts and poor harvests. For all or some of these reasons, Terah decided that he would emigrate with his family. The destination was Canaan and the route was along the great Euphrates River so that they would have water and food as they travelled. From Ur, in south east Mesopotamia not far from the Persian Gulf, they made it all the way to Haran, not far from the Mediterranean Sea. It was a journey of about one and a half thousand miles and probably took many months, if not years. It is possible that they named the town they came to Haran in memory of Abram's brother. Subsequently a nearby place was called Nahor, name of the third brother.

Most of Abram's family seem to have been content to remain in Haran because it had a culture similar to that of Ur. The moon god, Sin or Nanna, was worshipped in both places. There is a Jewish Rabbinic tradition[28] that while they were still in Ur, Abram smashed one of his father's idols and put a hammer in the hand of one of the others. Asked by his father what had happened, Abram said the god with the hammer had clearly killed the other god. Terah said furiously that this was impossible because they were simply man-made objects of wood and stone. Abram said that that was what he was trying to show. (The Rabbinic tradition is an oral tradition of sayings and interpretations by Israelite rabbis; it was not given literary form until about the second century A.D.)

CHAPTER 12:
AN EARLY PROPHECY OF THE MESSIAH

Nothing in chapter eleven, where Abram is mentioned as the son of Terah and the husband of the barren Sarai, indicates that he will be the founder of the Israelite nation and an ancestor of Christ.

---

[28] Midrash HaGadol Bereishis 11:28, 12:1; Bereishis Rabbah 38:8

It is at the beginning of chapter twelve that the real story starts, and the very first words show that Abram had encountered God and was listening to Him. God tells him, 'Go to the land I will show you' and 'all the peoples on earth will be blessed through you.' That this Messianic prophecy occurs in the very first words that we hear about Abram is significant.

Abram left Haran and with his wife, Sarai, and his nephew, Lot, and travelled towards Canaan but there was a famine in Canaan so they went to Egypt. The story of Abram's claiming that beautiful Sarai was his sister not his wife because he was afraid the Egyptians would kill him and give Sarai to Pharaoh, Gen 12: 11-20, shows him as both cowardly and deceitful, although his deceit was more by omission than commission. Sarai was his half-sister; they had the same father but different mothers. (The law against incest came only later into Israelite law.) This remains, however, a Bible story that I cherish because it depicts the people who loved God and who tried to obey his commandments as forever falling short, like us. What distinguished them was their love of God. There's a disarming honesty in the way the biblical writers acknowledge their weaknesses and it makes their writing more credible, the fact that they can be disparaging about their own people.

CHAPTER 13: SODOM

The Biblical account of Abram returning to Canaan and letting Lot choose where he wanted to live, which was near Sodom, while Abram headed for Canaan proper, has led to a startling new archaeological find at Tall el-Hammam in Jordan. Ruins have been uncovered that the discoverers are convinced is Sodom. They found it, they tell us, by following the clues in Genesis 13. (This is of course not the first time a Bronze Age city has been uncovered by carefully reading an ancient text. British archaeologist Frank Calvert found Ancient Troy by following the leads in Homer's *Iliad*.)

The archaeologist who thought that the Bible's geographical setting of Sodom is correct, is Professor Steven Collins of Trinity Southwest University, Albuquerque, New Mexico. In his talks, papers and book,[29] Professor Collins explains that the first thing he and his team did was to study all the Hebrew words in Genesis 13. One word stood out as having been incorrectly translated. It was the usual reason, translating a figurative word literally. In the tenth verse of chapter 13 one reads 'the plain of the Jordan.' The Hebrew word for plain is *kikkar*. But this is not the word that is used elsewhere in the Bible to express a flat piece of land. Usually the word is *mishor*, but there are three other words used for plain as well, none of them *kikkar*. Only here in the Genesis story is *kikkar* used. It means round or oval-shaped so it means the disk of the Jordan, rather than the plain of the Jordan.

The next clue was geographic; according to Chapter 13 Sodom had to be east of Bethel and Ai and visible from there. From the ruins of Bethel one can see the new site in the East. The third clue was environmental: The area had to be well watered and fertile. The Bible says it was like the Nile Valley or the Garden of Eden, green

---

[29] Collins, Steven and Scott, Latayne C *Discovering the City of Sodom*, Howard Books, Simon & Shuster, New York, 2013

and lush. So it had to be a part of the Jordan Valley that was small, circular, flat, well-watered, fertile and east of Bethel. With all the above in mind, Professor Collins and his team, together with the Department of Antiquities of the Hashemite Kingdom of Jordan, began to examine a small, circular, fertile plain in the lower reaches of the Jordan that matched all the Biblical criteria.

The team found evidence of several Bronze Age towns in this area, one much larger than the others. Because Sodom was always described as the biggest city on the Disk of the Jordan, they started digging at the site in 2005 and began to uncover the ruins of a considerable Bronze Age city. From bits of pottery turned to glass (requiring intense heat) and from other residue that could have been produced only in heat of almost unbelievable intensity (such as from a nuclear explosion) scientists working on the site came to the conclusion that the city had ended in an appalling conflagration with a heat so intense that it turned pottery into glass, scorched foundation stones and produced several feet of ash. Both the city and its dormitory towns and villages, all destroyed in this conflagration, were to remain uninhabited for seven centuries in spite of the fact that the kikkar was fertile and well-watered. For all these reasons, scientists studying the finds believe that only an airburst of a small comet or an asteroid (one about half the size of the Tunguska airburst of June 30 1908) above the north east corner of the Dead Sea could account for the damage seen in the ruins of what they now believe was Sodom.

There are archaeologists and historians who do not like this new theory about the whereabouts of Sodom and who favour a site south of the Dead Sea, others think that the Dead Sea has covered the site, but neither of those meets any of the biblical criteria.

Chapter 14: Melchizedek

In Genesis 14 one reads that war broke out among the Canaanite tribes a year or two before the destruction of Sodom. An alliance that included Sodom and Gomorrah was defeated by a stronger alliance under King Kedorlaomer. Lot and his family were carted off into slavery. A message reached 'Abram the Hebrew' with the news. Abram mustered a force of 318 men and set out on a rescue mission which succeeded.

On his victorious return, a telling incident occurred. The best way to understand the story is to consider one of the Dead Sea Scrolls, the famous 11Q13, or as it is sometimes called, 11Q Melchizedek. This scroll has thrown the cat among the pigeons for both Jewry and Islam because it emphasizes the concept that God is more complex than a single entity, and can allow an aspect of himself to subsist in human form if he so chooses. There are faiths outside the Abrahamic beliefs, like Hinduism, that embrace this idea but it has always been thought that of the three Abrahamic faiths only Christianity believes in the incarnation and in the Trinity.

The author of Scroll 11Q13 suggests that Melchizedek was an incarnation of God. He first appears in chapter fourteen of Genesis, then in the Psalms and finally there is quite a lot about him in the New Testament letter that was addressed by an early Christian writer to the Hebrews. In the Genesis story one reads that after

Abram defeated the forces of Kedorlaomer, recovered his relatives and all their possessions and took them safely back to Canaan, he was welcomed on his return not only by the King of Sodom but also by Melchizedek, king of Salem, who brought out bread and wine. He was priest of God Most High, and he blessed Abraham, saying, 'Blessed be Abraham by God Most High, Creator of heaven and earth. And blessed be God Most High, who delivered your enemies into your hand.' Then Abraham gave him a tenth of everything.

That's it. Melchizedek disappears from the story and is not heard about again until the psalms, and then it's just a brief allusion to this account in Genesis. But short though the Genesis story is, there are some extraordinary elements in it. Melchizedek appeared from nowhere. There is no information about his genealogy; simply that he was king of Salem. Salem means peace, and is a shortened form of Jerusalem. The word Melchizedek means King of Righteousness. So Melchizedek was both King of Peace and King of Righteousness. He offered Abraham a very ordinary meal of bread and wine, but one cannot help remembering the importance of these two elements in the ministry, life, death and resurrection of Jesus. The significance of his name can have escaped nobody. Jesus is often referred to as King of Peace and King of Righteousness. The last point in the story is that Melchizedek was 'priest of God Most High,' yet he was not Hebrew.

The author of 'Scroll 11Q Melchizedek'[30] pictures Melchizedek as identical with God, but also as distinct from him. It describes

---

[30] Vermes, Geza: *The Dead Sea Scrolls*, The Folio Society (by arrangement with Penguin Books Ltd.,) London, 2000; page 303, *The Heavenly Prince, Melchizedek*.

Melchizedek as the one who ultimately judges and atones but this is generally ascribed to only God, so this scroll, written by a Jew, powerfully indicates that God has a complex nature and that Christians didn't just dream up the concept of the incarnation and the Trinity; it was written into Judaism, not only in the first three verses of Genesis, but also in this Dead Sea scroll. Also interesting is that Abram gave Melchizedek a tenth of all the booty he brought back from the battle, the first Biblical allusion to a tithe. That the Jewish scribes included this incident in their writings, and chose never to eradicate it, shows that even if they remained unaware that Melchizedek was a manifestation of God, they did not believe that God was a tribal god, only for the Israelites. Melchizedek, his first priest, was not an Israelite.

Chapter 15: Covenant and Promise

Almost all of chapter fifteen is devoted to Abram in deep prayer, at a level in which he encountered God and heard his voice. God led Abram outside and bade him count the stars, promising that his descendants would number more than the stars that he could see; about 5 000 stars can be seen with the naked eye on a clear, dark night. Then, in verse 12, it says, 'As the sun was setting.' This is held to be a contradiction of verse five where Abram was counting the stars. The truth is that nowhere does one read how long this mystical experience lasted; it could have been days, or even weeks. In the next book, Exodus, one reads that Moses spent so long in close communion with God that the Israelites thought he had died on Mount Sinai, lost faith in God, and made themselves a golden calf as an image to worship. So there were and are occasions when God and man can be in such deep and sustained communion that it causes time to telescope for the human involved in the encounter.

Chapter 16: Hagar and Ishmael

By this time old and barren Sarai had given up any idea of bearing Abram a family. She suggested that Abram sleep with her Egyptian servant, Hagar, so that he could father the family he longed for and that God had promised. Hagar became pregnant and was contemptuous of the barren Sarai who promptly mistreated Hagar to the extent that she ran away. An angel of the Lord appeared to Hagar, told her to go back to her mistress and said she would bear Abram a son, a 'wild donkey of a man' whom Hagar was to call Ishmael. God promised that he would have many descendants, but he also said, 'His hand will be against everyone and everyone's hand against him.' It is from Ishmael that Muslim Arabs claim their descent. It should be noted that the description of Ishmael as a wild 'donkey' comes from the Masoretic text which was compiled by Jewish scribes after the Muslims had conquered Jerusalem. In the Septuagint, translated a thousand years before the Masoretic Text and before either Christianity or Islam existed, the Angel's words to Hagar were: 'He shall be a wild man, his hands against all, and the hands of all against him, and he shall dwell in the presence of all his brethren.' There was nothing about a donkey! But one can understand the hatred and fear of the Jews who when they compiled the

Masoretic Text had just seen the Muslims capture their beloved Jerusalem from the Christians, and who were contemplating the possibility that Jerusalem would never again be theirs. The prophesied antipathy between Ishmael's descendants and all other people gives me a cold shiver.

Chapter 17: Circumcision and Abram becomes Abraham

When Abram was 99 years old, God appeared to him and told him he would have a legitimate son. Abram laughed in disbelief; Sarai was 90. God added that Abram's name was to be changed to Abraham. Abram means 'exalted God.' His new name meant 'father of many' but contained 'exalted God' within it. God said that he would give the whole of Canaan to Abraham, and that he intended to have a special relationship with Abraham and his descendants. The physical sign of this relationship would be circumcision. God said Sarai (meaning my princess) was to be called Sarah (meaning everybody's princess.) Abraham begged God to bless Ishmael as well. God said Ishmael would be the father of kings but he reiterated that it would be through Abraham and Sarah's son, Isaac, that he would establish his covenant and make the Israelites a chosen people. Immediately 'On that very day' Abraham had himself and all the boys and men in his household circumcised.

Chapter 18: Mysterious Visitors

Abraham was resting in the shade near his tent, which he had pitched under one of the great trees of Mamre when he looked up and saw three men 'standing nearby'. He rose immediately, hurried towards them, bowed, addressed them courteously and offered them food, drink and rest. It seems that two of the men were angels and that the third was God Himself. He told Abraham again that he and Sarah would have a son. Sarah overheard and laughed because she was past the age of child-bearing. God told her that with God nothing was impossible. When the men got up to leave, Abraham accompanied them to where they could see Sodom in the distance. God told Abraham that there was so much wickedness in the city that he intended to destroy it. Abraham pleaded lengthily with God to spare the city, finally asking that it be saved if only ten good men could be found there. God agreed to this. Abraham had been promised his heart's desire by God, a son, but this did not mean that he was impervious to the needs of others. Lot lived in Sodom. Abraham, loving Lot, pleaded for him. And God responded to Abraham's love. On all occasions in which God appears to change his mind, it is love that causes the change.

Chapter 19: Destruction of Sodom

In the same way that the angels visited Abraham, they went to Lot, but this time only two of them. God was not with them. It seems there were not ten righteous men in Sodom, and God intended to destroy it. But He knew how much Abraham loved Lot, and he was going to give Lot and his family a chance to escape. Lot offered the two strangers the same hospitality that his uncle had. They declined, saying that they would spend the night in the town square, but Lot insisted that they stay with him, and they finally accepted his offer.

Whichever way you look at it, the story of Lot is horrific. It reads like a myth, and has much in common with some of the Greek myths. There was an incestuous relationship between Lot and his daughters. The Genesis story puts the blame on the daughters; they got their father drunk and slept with him in turn because they claimed that there were no other men around and they needed to continue the family line. But in the context of Sodom, it looks as if it was Lot himself who had been carrying on an incestuous relationship with his daughters. He chose to live in Sodom after all, and he offered his daughters to be gang-raped so that he could maintain his position as a protective host of his two male visitors. (There are authorities who feel that there was no risk of the daughters being raped. Whereas homosexuality was not only allowed but encouraged, rape of a woman was punishable by death.) However, the gang outside Lot's house did not want the women. They wanted to have sex with the two good-looking young men. Lot said no and the angels helped him by blinding the men outside so that they could not locate the door of the house. Is Lot really an ancestor of Jesus? According to this story, the elder daughter had a son, by her father, whom she called Moab. Moab became the founder of the Moabites, of whom one was Ruth, an ancestress of David and ultimately of Mary and of Jesus.

Lot and his family followed the angels to safety but the young men betrothed to the daughters rejected the opportunity to escape and remained behind. They could have been involved in the paederastic system, which demanded that they remain faithful to their male lovers until they reached their twenties and only then could they take wives. But that is speculation. According to the Genesis account, the angels grabbed the hands of Lot, his wife and daughters and ran them out of the city. Lot, pointing out that he was old and incapable of reaching the mountains, asked if he could turn aside into a small town called Zoar. The angels agreed. No sooner had Lot reached Zoar, just after sunrise, than the disaster happened. Was Lot's wife really turned into a pillar of salt merely because she looked back? Perhaps she *turned* back to see if something really would happen to Sodom, and standing in full view of Sodom was herself impacted by the shock wave, becoming a pillar of, maybe *ash,* which is another translation of the word usually translated as salt. Sodom, Gomorrah and other towns on the Disk of the Jordan were destroyed.

Chapter 20: Not Again!

Chapter 20 gives a second version of the story of Abraham lying about Sarah and claiming that she was his sister. In this account the king of Gerar, Abimelech, took Sarah into his harem. I am sure this wouldn't have happened twice in Abraham's life and that this is therefore another occasion in which two accounts of one incident have been included in the Israelite writings. This version does not fit into the story very well; Sarah must have been very old at this time and not likely to have drawn this kind of attention to herself. Furthermore, it interrupts the story of God's promise to Abraham that he would have a legitimate son.

Chapters 21 and 22 – The Birth and Near Sacrifice of Isaac

In spite of the fact that she must have been beyond menopause, Sarah became pregnant and bore a son, Isaac. The name means 'He laughs.' It introduces the lovely sixth verse of chapter 21 in which Sarah says: 'God has brought me laughter, and everyone who hears about this will laugh with me' It reminds one that both Abraham and Sarah had laughed in disbelief when God told them they would have a son. God had the last laugh! It is also important to note that this is a supernatural birth; Abraham and certainly Sarah were long past the age at which they could conceive and produce children.

For many readers of the Bible the almost-sacrifice of Isaac is a difficult if not a preposterous story. Why would God demand that Abraham make a human sacrifice of the promised and long-awaited Isaac? Most commentators feel that God was testing Abraham's faith. Some feel that the inclusion of the story is to demonstrate that God did not want child sacrifice: it was a common practice in the Middle East at that time, and one that the Torah speaks against several times. For Christians, however, the story has far deeper significance. Like Abel and Melchizedek, Isaac points towards Christ. Isaac was Abraham's only legitimate son; Jesus is the only son of

God. The hill in Moriah where Isaac was placed on an altar, and the hill where Jesus was nailed to a cross, are close and may even have been the same hill. A donkey was involved in the journeys towards execution of both Isaac and Jesus (who rode a donkey into Jerusalem a few days before the Crucifixion.) Two servants went with Abraham; Jesus was accompanied into death by two thieves nailed to crosses on either side of him. The number 'three' featured in both stories. It took Abraham and Isaac three days to reach the place of execution. Three were executed at the Crucifixion of Jesus. Jesus rose from death on the third day. Isaac carried on his back the wood on which he was to be sacrificed. Jesus carried on his back the wooden cross on which he was sacrificed. God provided the lamb on both occasions, a ram whose horns were locked in a thorny thicket in place of Isaac, and in place of sinful humanity his only son, the Lamb of God, bearing a crown of thorns. This story shows how much Christians lose who dismiss the Torah as not having much to do with Christ. The Old Testament is the beginning of the story of Christ.

A lovely and significant end to the story is that Abraham called the place where it all happened: 'The Lord will provide.' The editor of the story, who might have been Moses, added a telling postscript, saying that it was still said that, 'On the mountain of the Lord it will be provided.' For Christians the words are an amazing prophecy. On the mountain of the Lord, the salvation of the world and resurrection from death would indeed be finally provided, by Christ.

Chapters 23 – 25:
Deaths of Sarah and Abraham; Isaac marries Rebekah; Esau and Jacob

At the age of 127 Sarah died. A grief-stricken Abraham haggled with Ephron the Hittite for a cave in the field of Machpelah near Mamre, Hebron, in which to bury her. He secured the cave for a hugely inflated price. Several patriarchs and their wives would be laid to rest in the caves; Abraham with Sarah, Isaac and Rebekah and Jacob and Leah. The tombs are currently under Israeli control but they are in a largely Muslim area and the Muslims still use the Mosque built above the caves, except for certain Jewish religious festivals when Jews may worship there. The Jews feel strongly that Abraham bought the land legitimately and that they have a strong claim to it.

Abraham married again, a woman called Keturah; one reads in Chronicles that she had been his concubine. When he felt that death was approaching, he set about the business of finding a wife for Isaac (Chapter 24.) There is the curious incident of the oath that Abraham demanded of a trusted servant, who had to swear to carry out Abraham's instructions by placing his hand under Abraham's thigh. Many theories have been propounded about this but the most likely one is that the servant had to place his hand close to the source of Abraham's seed and the circumcision that marked his covenant with God. God had promised that the world would be blessed through Abraham's progeny so the task with which the servant was being entrusted, finding a wife for Isaac and thereby ensuring the next generation, was intimately connected with the source both of Abraham's covenant with God, and with the descendants through whom God had told him the world would be blessed. Abraham made it clear to his servant that Isaac's wife could come only from Abraham's own people in Haran. Abraham's instructions to the servant are the last words that he speaks in the Bible, suggesting that when he sent his servant on this vital errand, he was close to death.

Good and honest man that he was, the servant set out immediately and did not stop until he reached Aran and the town of Nahor, just as the women of the town were approaching the well to draw water. Praying that when he asked a girl to put down her pitcher so that he could have a drink she would offer to draw water for his camels too, the servant approached the well. He was clearly looking for someone who was not only attractive, but who was also kind and generous.

Beautiful Rebekah met all the requirements. She lowered her pitcher so that the servant could assuage his thirst, and then offered to fill the trough so that his camels could drink. Pitcher after pitcher she emptied into the trough, until all the camels had had enough. The servant asked who she was and she said that she was the granddaughter of Nahor (Abraham's brother) and Milcah. (That made Rebekah a first cousin once-removed of Isaac.) Giving her some of the beautiful jewellery that Abraham had provided, the servant asked whether he could spend the night at her home. She said yes immediately and ran back to tell her parents to expect a visitor while the servant knelt to pray, thanking God for letting him meet Rebekah. Rebekah's brother, Laban, was clearly impressed by the rich jewellery. He called the servant, 'Thou blessed of the Lord.' The negotiations went well and within a short space of time, Rebekah, with her nurse and some other personal servants, set off to accompany the servant back to Canaan. Isaac was in a field 'meditating' when the servant returned with Rebekah. He was probably praying, but was also still grieving for his mother. The servant told Isaac all that happened and who Rebekah was. I'll let the King James writers complete the story: 'And Isaac brought her into his mother Sarah's tent, and took Rebekah, and she became his wife; and he loved her; and Isaac was comforted, after his mother's death.'

Abraham died soon afterwards, leaving everything to Isaac. Ishmael came back and he and Isaac buried their father together, the last time that they worked together because in the 18th verse of chapter 25, it says that Ishmael's descendants (traditionally the Arabs) 'lived in hostility towards their brothers' (traditionally the Jews.) After some years of being barren Rebekah became pregnant. It was an uncomfortable pregnancy, and God told her that there were twins in her womb who would father two nations; the descendants of the older would serve the descendants of the younger. The first born, Esau, was covered in red hair. He was followed by Jacob, who was holding onto Esau's heel. As the boys grew up, the differences between them became marked. Esau was a powerful, muscular, man's man, wanting instant gratification and not much given to intellectual pursuits. 'A man of the open country,' hunting was what he enjoyed. Jacob was slighter, more intelligent and sensitive, more conniving, and able to strive patiently towards a goal. The King James calls him 'a plain man' but the NIV says he was 'a quiet man.' I prefer the NIV translation. 'Plain' suggests open and honest, whereas as the story unfolds it shows that Jacob was anything but.

He did not like the open country like his brother did. He preferred to remain among the tents. Not surprisingly, Esau was his father's favourite, Jacob his mother's.

Jacob's scheming is revealed in the matter of the stew that he was cooking when Esau returned home after a long spell of hunting. Ravenous, Esau demanded some of the stew. Jacob said Esau could have some, provided he sold Jacob his birthright, which meant all the inheritance rights that would have been Esau's when Isaac died. Telling Jacob that he was almost dead from hunger and that a birthright meant nothing to him, Esau agreed. This was considered a 'godless' thing to do and was referred to as a grievous sin by the New Testament writer of the letter to the Hebrews (Hebrews 12:6.)

Chapters 26 - 28: Jacob deceives Esau and flees for his life

In chapter 26 is yet another instance of two copies of an original document being arbitrarily included, because one reads *for the third time*, how one of the patriarchs pretended that his wife was his sister because he was afraid that he would be killed by a king who desired her. This time it was Isaac lying to Abimelech, King of the Philistines. Since Abimelech is the name of the king that Abraham lied to as well, it is clear that this is a third version of an original story.

The chapter goes on to show Isaac becoming increasingly wealthy and arousing envy among the Philistines who urged him to leave their area. There were also disputes among the Hebrews and

Philistines about the wells, not unnatural in a dry and arid region. A treaty was signed between Isaac and Abimelech at Beersheba but an identical one had been signed between Abraham and Abimelech, at the same place, (chapter 21:31) and that's not very likely. So again we have a clear indication that we are dealing with two copy streams of an original document.

Esau's rejection of his birthright absolved Jacob to some extent when in chapter 27 he and his mother deceived Isaac into believing Jacob was Esau, so that Jacob could receive the firstborn blessing. In a sense Esau had already given this blessing to his brother. The biblical writer makes this clear by deliberately linking the two incidents around a pot of stew, a neat literary device. The story of how Rebekah disguised Jacob and got Isaac, who had gone blind, to pronounce the first-born blessing on his younger son, is well known. Rebecca clearly got on much better with Jacob and probably intended to live with him one day so she wanted as much of Isaac's wealth as possible to go to him. When Esau returned and the plot was uncovered, Esau uttered a bitter cry and begged his father for a blessing too, but Isaac said that his brother had deceived him and that the blessing and prayer had been made. They ensured that Jacob would be lord over Esau and would inherit most of Isaac's wealth. In the Bronze Age such a blessing had the nature and importance of a last will and testament and could not be altered.

Esau vowed to kill Jacob when Isaac died. As usual, Rebekah overheard and quickly devised a scheme to separate the twins. She told Isaac that Esau's non-Israelite wives had made her unhappy and that if Jacob also took a wife from among the Hittite women, her life would not be worth living. So Isaac summoned Jacob and ordered him to go to Haran and find a wife there. Poor Jacob! He'd been a mummy's boy all his life. Now he had to undertake a dangerous journey, about 450 miles, all by himself, and if his ailing father died he would have his murderously irate and much stronger elder brother in hot pursuit.

Reading between the lines, I don't think Isaac and Rebekah had done a very good parenting job. Each had a favourite son and ignored or despised the other child. The result was that Esau, favoured by his father, became a rough, unkempt, thoughtless hunter pursuing his physical needs. He married three women against his parents' wishes. Jacob, on the other hand, was his mother's favourite, stayed home all day, cooked what his brother caught, and clung to Rebekah for protection and advice. The relationship between the parents would almost certainly have been strained by their arguments over their sons, hence Rebekah's continual eavesdropping and her preparedness to hoodwink Isaac to gain advantages for Jacob.

Jacob probably cast many a look behind to see if Esau was following him as he hot-footed it across the desert. He must have been frightened and lonely. As the second day drew to a close, he curled up and went to sleep. In all probability he had not stopped the previous night and this was his first giving into exhaustion. One would have expected him to have nightmares. He didn't. What he had was a life-changing dream.

A Hard Pillow

In the dream he saw a stairway going up to heaven. There were angels ascending and descending the stairs. At the top was

God. He told Jacob that He was the God of Jacob's forebears and that He would give Jacob the land on which he was lying. Jacob's descendants would be like 'the dust of the earth' and 'all people on earth will be blessed through you and your offspring. I am with you and will watch over you wherever you go, and I will bring you back to this land. I will not leave you until I have done what I have promised you.' For one who can have had little faith in himself and who was filled with all sorts of fears and terrors and I hope some guilt, it was an extraordinary vision. For today's reader it is the still, small voice again, mysterious, undeviating, enduring, assuring mankind that all will be blessed through Jacob's offspring. It is not surprising that when Jacob woke up he was filled with awe and reverence, and a feeling that he was in a sacred place. 'The Gate of Heaven' he called it. He sort of missed the point of God's promise that God would be with him 'in all places whither thou goest.' He thought the place where he had the dream was special and holy, a thin place, where one could encounter God. So he upended the stone on which he had rested his head, so that it became a small pillar, and poured oil on it. He called the place Bethel meaning 'House of God.' It had been called Luz before. Jacob vowed that if God would watch over him and bring him safely home, he would believe in Him, again missing the point! He is saying to God, 'If you look after me, I'll believe in you.' If God could go on loving Jacob there's hope for the rest of us. I've heard this story umpteen times and have always wondered about that stone pillow. I can't think of anything more uncomfortable. Perhaps he simply leaned against it.

Chapters 29 - 31: Deceiver Deceived

When Jacob reached the land from which many years before his grandfather Abraham had trekked away, he had an experience similar to that of the servant sent to find a wife for Isaac. Again, the scene was a well where some animals were waiting to be watered. (Two versions of a single story again?) Jacob saw some shepherds arrive but they made no move to lift the heavy stone that covered the well. Instead they lazed around waiting for the rest of the shepherds. Jacob asked them about his Uncle Laban and discovered that they all knew him. A shepherdess approached with her herd, and the men informed him that she was Laban's daughter, Rachel. Because the shepherds refused to remove the stone from the well so that Rachel could water her sheep, Jacob himself removed it. He introduced himself, kissed her and cried, probably in relief, because his cousin was beautiful and he had partly come all this way to find a wife. Rachel ran back to tell her family about Jacob, and Laban hurried out to meet his nephew, again, too many similarities with the earlier story.

Jacob stayed with the family for a month, after which Laban said he would pay Jacob if he worked for him. Jacob said all he wanted was Rachel as a wife. Laban agreed provided Jacob worked for him for seven years. But Jacob, the deceiver, was now deceived. After seven years the marriage duly took place, the bride was unveiled, and it was not Rachel whom he had married but her sister, Leah, a much plainer woman. Laban said he would give Rachel to Jacob after the bridal week, as a second wife, on condition that he stayed to work for another seven years. Jacob agreed.

It is because Jacob did not love Leah, one reads, that God let only Leah have children. She had four sons, Reuben, Simeon, Levi and Judah. Mortified at not having children of her own, Rachel asked Jacob to sleep with her servant, Bilhah, so that she could have a surrogate family. Jacob duly slept with Bilhah and had two more sons, Dan and Naphtali. Meanwhile Leah was unable to fall pregnant again, so gave her servant, Zilpah, to Jacob. By Zilpah Jacob had two more sons, Gad and Asher, eight sons so far. By choice Jacob usually slept with Rachel, the woman he really loved. One day Rachel asked Leah's son, Reuben, for some mandrakes that he had found in a field. Leah said Rachel could have them (they were supposed to have pregnancy-inducing properties) provided she let Jacob sleep with her. Rachel agreed. Leah had two more sons, Issachar and Zebulun. She also had a daughter, Dinah. God finally had pity on Rachel and she bore a son, Joseph. Jacob now had eleven sons.

Perhaps it was because they were both deceitful by nature that Laban and Jacob concocted the weird pact about the livestock. Each thought he had got the better of the other but in fact the writer of Genesis says that it was God alone who determined the outcome. Jacob suggested that they divide Laban's flock into two groups. In the one group they would put the usual brown and black goats and white sheep. In the other would be striped and spotted animals. Jacob would take any spotted and striped animals born to the ordinary looking group during the next few years. Laban was delighted with the scheme. He sent the spotted and striped animals a three days' journey away, leaving only the normal-looking animals in Jacob's care. Laban must have laughed to himself; the normal ones were not likely to produce unusual ones. He would be richer than ever when the flocks were finally counted, and Jacob would have hardly any animals.

Jacob now resorted to a superstition that he believed would affect the outcome in his favour, the belief that whatever a ewe saw at the moment of conception would affect the lamb or kid that she bore. It's completely fallacious. Cutting down some poles, Jacob peeled the bark from them so that they looked striped. Then he placed these wherever the sheep and goats mated. Soon striped and spotted lambs and kids began to appear. He made sure that the stronger animals would always be pointed in the direction of the striped and spotted ones when they mated. His 'different' herds began to increase in size, and the animals became increasingly stronger, because God willed it so and not because of Jacob's shenanigans with striped poles.

Not surprisingly, when Laban and his sons saw their father's herd, their inheritance, diminishing in comparison with Jacob's, they became increasingly cold and angry towards Jacob, who realized that it was time to go. He sent for Rachel and Leah to go to him in the fields; he obviously couldn't discuss his plans in Laban's home, and told them that in spite of the fact that Laban had cheated him time and again, he had grown wealthy. Telling them that this was God's doing (an angel had appeared to him in a dream and shown him that the male goats that were mating were all speckled and striped) he urged them to get ready for a quick departure. I imagine that Rachel and Leah had a hasty discussion before informing Jacob that as they would have no share in what was left of Laban's wealth, they were perfectly content to go with him. They said, 'whatsoever God has said unto thee, do.' Jacob did. He loaded up his wives and children and headed for the hill country of Gilead on the first stage of his journey back to Canaan.

But Rachel had stolen her father's household gods. When Laban discovered the loss he set off in pursuit and overhauled the fugitives in the hills of Gilead. God told him in a dream to speak neither good nor bad to Jacob. So Laban controlled himself and asked Jacob why he had run off without giving Laban a chance to say good-bye to his family, and why he had stolen his household gods. Jacob denied that he had the household gods. He invited Laban to search for them, promising that whoever had taken them would pay with his life. Overhearing this, Rachel went into her tent, sat on the household gods and pretended she had her period and couldn't stand up. Laban gave up and said Jacob could return to his own country in peace. About Rachel's deceit and ruse, no comment, except – household gods? Idols? Jacob clearly did not know she had them because he would never have suggested that Laban kill the thief if he had had any notion that it was his beloved Rachel. She must have owned up to Jacob afterwards. The story makes it clear that while Jacob remained faithful to God, the family in Haran were worshipping idols.

Chapters 32 - 33: Jacob becomes Israel

Jacob was terrified at the prospect of meeting Esau. As he neared his homeland, he split off considerable portions of his flocks and sent them on ahead in the charge of servants. He commanded them to say, when accosted by Esau, that the flocks were presents from his brother, Jacob, who was coming on behind. Jacob was trying to buy Esau's forgiveness. He also prayed fervently that God would protect him.

When he reached the Jabbok River (tributary of the Jordan) Jacob sent his wives, children and servants across while he remained on the other side, to pray. In the Biblical account of the early history of Israel the night that Jacob spent on the Jabbok River bank is one of the most momentous. Jacob, a weak and sinful progenitor, was accosted by God and as a result became one of the early founders of a race of people who knew God but who endlessly struggled with him. That's what Israel means: 'He struggles with God.'

The tight economy of the Biblical words hides the enormity of what happened (Gen. 32: 24-30.) The King James Version is not at all clear because it describes Jacob being accosted by God but a confusion of pronouns makes it difficult to determine who is fighting whom. The NIV makes it much clearer showing that this is not an account of a man wrestling with God as at climactic moments in our lives, some of us do. This is an account of God struggling with man. God wanted Jacob to trust him and to follow a certain course of action but Jacob was loath to do so. God never interferes with his gift of free will. He will do all he can to persuade one to do what is right but ultimately one has to make the choice oneself. What God wanted Jacob to do was to enter the Promised Land and put the meeting with Esau in God's hands.

The trouble was that Jacob's nature was to take things into his own hands. He had conned his father into giving him the all-important inheritance blessing. He had not understood the omni-presence of God and had put up a shrine to mark the place where He'd met God. He thought his cleverness with the streaked poles had made him wealthy. Jacob had still not learned. All night he resisted God. In the end God beat him down physically. He touched Jacob's hip (NIV translation) and put it out of joint. It is a major joint in the body and Jacob was instantly crippled, and must have been in considerable pain.

Pain and suffering! One of the great problems of Christianity and theism. This incident provides a partial answer: Sometimes it is only when God chastises and inflicts suffering that one understands and accepts. With Jacob in considerable pain, God, surprisingly, announced his intention to withdraw from the fray, and told Jacob to let him go. How often, in moments of pain and distress, one thinks that God has abandoned one. So with Jacob. He sensed God's withdrawal. For all his faults, however, Jacob had an unshakeable trust in God. He would not let God go. Interestingly, God did not tell Jacob his name. He knew that Jacob knew who he was, as one always knows when one hears that still, small voice, even when one tries to drown it out in the noise and busyness of life and its problems. For Jacob that was a turning point, and a huge lesson for all, not to close one's ears, not to let God go, not to turn from him, even when one is bowed down with pain, incomprehension and a sense that God has abandoned one.

What a victory Jacob achieved for himself and ultimately for everybody! While he was hanging on, he sensed God looking directly at him and asking him his name. Obviously God knew who Jacob was, but he needed Jacob to identify himself because he was about to change Jacob's name. It is always in one's moment of not letting go, that God can change who one is. He doesn't change one's character or one's personality, but when one puts oneself under his authority, he can use one's character and personality in ways that bring blessing to oneself and to others.

God told Jacob that he had prevailed. That's a wonderful moment. For all his wrong ideas and deceitfulness, Jacob had remained faithful to God. And God changed Jacob's name to Israel, meaning *he who struggles with God*. What a struggle, lasting centuries! Even when the whole purpose of it is made manifest in Jesus, most of Israel still does not understand, and, as their name and the name of their country imply, they continue to struggle with God. Jacob continued his journey towards his old home, limping. When he saw Esau coming towards him, he put his wives, concubines and children behind him and went ahead to meet the brother he had wronged. Clearly frightened, he nevertheless stuck with what God had ordered him to do and kept advancing, albeit with repeated bowing. In the end though, it was not the lame, frightened Jacob who behaved well, but the abused Esau. Esau appears the more 'Christian' of the two brothers; he rushed up, threw his arms around Jacob and welcomed him with tears of joy.

It does make one wonder. Why was Jacob the chosen one? The reason, it seems to me, is that for all his faults, Jacob was the one who walked with God. He thought of God a great deal, and that's a kind of praying, or, more correctly, it spills over into prayer very easily. Jacob did not deny the spiritual aspect of his being. That's why he had those two momentous dreams, first when he saw the stairway into the kingdom of heaven, and second when he grappled all night with God to such an extent that he emerged physically injured.

Of course, for all his geekiness and deceitfulness, Jacob did have some positive traits. He was in for the long haul. He had endurance. His years of working for Laban prove that. Instant gratification was not in his nature, as it was in Esau's. Esau was much more emotional, living for the moment, impulsive, not given to praying about things. Although he enthusiastically welcomed Jacob back, he could as furiously have rejected him. Jacob realized this. It would appear that Esau did not harbour grudges, but this seems more from thoughtlessness (and from gratitude for all the flocks) than from any moral sense.

Before I leave chapter 33, there is another verse that I find significant, verse 10. Jacob is speaking to Esau: 'For to see your face is like seeing the face of God, now that you have received me favourably.' Jacob, who had seen God's face in his dream, now saw the face of God in Esau. He saw God in kindness, forgiveness and generosity, wherever these may be found. Jacob was beginning to realize that every brother, race, nation, religion and cult, all are God's, and God is in all. The Israelites are not more beloved by God than others, but they are the ones who first recognised God, who first wrote about God, who made God known to others, and from whom Christ would come.

Although Esau asked Jacob to accompany him to his home in Seir, Jacob declined (diplomatically.) Esau set off, with his new herds, and Jacob and his family followed on slowly with the remaining herds, but they gradually turned away and moved towards Shechem in Canaan. Instinctively Jacob knew that to live close to Esau was not a good idea. The chapter ends with Jacob building an altar to God at Shechem.

Chapters 34 – 38:
Dinah and the Twelve Sons of Israel

The story of Dinah in chapter 34 is a lurid and violent one that reflects appallingly on the Israelites. There is only one positive element to be drawn from the repulsive story: It shows the Israelites in a horribly bad light. That they can describe their own treachery and viciousness in such clear, unambiguous terms, gives one confidence in their general truthfulness and objectivity. There is of course an opposing view, that as a patriarchal society they did not think their behaviour particularly immoral. I find it difficult to accept that their vicious brutality can be seen in any other way than wicked, and certainly their father, Jacob, now known as Israel, was appalled by it.

Dinah was Israel's daughter by Leah. When Israel (I'll stick with the new name now) and his family arrived in Canaan, Schechem, the son of Hamor the Hivite, saw Dinah, was instantly enraptured by her, 'took her and violated her.' One immediately thinks that this was rape. But the next few lines suggest that it was more likely a case of pre-marital sex. 'His heart was drawn to Dinah, daughter of Israel, and he loved the girl and spoke tenderly to her.' Schechem's father, Hamor, asked Israel if Schechem could marry Dinah. When Israel told his sons what had happened, they were absolutely livid. They agreed to the wedding but demanded that all the Hivites be circumcised. The Hivites accepted this but while they were still in a weakened and painful state, Israel's sons, Simeon and Levi, fell upon them and murdered them all. With the help of their other brothers, Simeon and Levi then looted the city and carried off the women, children, flocks and herds. When he heard what had happened, Israel told his sons: 'You have brought trouble on me by making me a stench to the Canaanites and Perizzites, the people living in this land.'

It's a dreadful story of deceit, murder and pillage. And not once in the entire chapter is God mentioned. He comes into the story again in the first verse of the 35th chapter, telling Israel to leave the area and settle at Bethel, which Israel did, after ordering his people to get rid of the foreign gods that they had with them. Once again truth is found in the almost throw-away lines; the people had been worshiping idols, hence God not being mentioned in the story of Dinah.

The deaths of Rachel and Isaac are recorded in chapter 35. Then in verse 22 one reads that Reuben slept with his father's concubine, Bilhah. His father never forgave him. It is followed by 'begats' showing the descendants of Israel. In chapter 36, the descendants of Esau are listed, and the chapter ends with the words, 'These were the kings who reigned in Edom before any Israelite king reigned' showing the hand of a later commentator or editor since Moses lived long before Israel became a monarchy.

Joseph and the Flamboyant Coat

Everybody knows the story of Joseph, his dreams and his brightly coloured coat. It is a story of parental favouritism and sibling jealousy. When Joseph is first encountered he is a sneaky teenage telltale. The reader has some sympathy for his brothers who are the victims of his constant tale-bearing, or 'bad reports' as the Bible puts it. Their father, Israel, added fuel to the fire by making it clear that Joseph was his favourite, probably because Joseph was his beloved

Rachel's son. Joseph's grandiose dreams started even before Rachel died. Needless to say the brothers hated him with a passion, and even Israel was angry when Joseph said he had had a dream in which his parents and his siblings all bowed to him. But, says the Bible, even though he was irritated, Israel, who had himself had two amazing dreams, consciously sought to remember Joseph's.

The brothers' chance to get their own back came when they were grazing their flocks at Dothan, and Israel sent Joseph to find out how they were doing. The brothers had no difficulty spotting Joseph when he was still a long way away because he was wearing the 'richly ornamented robe.' They decided to kill him and tell Israel that a wild animal had 'devoured him.' Only Reuben, the oldest, demurred. He persuaded the brothers to dump Joseph down a well, meaning to rescue him later, but while Reuben was out of sight, a caravan of Midianites (Ishmaelites) came by, and Judah persuaded the brothers to sell Joseph to the Midianites, because Joseph was their 'own flesh and blood.' So Judah also emerges well from the story.

When he found out what they had done, Reuben was distraught. The brothers killed a goat, smeared Joseph's coat with blood and took it back to their father, plunging Israel into bitter and despairing grief. 'All his sons and daughters came to comfort him,' the Bible tells us, and this instantly involves the reader in yet another mystery. Daughters? Israel had only one daughter, Dinah. Some have suggested that it might be referring to daughters-in-law (the eldest of the brothers had reached marriageable age) and others think some of Israel's sons had twin sisters. (Israel was himself one of a pair of twins.) Meanwhile the Midianites took Joseph to Egypt and there sold him to Potiphar, one of Pharaoh's officials.

A Feisty Ancestress of Jesus

The story of Tamar seems an irrelevant sub-plot; Yet Judah and Tamar were the parents of Perez who became the head of the leading clan of Judah, and an ancestor of David and Jesus. It is Tamar's part in the story that is so absorbing; she must have been a feisty, clear-headed, intelligent and beautiful woman.

My NIV study notes call it an unsavoury story, largely because Judah left his brothers to seek his fortune in Adullam, a Canaanite city south west of Jerusalem, and because the story deals with contraception and prostitution. I disagree with the note compilers, who are obviously of the belief that nothing good can come from the Canaanites. The fact is that Jesus comes as much from them as he does from the Israelites, because both he and David, says the Bible, were descended from Tamar.

On with the story. While Judah was in Adullam, he married a Canaanite woman by whom he had three sons, who were therefore half Canaanite. When they grew up, Judah married his first-born son, Er, to a young woman called Tamar. Er was wicked, says the Bible, so God caused him to die young. Judah resorted to the Jewish levirate law, by which a brother or other near relative slept with a widow so that she could have offspring to carry on the name of the one who had died. The second brother, Onan, was so angry that if Tamar conceived, the baby would not in law be his, that he spilled his semen on the ground, a contraceptive technique still sometimes called Onanism. God disapproved of this, so Onan died too. Judah was afraid that his youngest son, Shelah would also die if he married Tamar, so he kept Shelah at home, disobeying the levirate law. Judah's own wife died a short while later, and when he had recovered from his grief, Judah went to Timnah on business. Tamar, told that he was on the way and knowing that he was not going to allow Shelah to marry her, dressed herself provocatively, wore a veil to hide her face, and stationed herself on the road like a temple prostitute. The inevitable happened; Judah spent a night with her and promised her a goat for her services. She accepted this, provided he left his seal with its cord, as a pledge.

Three months later Judah was informed that Tamar was pregnant and guilty of prostitution. He ordered that she be burned to death. Tamar, however, had known this would happen. She sent the seal and cord to Judah telling him that it was their owner who had slept with her. On receiving the tokens, Judah said, 'She is more righteous than I since I wouldn't give her to my son Shelah.' As a result of their night together, Tamar had twins, Perez and Zerah. Perez became the ancestor of David (Ruth 4: 18-22) and ultimately of Christ. It is interesting that the Bible makes clear that in the ancestry of David and the Messiah is this outrageous, courageous and clearheaded non-Israelite woman, whose actions pulled the Israelites back into covenant obedience, not only about the rights of childless men but also about the care of widows (who would need the next generation to support them in old age.)

THE STORY OF THE TORAH
Good-looking Joseph

After the digression about Judah and Tamar, Genesis takes the reader back to Egypt and to Joseph who was a slave in the household of Potiphar. This worthy soon discovered that the well-built and handsome Joseph was an intelligent man whom he could trust. In a short space of time he had appointed him manager of his house and business. Potiphar's wife also saw that Joseph was well-built and handsome, and tried to get him to sleep with her. He refused. She enticed him into the house one day when the servants weren't there, caught him by his cloak and tried to inveigle him into going to bed with her. Pulling himself away, Joseph ran off, leaving his cloak behind. When Potiphar returned, his wife told him that Joseph had tried to violate her, and that he had run away when she screamed, leaving his cloak. Potiphar threw Joseph into jail – where he immediately became so liked and trusted by the chief warder, that he was put in charge of the other prisoners. Two of the prisoners, Pharaoh's cupbearer and baker, asked Joseph if he could interpret some strange dreams that they had had. Jacob told the baker he would be executed and the cup-bearer that he would be freed and to tell Pharaoh about his unfair imprisonment. What Joseph said happened. The cupbearer was freed, but forgot to mention Joseph's plight to Pharaoh.

For two long years, Joseph remained in prison. Then Pharaoh dreamed that seven lean cows ate seven fat cows and seven withered grain heads consumed seven plump ones. Nobody could tell him what this meant, until the cupbearer remembered Joseph, who was sent for. Pointing out that only God could interpret dreams,

Joseph told Pharaoh that seven years of good harvests would be followed by seven years of famine. He said Pharaoh should appoint a trustworthy man to save a portion of the good harvests for the years of famine. Pharaoh saw that Joseph was 'discerning and wise', and appointed him to supervise the storing of the food.

Attired in rich clothes and in charge of the whole of Egypt, Joseph carried out Pharaoh's instructions. He married Asenath, daughter of Potiphera the priest, and they had two sons, Manasseh and Ephraim. The seven years of plenty ended and the famine began. Joseph opened the store houses and rationed the grain to the hungry.

Chapters 42 – 50: Israel's Sons in Egypt and the End

The famine spread and Joseph's brothers arrived in Egypt to buy grain. Joseph recognized them but they, not surprisingly, did not see in the Egyptian governor the brother they had sold into slavery. Joseph demanded that they bring their youngest brother to him. Leaving Simeon behind as a hostage and then finding to their horror that their money had been returned, the brothers continued home and reported to Israel that the Egyptian governor wanted Benjamin. Israel refused but when the famine continued, the brothers made another trip to Egypt taking Benjamin and double the silver.

Joseph treated them all royally but this time on their return they were pursued by Joseph's steward who found their silver still in their bags and an incriminating silver cup hidden in Benjamin's. Distraught, the brothers returned to Joseph who ordered that Benjamin become his slave. Judah explained that their aged father had only two sons by the wife he had loved. The elder was dead leaving only Benjamin, whose loss would kill their father. Joseph, perceiving that the brothers felt remorseful, identified himself and told his brothers to bring their father to Egypt while the famine lasted.

After a moving reunion with his father Joseph installed his family in the Nile Delta, where their descendants were to remain for centuries. Before he died Israel blessed his sons and grandsons, insisting on giving his younger grandson, Ephraim, the elder-son blessing, and making it clear that he was adopting Joseph's sons. After his father died Joseph took the embalmed body back to Canaan and interred it in the cave where his ancestors were buried. After several years Joseph too died, after securing a promise from the Israelites that they would take his bones back to Canaan when God took them 'to the land he promised you.'

End of the Beginning

We've come to the end of the beginning, with Israel in Egypt, many questions raised, and few answered. What does a 21st Century reader make of it all? As I said at the start, it depends on who you are and what your beliefs are. What we've seen is that Genesis falls into two distinct sections. First is the attempt by a Bronze Age people to account for the existence of the world and everything in it. They come to the conclusion that we inhabit an orderly universe and that God created it. There is an attempt to grapple with the problem of evil and suffering, and the beginning of a realization that it is a spiritual problem and will finally have to be resolved on that level.

The people who produce this account are Israelites, and the second section of the book is their attempt to record their own early history. Their stories and meditations appear at the dawn of man's ability to write, and although some at least of the book derives from the oral tradition, there are indications that some very ancient writing may lie at the heart of Genesis. One has to keep reminding oneself that those ancient languages had limited vocabularies compared with the enormous vocabularies that modern languages enjoy. It must have been difficult for those early writers to express complex philosophical ideas with a limited range of words. Yet they managed to produce an astonishing piece of writing.

There are those who criticise the Bible in general and Genesis in particular for being partly responsible for the world's misogyny. They say Genesis blames Eve for the fall of man, resulting in centuries of women being denigrated and given inferior status by adherents of the Abrahamic faiths. I find that an absurd reading of Genesis. This was a dangerous period in human history; civilisation was collapsing. If a people were to make it through the destructive horror that surrounded them, there had to be a clear division of labour with men protecting the tribe and women caring for the next generation. Much that seems like misogyny was merely the attempt by a small and dispossessed people to ensure their survival. Apart from everything else, the beginning of Genesis does not answer all the questions. It asks them. Could there have been an ideal existence before this fraught one of evil and suffering, and was that a realm to which spiritual man can aspire? The prophecy that through the offspring of Abraham all the world will be blessed, introduces the concept of the Messiah, the one who will open access to that ideal world for all. For Christians, Genesis opens with three of the most profound verses in the Bible, the revelation of God the Holy Trinity, before space, before time, in the beginning. This is the supreme revelation of the Bible: That God is, that he exists as creative Father of the Universe, verse one, as life-permeating Holy Spirit, verse two, and as Light of the World and Redeemer, verse three. I know that if natural scientists happen to read this they will throw their hands up in horror.

Yet I was listening to some of them on Melvyn Bragg's Radio 4 programme 'In Our Time' recently, the one about the cell, basic building block of life[31], what the atom is to physics. Melvyn Bragg's guests were Steve Jones, Professor of Genetics at University College, London, Nick Lane, Senior Lecturer in the Department of Genetics, Evolution and Environment, also at University College, London, and Cathie Martin, Group Leader at the John Innes Centre and Professor in the School of Biological Sciences at the University of East Anglia.

From what they said it seems that to produce a single living cell, there had to be the right chemistry and a non-oxygen environment, which they said was exactly how it was on earth some three and a half to four billion years ago. But even with chemical conditions perfect, 'you need *a driving force* to force these things into existence,' said Steve Jones. Vital too, said Cathie Martin, was that a cell had to have a bubble-like cover, a cell membrane, to separate its speck of life from the muddy soup of chemicals around it. A member of the panel quoted Erwin Schrödinger who said that life was a little patch

---

[31] BBC Iplayer Radio 4 Melvyn Bragg *In Our Time, The Cell*

of order in a sea of chaos. Order from chaos! An ancient description of how God created the world.

For millennia it seems that life remained at the single-cell stage. Steve Jones took up the story and said that what happened then was a quantum jump! Single-cellular organisms couldn't develop into multi-cellular organisms because they were too energy deficient. But suddenly something occurred, a once-off. It's never happened again. (No-one asked why it hasn't happened again. Why isn't it still happening?) Apparently one cell engulfed another and made use of its energy. From that single event, every form of multi-cellular life developed, and nobody knows why. This is not a God-of-the-gaps argument. It is an argument from the known. These scientists tell us that this happened, and it happened only once, like the Big Bang. It's the answer to *why* it happened that they are unable to give.

'This is one of the most fascinating mysteries at the heart of Biology,' said Nick Lane. 'It happened just once but every single form of multi-cellular life can be traced back to that single event – fungus, ferns, plants, trees, fish, mammals, man.' The new cell that formed from the merger is known as a Eukaryotic Cell. All multi-cellular organisms on earth contain Eukaryotic cells. So how life originated is more complex than anybody ever imagined. To hear those front-line scientists say they do not know what the *driving force* was, or *why* multi-cellular life came into being the way it did, that it happened only once and never again, that when life first began, oxygen would have killed it, so there was no oxygen, and when life began to need oxygen, there it was, all this points towards God, the author of life. By what those scientists revealed, God is more awe-inspiring than anybody has ever imagined. In the same way that He created multi-cellular life in that blinding once-off moment of love and union, so in an equally mysterious, quantum-leap moment, his holy spirit invaded a species of physical life, granting it language and conscience and knowledge. Nobody can know what God gained by doing this. What I do know is that without the mysterious driving force that empowers both the physical and spiritual aspects of my being, I would not be me.

Part Three
Entrance to Exodus

The Ten Commandments

Introduction

If it were merely an account of how the Israelites escaped from bondage in Egypt, then Exodus, the second book of the Bible, would be of little more significance than, say, Homer's Odyssey. I'm not trying to belittle the Odyssey, which is also an epic account of a long journey home, but Exodus is more than that. For one thing, it contains one of the world's first great moral codes, the Ten Commandments, an astonishing achievement for a Late-Bronze-Age people. For another, Exodus continues to explore the Israelites' evolving understanding of a God who is light years more complex and awesome than the gods of the Greek pantheon. Genesis introduced God the Trinity, creator of the universe. Exodus continues the revelation showing God as outside time and space but as the immanent and spiritual source and sustainer of life. A third reason for reading Exodus is that it begins the story of Moses. Whatever one thinks of Moses, whether one regards him as a mythical or an historical character, he strides out of ancient writing like a Colossus. Of all the B.C. heroes of Ancient Greece and the Middle East, there is none more powerful, more moral, more wise or more courageous than Moses. Finally, like the Odyssey, Exodus tells a darn good story, describing a miraculous escape of a people who after many struggles, like Odysseus, find their way back home. (Of course they don't get back until the end of the Torah and don't begin to settle down in

Canaan until the Books of Joshua and Judges but much of the story occurs in Exodus.)

As to who wrote Exodus, and when, the same thing can be said about it as about Genesis. It may have been written by Moses – or parts of it may have been. Some parts were certainly inserted afterwards. What cannot be denied is that towards the end of the second millennium B.C. the Israelites were established in Canaan, and somehow they must have got there, and someone must have led them. The Biblical version may well be the answer to both those questions.

Chapter 1: Israel in Egypt

'These are the names of the sons of Israel...' are the first words of Exodus, and that is what the Hebrews call the book: *Sh'mot* meaning *These are the Names*. The name *Exodos,* meaning exit or departure, was given to the book in the third century B.C. by the Septuagint translators. Israel's sons 'were fruitful and multiplied greatly,' says Exodus, so much so that the Egyptians began to fear them, and a new king enslaved and oppressed them. There are many questions that arise right here, at the beginning of the book. Among them are:

- Can archaeology or ancient Egyptian texts prove that the Israelites were ever in Egypt?
- Were they enslaved?
- Did the Egyptians in fact have slaves at all?

- Did Hebrew slaves help to build the pyramids or any other ancient Egyptian structures, as claimed in some famous – or infamous – Hollywood films?

First, the slavery issue. Yes, the Egyptians did have slaves; they are referred to in some ancient Egyptian writings[32]. The Great Harris Papyrus (it is 41 metres long and is in the British Museum) gives an account of Rameses III of the 20th Dynasty adding up his spoils of war which included '295 male and female slaves.'

Next question: Among the slaves in Egypt was there ever a large body of Israelites? What the Bible says is that when Israel escaped from Egypt, Israel had more than half a million fighting men. Extrapolated from this, the Israelites would have numbered about two million. The entire population of Egypt was only about three and a half million at that time, so the number of Israelites doesn't sound very likely, until one remembers that throughout history when the citizens of wealthy and powerful countries do not want to do menial or low-paid work, slaves or cheap-labour immigrants do it. It is in the nature of things that these inevitably hard-working labourers begin to increase in number, and some even bring their relatives from abroad, until there are so many of them that they become a 'problem.'

Did Israelite slaves help to build the pyramids? No. There is no indication in the Bible that they did, and the best date for the

---

[32] Breasted, James Henry, Translator: *Ancient Records of Egypt, Vol 4, The Twentieth to the Twenty Sixth Dynasties,* paperback edition, University of Illinois Press, Chicago, 2001, The Great Harris Papyrus from page 151

Israelites' presence in Egypt was 800 years after Pharaoh Cheops built the pyramids. What the Bible does say is that the Israelites were made to build the store cities of Pithom and Rameses, supporting Joseph's being appointed by Pharaoh to provide storage facilities for grain.

There are currently two possible dates for the exodus. The first is suggested by 1 Kings 6:1 that says the exodus occurred 480 years before Solomon built the temple, putting it somewhere between 1450 and 1440 B.C when Thutmosis III was Pharaoh. The second date is about 1290 B.C. when Rameses II (1279-1213 B.C.) was Pharaoh. Moses was an old man when he led the Israelites out of Egypt, so if Thutmosis III was the exodus king, Moses probably grew up in the reigns of Thutmosis I and II. Thutmosis is often spelled Thutmose, similar to Moses's own name, which is Egyptian, although some authorities think it has a Hebrew root. It seems that the Israelites were in Egypt at the time that the country was a colony of the Hyksos, a Semitic people who overran northern Egypt at the time of the decline of the Middle Kingdom. It was a confused time which produced hardly any monuments or records. This would explain why almost nothing about the Israelites was recorded. The Hyksos conquered the delta region of Egypt, where Joseph had settled his family. They were never much concerned with southern Egypt, the Nile Valley area.

It seems obvious that a Semitic king, or pharaoh, would have been well disposed towards the Hebrews, also a Semitic people. Exactly what proportion of the Semites were Israelites one cannot know. Some authorities think all the Hyksos were Israelites and that the Exodus happened when Pharaoh Ahmose drove them out.

Perhaps the truth lies somewhere between; it might have taken the Egyptians a while to drive out all the Semites (Hyksos, Phoenicians and Israelites) beginning with Ahmose's persecution of the Hyksos and not finishing until the plagues. It seems increasingly likely that the Israelites migrated from Egypt to Canaan from the 1400s B.C. until the 1200s. Somewhere in that time a fairly substantial group left, the Exodus.

The recent deciphering of the Hieroglyphic inscriptions on an ancient Egyptian granite block, acquired in 1913 by German archaeologist Ludwig Borchardt and now in the Egyptian Museum of Berlin, supports the theory that the Israelites arrived in Canaan from about 1400 B.C. The inscriptions have been conclusively deciphered as mentioning three races 'falling', Ashkelon, Canaan and Israel, proving that Israel was already in existence by then. Dated to the thirteenth century B.C. it is the oldest extra-Biblical support for the existence of Israel yet found. (Borchardt is the archaeologist who found the famous bust of Queen Nefertiti.)

Chapters 2 – 3: Drown all the Boy Babies

According to the first chapter of Exodus a new king who did not know about Joseph feared the rate at which the Israelite numbers were increasing and ordered that Israelite boy babies be drowned. A Levite mother, Jochebed, placed her baby, Moses, in a papyrus basket waterproofed with pitch and launched it on the river. There is a similar story about the babyhood of Sargon of Akkad who lived long before Moses, but the tablet on which the Sargon story was found (in the library of Ashurbanipal) has been dated to centuries after Moses.

Moses's elder sister, Miriam, saw the Egyptian princess come down to the river to bathe, see the little boat among the reeds and send one of her maids to fetch it. That it was a princess who found the baby meant that not only did she have the authority to override the execution order, but also that she was able when he was weaned to have him with her at the royal court where he was assured of the best education available at the time. He would almost certainly have been taught to write.

Manslaughter and Escape to Midian

In spite of his privileged upbringing, Moses continued to feel deep sympathy for his enslaved family and for the rest of the Israelites. It led to his killing an Egyptian who was abusing an Israelite. When the killing became known and he realized that he was in danger of being arrested and executed, he escaped into exile, reaching the country of Midian. There he helped a group of seven sisters who, when they tried to water their flocks, were being driven away by some shepherds. The sisters were the daughters of a priest, Reuel, which means 'Friend of God'. Reuel was also called Jethro, which might be a title meaning 'Excellency.' This is another case of a priest of God who was not an Israelite, reminding one of Melchizedek.

Reuel invited Moses to stay and gave him his daughter, Zipporah, as a wife. They had a son, Gershom, meaning 'alien in a foreign land'. Nobody knows exactly where Midian was; some authorities believe it was in the southeast region of the Sinai Peninsula, and some that it was in the western section of Saudi Arabia. So the location of Mount Horeb is not known, but it was at the base of this mountain, when Moses was tending his father-in-law's flocks, that an astounding revelation about the nature of God was made.

THE BURNING BUSH AND THE NAME OF GOD

It happened when Moses, perhaps sitting on a rocky outcrop, was idly watching the sheep grazing below him. He noticed something really weird, a bush on fire but not burning up. Mystified and uncomprehending, he continued to watch it, unable to understand why it did not turn to ash. Sceptics deny that Moses could have seen any such thing. One explanation is that he had partaken of a hallucinogenic substance; the one most commonly cited is *Amarita Muscaria,* the traditional white-spotted red toadstool which is hallucinogenic but also poisonous if not cooked long enough in masses of leaching water. There is absolutely no indication in the Bible that Moses was either ill or under the influence of drugs. I think one can safely jettison that idea. Another explanation is that Moses came across a flowery shrub called *Dictamnus Albus,* also known as dittany or fraxinella and even Burning Bush. It exudes volatile methane gas and if you hold a match or a lighter to a flower stalk, flames whoosh up it; but it lasts only an instant, whereas what Moses encountered was a bush that burned and burned but did not shrivel up.

After watching it for a bit, Moses carefully approached it, and that was when God called him by name. God chose for Moses to see something, consciously or subconsciously, that would focus his attention completely, sweeping everything else from his mind, enabling him to hear God's voice. What followed is one of the most significant incidents in the Old Testament. Moses learned not only the name of God but also something about God's essential nature. God told Moses to take off his shoes because he was standing on holy ground. That is an absorbing detail, the need to feel the earth beneath one's feet, not a floor, not a road, not the leather of shoes or sandals, but the earth, made by God and from which all humans are made; the earth is holy ground. One needs at times to feel it beneath one's feet, to surrender to the moment, to reconcile with the origin of one's being and to feel the presence of God.

As Moses stood there, the desert sand and rock beneath his feet, deeply immersed in the world of the spirit, God told him that he had seen the suffering of his people in Egypt and he wanted Moses to go back to Egypt and to tell pharaoh to let his people go. The first thing Moses felt was that he was not the right person for the job, but God said he was and that when he brought the Israelites out, he would bring them to this very mountain where they would worship Him. Moses said that the Israelites would want to know what God's name was. It seems that Moses was aware that his fellow Israelites were worshiping the pantheon of Egyptian and Mesopotamian gods. Here is God's reply from the King James Bible: And God said unto Moses: 'I am that I am.' And he told Moses to tell the Israelites that 'I am' had sent Moses to them.

In God's own still, small voice comes this amazing revelation of his being. When God speaks of himself, he calls himself 'I am' and when people speak of him, they call him 'He is,' which is what JHWH (or YHWH) Jahweh, means: 'He is.' God exists in eternity, outside time and space. He, quite simply, is. It is astounding that a seer of the Bronze Age could have gained such an insight into the nature of God, a realization that he is beyond birth and death, eternal, outside time, and it is striking that this understanding was derived through the power of the word, through language, through grammar. The first person singular of the verb 'to be' is the name of God. It expresses eternal existence, 'I am.' It's a revelation that came from the creator of the word, from God Himself. And it explains why the Temple authorities were so furious when someone asked Jesus if he was a reincarnation of Abraham and he replied: 'Before Abraham was, I am.' (John 8: 58) He was claiming co-existence, co-being, with God. He had just told them that he was, 'The light of the world,' (John 8: 12) reminding one of the opening of Genesis which shows him as the creator of light. To the temple authorities, his final claim that he was in some mysterious way in co-being with God was the ultimate blasphemy and they picked up stones to kill him there and then but as they were bending down to find stones, he disappeared

An obvious question is why God chose Moses as the first recipient of such a revelation? And a possible answer is that in this world of freedom of choice, Moses was one who devoted time and energy to search deep within himself for the source of his being. As he watched over Jethro's flocks on the far side of Mount Horeb, deep in thought and meditation, God set not only the bush alight, but also the flickering spirit within Moses himself. Moses became God's chosen instrument in His rescue plan for man's immortal soul. When Moses finally understood and accepted what God wanted him to do, and in spite of his fear that he was unequal to the task, he never again wavered in his commitment to carry out God's instructions in spite of all that was hurled against him. Looking back on this incident from more than three thousand years later, it is easy for a twenty first century reader to see that everything about Moses made him the right person to negotiate the Israelites' exodus from Egypt, and to write down the revelations about God. Moses could easily have been well acquainted with the new king because they would have been boys together at the royal court. He spoke the language and understood the customs of the Egyptian court. He had received the best education available in the world at that time. He could write. He was a Hebrew. He was the right man.

It is interesting that God told Moses that Pharaoh would not immediately comply when Moses asked him to let the Israelites go. He was warning Moses that there was an uphill struggle ahead, and stiffening his resolve.

Chapter 4: Another Serpent

In Chapter four one reads that God gave Moses some notable assistance for the huge task ahead – the ability to work miracles. God changed the everyday staff that Moses was carrying, probably a shepherd's crook, into a powerful symbol of authority. When Moses, ordered to do so by God, threw the staff onto the ground, it became a snake and Moses fled from it. God ordered him to go back and pick it up and when he did so, it reverted to being a staff. One has to wonder why it became a snake. It seems that from the beginning, the Bible warns against judgmentalism by showing that goodness and evil are linked in every human psyche. One should restrict one's battle against evil to that which lurks in one's own soul and not concern oneself with the evil that one thinks exists in the souls of others. So Moses's staff had both good and evil twisted into its substance; on the one hand it was able to part the Red Sea so that the Israelites could cross in safety and on the other it could become a death-dealing serpent poised to attack. This linking good and evil in a snake appears elsewhere in the Bible.

The Ancient Israelites use three different words for 'serpent' in the Torah. For the one in the Garden of Eden and here in Exodus they use the word Nahash, clearly an onomatopoeic word, and in fact it does also mean hiss or mutter or whisper. It also means to enchant or mesmerise, as a snake often does with its prey, and as the serpent in Genesis seems to have done with Eve. Then there's the word 'seraph' which means 'fiery, flying serpent.' A third word is 'Tanniyn' which translates as dragon, serpent, crocodile or sea monster. Later in the story one reads that God ordered Moses to make a bronze snake, fix it to a staff, and hold it high over the heads of the Israelites so that they could look on it to save themselves from a plague of snakes that had attacked them in the desert. The Hebrew word for the brazen serpent or bronze snake was Nehustan.

Moses Returns to Egypt

In spite of the miraculous powers being given to him, Moses pointed out to God that he had a weakness that would compromise his ability to lead the Israelites. He was not a good speaker; he was slow of tongue, not eloquent. It's almost certain, of course, that having been brought up in the Egyptian court, he did not speak

Hebrew very well. God said that Aaron, his brother, could be his speaker. Finally Moses agreed to embark on this enormous quest. He picked up his staff, and returned to Jethro to tell him what had happened and what God had commanded. Jethro blessed him and told him to obey God and do what he had been ordered to do, so Moses left for Egypt with his wife, Zipporah and his sons, Gershom and Eliezer.

There's a disturbing idea in the twenty first verse of the fourth chapter when God says about Pharaoh, 'But I will harden his heart so that he will not let the people go. Then say to Pharaoh, 'This is what the Lord says: Israel is my firstborn son, and I told you, Let my son go so he may worship me. But you refused to let him go; so I will kill your firstborn son.' If the hardness of Pharaoh's heart came from God, is God responsible for evil? And doesn't it show a vengeful nature in God to kill Pharaoh's firstborn son because Pharaoh wouldn't let God's firstborn son (Israel) go? As always, it's easy to give glib answers to this, or duck the question altogether, but neither of those will do. One really has to grapple with it.

Probably the most acceptable response is that people act within the parameters of their beings, and God, standing outside time and space, is aware of their thoughts and allows them to act as they choose. God knew that Pharaoh was a dictator who employed slaves and was unlikely to want to let them go. He didn't make Pharaoh like that – Pharaoh chose to be like that.

In support of this is an idea from E W Bullinger[33] who in *Figures of Speech in the Bible,* points out that in both Hebrew and Greek there is a figure of speech whereby the active form of the verb means to *allow* something rather than actually to do it. An example is in the Second book of Samuel, ninth verse of the twelfth chapter: The prophet Nathan is explaining to David how he has sinned, and he says: 'You struck down Uriah the Hittite with the sword.' Of course David did not do that himself. He contrived to have Uriah placed in a position where it could happen. So when God says he will harden Pharaoh's heart, it could mean that God knows how Pharaoh will act and will allow him to do so. He will not impose His will on Pharaoh. Never, in the Bible, is God's gift of free will compromised. Not for Pharaoh. Not for Judas. Not for the High Priest Caiaphas. Not for Pontius Pilate. Not for you. Not for me. It is an absolute gift. God appeals to one and tries to persuade one, as he does with Pharaoh, but ultimately, the choice is one's own.

Now for another extraordinary bit in the Exodus story. Having chosen Moses to lead the Israelites out of Egypt, God stopped Moses and his family on their journey to Egypt and threatened to kill Moses! (Chapter 4, verse 24) Zipporah, the wife of Moses, thought she knew why God was angry with Moses. As a Hebrew Moses would have wanted his firstborn son, Gershom, circumcised, but Zipporah had not wanted this inflicted on her son. When, however, she saw that God was going to take the life of Moses (perhaps he had some dreadful disease and was hovering on the very edge of

---

[33] Bullinger E W *Figures of Speech Used in the Bible,* Cornell University Library, Internet Archive, accessed 2016

life) she relented, and herself performed the operation on Gershom. She laid the foreskin on the feet of Moses to prove she had done it.

In Rabbinical literature is an interesting postscript to this story. The Talmudists have a belief that Jethro gave Zipporah to Moses on condition that their first son be brought up worshiping idols, and that Moses swore to respect this condition[34]. Hence God's anger with him. But it could be that the Talmudists created this story to be disparaging of the non-Hebrew Jethro. (The Talmud contains the opinions of thousands of rabbis on subjects pertaining to their history, religion and culture.) The Bible does not support this interpretation; it describes Jethro as a holy man, not an idol worshipper. He had come to know God himself (one reads later how important a part he played in the writing of the Ten Commandments.)

The Samaritan Pentateuch (the first five books as they developed in Northern Israel, Samaria) has a very plausible rendition of this story, and it has nothing to do with circumcision. It says God did not want Zipporah and her two sons to accompany Moses when he set out for Egypt. When he hovered on the brink of death, she knew why God was angry. So she mutilated herself, not her son, to express her guilt and remorse. There are two ancient Hebraic words at issue here: The Masoretic Text has 'b'nah' (her son) while the Samaritan Pentateuch has 'binnah' meaning 'her understanding' or 'blocked heart.' According to the Samaritan Pentateuch, Zipporah returned to her father with the children while Moses went on to Egypt. This actually makes more sense of even the Masoretic Text because one

---

[34] *Jethro in Rabbinic Literature,* Mek.l.c.; Yalk.,Ex 169

does not hear of Zipporah or her sons again until much later in the story when the Israelites were at last approaching the mountain where God had said they would worship him. On hearing that they were coming, Jethro took Zipporah and the two boys to be re-united with Moses. But when had Moses parted with his family? Without the Samaritan Pentateuch one would have no idea.

Immediately after this story one reads that God appeared to Aaron, Moses's brother, and told him that Moses was on the way and that Aaron should go to the desert to meet him, which Aaron duly did and kissed his brother after what must have been a long separation. Moses told Aaron that God wanted him to lead the Israelites to freedom. Aaron undertook to tell the people, so the brothers returned to the Israelite quarter and called the elders together. With Moses standing by and prompting him, Aaron told them that God had seen their misery and had sent Moses to deliver them.

Chapters 5 - 6: Three Days or Forever?

The brothers' first move, described at the beginning of chapter five, made things worse for the Israelites, not better. They sought an audience with Pharaoh and asked if he would allow the Hebrews to go into the desert for three days to worship God, an idea first propounded by God in chapter three. Three days? The Israelites intended to leave for good. Did God suggest they lie to Pharaoh as a means of escaping? Generations of scribes must have thought about this, yet they were never tempted to remove this bit from the story. Some commentators feel that in the Bronze Age tricksterism was an acceptable way of dealing with corrupt power and tyranny, and certainly in the books ahead one will read that Israel's great military commanders, Joshua and David among them, regularly used surprise, diversion and ambush as strategies. Could Israel's struggle to escape from Egypt be seen in the same way? What is certain is that God knew that there was no way in which Pharaoh was going to allow his entire work force to leave Egypt for good, but there was a possibility that he would let them go on a pilgrimage for three days although initially he would not allow even that. He refused angrily when Moses asked, accusing them of laziness and of trying to get out of work. He said he would make things more difficult for them; in future no straw would be provided for the Israelites' brick-making. In spite of all their efforts the slaves were unable to fill their quotas, and Pharaoh refused to relent. The Israelites accused Moses and Aaron of making their people 'a stench' to Pharaoh. Moses cried out to God that he had not rescued his people at all but had brought worse trouble on them.

God told him that He was the God of Abraham, Isaac and Israel, and that he would give to their descendants the land that he had promised. Strengthened by this reminder of their history and of God's promises to his ancestors, Moses tried again to persuade the Israelites to believe that God would free them. They refused to listen to him. Holding firmly to God's promises, Moses decided that he and Aaron would go to Pharaoh and repeat the request that he release the Israelites, although part of him did wonder why Pharaoh should listen to him when the Israelites themselves wouldn't.

Chapters 7 – 11: The Plagues

Still apprehensive 'I speak with faltering lips' but determined to obey God, Moses approached Pharaoh, wondering whether he would even be given a hearing. At this stage God gave Moses a strange piece of encouragement. 'See,' he said, 'I have made you like God to Pharaoh.' Humble and quiet by nature, Moses had no idea how he appeared to others; however, the Pharaohs' belief that they were gods predisposed them towards the possibility of encountering gods in human flesh, and it seems that Pharaoh did indeed see something godlike in Moses. Instead of throwing the two brothers out, he asked them to show him a miraculous sign. Aaron threw his staff on the ground, and it became a snake. The Hebrew word for 'snake' here is *Tanniyn*, which translates as serpent, dragon, sea monster or crocodile. Almost certainly crocodile is meant, because the Egyptians believed in a crocodile god called Sobek. When Pharaoh's own magicians were also able to convert their staves into crocodiles, Aaron's crocodile swallowed theirs, suggesting that the God of the Israelites was more powerful than the Egyptian gods and would in the end defeat them. Pharaoh did not think that the magical demonstrations were particularly impressive. He hardened his heart and refused to set the Israelites free.

Now began the plagues. One cannot read about them without remembering that all this was happening at the time of the Bronze Age Collapse. The dreadful droughts, dried up rivers and devastating storms that one reads about in the Torah description of the plagues suggest a time of volatile weather that may have been precipitated by volcanic activity, earthquakes and/or a bursting asteroid, all of which would have caused a deep disturbance in the earth's atmosphere.

The Ipuwer Papyrus

Reading about the plagues is an opportune moment to consider the Ipuwer Papyrus[35] which was acquired in 1828 by the Dutch Government from an Armenian collector of Egyptian antiquities. The date of the papyrus now in the Leyden Museum in Holland is disputed but it seems to be from somewhere between the beginning of the Ancient Egyptian Middle Kingdom and the Second Intermediate Period. It was translated by Alan Gardiner and describes a chaotic time in Egypt when there was starvation, drought and an escape of slaves. As usual there are Egyptologists who say the Papyrus refers to earlier events, and some who say it refers to later events, than the plagues of Exodus. Others say that the similarities are too marked to be ignored.

The first plague was the turning to blood of all the water in Egypt. The Ipuwer Papyrus says there was plague throughout the land, that blood was everywhere, that the river was blood, that all was ruin. Whatever else, it seems that either the Nile was infested with red algae or it was low and contaminated and the waters instead of flowing clean and strongly were stagnant, stank and were the dark brown colour of old blood. Exodus says that Pharaoh turned his

---

[35] Papyrus Leyden 1344, Egyptian hieratic, Dutch National Museum of Antiquities, Leyden, translated By Alan Gardiner (1879-1963)

back on everything and 'went into his palace and did not take even this to heart.'

None of the three plagues in chapter eight, frogs, gnats and flies, finds a direct echo in the Ipuwer Papyrus. It seems likely, however, that such disasters would have followed contamination of the river; frogs would have left the stinking water, and gnats and flies would have erupted from maggots as small animals began to die of poison and thirst. In the ninth chapter larger animals began to die. The papyrus states that all the animals wept in their hearts, and the cattle moaned. 'Behold cattle are left to stray and there is none to gather them together.' Because the next plague affected humans, perhaps a human form of anthrax or bubonic plague.

Pharaoh still refused to let the Israelites go, and a plague of hail destroyed the harvest. In Chapter 9, verse 23, one reads that the Lord sent thunder and hail, and lightning flashed down to the ground. The Ipuwer Papyrus says gates, columns and walls were consumed by fire. Such a devastating hail storm would of course annihilate the crops. I have watched many a severe hail storm in South Africa come sweeping down from the peaks of the Drakensberg in ominous-looking navy blue or deep green clouds, with crashing thunder and bolts of lightning looking like columns of fire linking heaven and earth. Enormous hailstones batter cars into wrecks, flatten fields of cereal and strip branches and leaves from trees. When after the storm one ventures outside the smell of battered greenery is as if all the world's aromatic herbs have been pounded to pulp in a giant mortar and pestle. In the Ipuwer Papyrus one reads, 'That has perished which was yesterday seen. The land is left over to weariness.' With the vegetation stripped away, the flax and barley harvest ruined and hardship staring his people in the face, Pharaoh finally yielded and agreed to let the Israelites go, but when Moses stretched out his hands in prayer and the dreadful storms abated, Pharaoh hardened his heart again, and forbade them to leave.

The next plague was locusts. Now it was the turn of the wheat and spelt, both of which ripened after the flax and barley, to be destroyed as only a swarm of locusts can do. I've seen this too in Africa, the sudden emergence after the first rains of the 'voetgangers' literally foot goers, the pre-flight stage in the locusts' development. When eradication of the voetgangers is not adequate, the great swarms take to the skies, and where they descend comes complete destruction of every leaf and blade. The locusts came down in Egypt. The Ipuwer Papyrus says that neither fruit nor herbage can be found.

With the last bits of harvest annihilated, Pharaoh agreed to let the Israelites go, and again Moses prayed for the plague to stop. A strong wind carried the locust swarms towards the Red Sea. Pharaoh went back on his word, precipitating the penultimate plague, darkness. This was possibly a sand storm; they blow across Egypt each spring. With the topsoil in the valley and delta dry and loose after the failed harvests, this one must have been particularly severe. In the Ipuwer Papyrus it says: 'The land is without light.'

The Ipuwer Papyrus says nothing about the final plague, the deaths of the firstborn. There is a theory that after the first nine plagues the Egyptians resorted to sacrificing their first-born children. The Israelites marked their homes so that the sacrifice would not be demanded of them. Perhaps. One can only speculate. What Exodus says is that God told Moses to prepare the people for imminent escape, firstly by asking their long-suffering Egyptian neighbours for silver and gold. Now there's an odd notion. When you think about it, however, it makes sort of sense. The Israelites would have made no secret of the fact that it was their God that was responsible for the succession of disasters that had befallen Egypt, so one can well believe that the Egyptians were prepared to pay them to go.

CHAPTER 12:
THE PASSOVER

Moses told the Israelites that so important was the night that lay ahead of them that God said they had to set their calendar by it. The first Passover was to be the first day of the first month of the first year. In the same way Christians would set their own calendar by the birth of Jesus. God's instruction concerning the Passover was that only the Israelites themselves and foreigners who had been circumcised could commemorate it. There could be no mixing of this festival with those pertaining to man-made or natural deities. To commemorate it they had to eat only unleavened bread for a week and then they would be able to partake of the Passover festival at which lamb would be served.

The Israelites began their preparations. At twilight the head of each Israelite family killed, seasoned with bitter herbs, roasted, carved and issued to his family portions of an unblemished year-old lamb. Small families had to share with one another and no waste was allowed. Any parts of the lamb not eaten were burned. They ate late at night, standing, ready to go, their sandals on and their staves to hand. There was no time for bread to rise; it was packed in kneading troughs to be carried on their shoulders. As ordered, they had painted some of the blood of the lambs they had slaughtered on their doorframes, a sign to the Lord to *pass them over*.

The obvious question is why on earth the Israelites had to do this last thing. God is omniscient. He knew which were Israelites and which were unbelieving Egyptians, although here, let it be said, some Egyptians, thinking it expedient, did exactly what the Israelites were doing. Many of them escaped from Egypt with the Israelites that night (Ex 12: 38). The best answer to the whole problem of why the blood of an innocent, year-old, unblemished lamb had to be painted on the doorways of Israelite homes comes from Christianity. In fact it is the only answer that makes sense. For Christians Christ is the Passover Lamb. When the Israelites (who were obviously no less sinful than the Egyptians) painted their homes with the blood of lambs that night, saving themselves from the angel of death, they unknowingly began the ministry of Christ. Clearly, omniscient God did not need this amazing bit of theatre to show him which people were Israelites and which Egyptians. But the Israelites and the Egyptians needed it. They needed to be part of a ritual enactment that would reach fulfilment only a thousand years later. God insisted that the Israelites re-enact the Passover every year for century after century, and date their calendars from it, and so they did, until Christ lived, died and rose. Only then did painting the doorway of a house with the blood of a lamb make utter and glorious sense. Christ is the world's Passover lamb. John the Baptist, St John and St Paul all called Jesus the Lamb of God. Like the lamb of the Israelite Passover, He offered himself in the early prime of his life. He was unblemished; even Pontius Pilate at his trial declared him innocent. The hyssop branch, with which the blood had to be painted on the door frames presages the Hyssop branch that lifted a sponge of moisture to the lips of the dying Jesus (John 19:28-29.) And Jesus was crucified at the time of the Passover Festival; all four gospels confirm this.

What Christians believe is that by having enough faith to apply the sacrifice of Christ to the portals of their lives, they can prevent God from dealing justly with their unrighteousness, thus enabling them to be passed over by spiritual death (the gift of mercy) and to be granted undeserved forgiveness and spiritual immortality (the gift of grace). It doesn't mean that Christians can sin with impunity. Those who love Christ try to lead lives of goodness and service, not to earn their way into heaven, they can't, but to express their endless gratitude to the one who alone saved them from deserved punishment and won for them spiritual immortality. Jesus achieved it with supreme personal sacrifice, and all He asked of humanity in return was that they loved and served one another, repented when they had done wrong, tried to do better, and left the rest to him.

Because Pharaoh refused to yield, Egyptian firstborn began to die at midnight. Appalled, Pharaoh summoned Moses in the middle of the night. He told Moses that the Israelites had to leave Egypt immediately. Here are Pharaoh's final words, from the King James: 'Also take your flocks and your herds, as ye have said, and be gone; and bless me also.' Why did Pharaoh ask for a blessing from the man that he believed was responsible for the dreadful scourges that had ravaged his country and taken the life of his son? All that I can think is that, as God had said would happen, Pharaoh had come to see that the God of Moses was indeed the Lord. One does not read that Moses blessed Pharaoh. It sounds as if he simply walked away. The incident remains one of those odd anomalies that give biblical accounts more credibility, not less, because it portrays Moses in an ambivalent if not a downright negative way, while showing Pharaoh in a sympathetic light. It is a pity that Moses did not respond to Pharaoh's request for a blessing, and it is an even bigger pity that Pharaoh's change of heart did not last long. Urged on by their distraught neighbours, and passed over by the Angel of Death, the Israelites fled (Exodus 12:51.) A last word from the Ipuwer Papyrus: It tells how the Egyptians 'lament that servants are leaving servitude and acting rebelliously.'

Chapters 13 – 14: Miraculous Crossing of the Red Sea

The first half of chapter thirteen repeats God's instruction that the Passover be remembered and celebrated by the Israelites as long as they lived in the land that God had promised them. This insistence on remembrance is because the Passover had to be enshrined in the national memory so that the Israelites would recognise the Messiah when He came to fulfil the law. The second half of the chapter has the Israelites leaving Succoth (whereabouts unknown.) They probably avoided the direct route to Canaan along the Mediterranean coast because it was well protected with Egyptian forts. More than likely they travelled down the Sinai Peninsula, which means they would have had to cross one of the two gulfs. The Red Sea splits around the Sinai Peninsula with the Gulf of Suez on the left and the Gulf of Aqaba on the right.

The Story of the Torah

As they fled, they were led by the Spirit of God in the form of a pillar of cloud during the day, and a pillar of fire during the night. Still frightened and unsure, the Israelites needed this mysterious and mystical revelation of the presence of God. It was while they were encamped near Pi Hahiroth, between Migdol and the sea (these sites have never been accurately identified) that they saw the Egyptian chariots advancing towards them. They were terrified and turned on Moses, asking him why he had brought them to the desert to die. Moses told the people to be still and to stand firm and not to fear because God would deliver them.

He did, but not in the way Moses envisaged. God told Moses that rather than getting them to stand firm Moses should order them to move towards the sea, fast. Moses was to raise his staff to divide the water so that the Israelites could march across to the far bank. The pillar of cloud moved to the back of the Israelites, giving daylight to them but darkness to the Egyptians. The Israelites moved steadily through the sea channel. Much has been written and speculated about exactly how the Red Sea could have parted. Some believe Red Sea is a mistranslation of Sea of Reeds, perhaps a marshy area north of the Gulf of Aqaba. Some believe it was a crossing of the Gulf of Suez and others that it was a crossing of the Gulf of Aqaba. Ancient chariot wheels have been found on the seabed of Aqaba, lending support to that theory but all is speculation. There are even some who believe that Moses had a knowledge of tides that enabled him to lead the Israelites across a ford. All that the Bible says is that Moses held his staff up and the waters parted, enabling the Israelites to cross. Behind them the Egyptians waited for sunrise. When the last Israelites had crossed safely, the pillar of cloud moved, morning broke for the Egyptians and they pursued the Israelites, but the wheels of their chariots sank into the wet sand and in some cases broke. Some Egyptians tried to go back, others to go on, and they were still in a confused jumble in the ford when from the far bank Moses stretched out his hand over the sea, it flowed back and the Egyptian host was drowned. The awed Israelites, staring at the sea that covered the Egyptian army, dared to believe Almighty God would get them home.

Chapters 15 -16: The Sinai Desert, Manna and Quail

As the Egyptians drowned, Moses and the Israelites sang a paean of praise to God, and Miriam led the women in a dance with tambourines. This is a very uncomfortable reading. From earliest times even the Israelites found it difficult to accept that their ancestors danced and sang for joy almost on the bodies of the dying Egyptians. There's an ancient Jewish story that when angels were about to break into song at the salvation of the Hebrews, God silenced them declaring, 'How dare you sing for joy when My creatures are dying?'[36] The Talmud also teaches that Jews should never in their gratitude to God for deliverance forget the misfortunes afflicting others.[37] The custom of breaking a glass at the end of a wedding ceremony is seen as a reminder to those who are joyous, that others might be suffering, and a similar explanation is given for the spilling of drops of

---

[36] Talmud, Megillah 10b and Sanhedrin 39b.

[37] Berachot 31a

wine on Seder night; the cup of deliverance and celebration cannot be full when others have to suffer. From earliest times Israelites have learned to mourn the loss of those who have had to die that they might live.

From contemplation and celebration of their extraordinary deliverance at the Red Sea, the Israelites turned and began their onward march. Ahead lay a long journey. As they trudged, more and more wearily, they kept looking for fresh water. For three days they found none. When at last they did, the water was too bitter to drink. They complained angrily to Moses. Again God came to their aid, showing Moses how to purify the water by throwing wood into it. At their next stop, Elim, there was plenty of fresh water. From Elim they travelled farther south to the Desert of Sin (probably the origin of the word Sinai but interesting that it should be 'sin'.) They did not find any fresh food for days and as usual were grumbling bitterly, wishing they had never left Egypt and telling Moses they were all probably going to starve to death. Again God intervened, this time by providing manna and quail. He told the Israelites not to collect manna and store it; they had to take only as much as was needed, except on the sixth day when they were to take twice as much so that they did not have to gather any food on the Sabbath. If they took too much on week days it would go rotten. Of course some tried to gather more than they were entitled to take, thinking not without reason that one never knew what the morrow would bring. The manna always went bad.

Some **ethno mycologists** have suggested that the description of manna given in Exodus could apply to the mushroom *Psilocybe cubensis,* magic mushrooms. They are highly attractive to insects and often contain maggots and larvae that cause them to decompose rapidly. What most causes the magic mushroom to be a contender in the age-long attempt to identify manna however is that it first appears as small fibres (mycelia) that resemble hoarfrost, and this fits the biblical description, but, this fungus has too little nutritional value and is too poisonous. It does not appear to be what fell from the skies to feed the Israelites. Others think manna was the desert truffle, the *terfeziaceae*. It is more common than the European variety, grows all over the deserts of the Middle East and is more prolific when there have been thunderstorms in the winter months. The trouble is they're not visible to the naked eye; one has to dig for them and they're seasonal so they cannot have been manna. No. One may have to accept that manna was a miracle food and that it fed the Israelites for a long time. No natural food found in the Sinai Desert, including the seasonal secretion of the Tamarisk Tree, would have been able to sustain life as long as manna sustained the Israelites. And quail? Quail, which migrate every autumn across the Sinai Peninsula from Europe to Africa are small members of the pheasant family, *Coturnix coturnix.* The spring migration is usually much farther west. (More about this later.)

Verse 34 in chapter sixteen has aroused some controversy. Here it is from the King James: 'As the Lord commanded Moses, so Aaron laid it up before the Testimony, to be kept.' What Aaron had just done was to place an omer of manna in the Ark of Testimony so that future generations could see the bread of life. The two problems are firstly that the omer of manna (just over 3½ litres) was not in the Ark when it was finally brought to Jerusalem and placed in the temple, and secondly, when Aaron did as he was bid, and laid 'it up before the Testimony,' the testimony did not exist! The Ark of the Covenant, often called the Testimony, came into the story only after the two stone tablets containing the Ten Commandments were placed in it, and that's still four chapters ahead at this stage. So what 'testimony' is Exodus talking about? Of course critics of the Bible love this; it proves that it was not written by Moses but a long time afterwards, they say.

What critics forget is that the Israelites came from the three areas in the world in which writing was invented and alphabetized (Mesopotamia, Egypt and Canaan) and they therefore almost certainly had, in addition to their oral tradition, some very early pieces of sacred writing. Moses would have made sure that the writings that they possessed were carefully preserved in some kind of box. The language in which the oldest parts of the Bible were written supports the contention that the Israelites were able to write this early in their history. The earlier section of Genesis contains more Akkadian and Sumerian-derived words and names, while the last fourteen chapters that deal with Joseph and his brothers settling in Egypt, contain Egyptian-derived words and names. Joseph himself, Pharaoh's minister of supplies and therefore almost certainly literate, may have recorded the latter part (pretty much his own story) whereas the earlier sections would have incorporated documents taken to Egypt by his father and brothers.

All this is speculation but it is the only assumption that makes logical sense. Anyway, whatever else, these writings would have been kept in a highly secure chest or Ark, the Testimony. It is obvious that from the beginning the Israelites carried such an early version of the Ark with them, containing not only all their sacred writings but also the bones of Joseph that they had promised to return to Canaan. As for the omer of manna, the 'bread of life,' it did not survive and was not in the Ark when it was placed in the Temple. Its absence was pointing towards the Messiah, who told his followers that *he* was the 'bread of life,' that he would arise from the awful death that lay ahead of him, and would ensure their spiritual survival forever. Manna was for the short term. Jesus is for the long.

So manna was another piece of theatre from the Israelites' dramatic history that enables readers of the Torah to strengthen their hold on the prophetic thread that leads to the incarnation. It is an integral part of Christian belief, that each has to partake of the bread of life for him or herself. There is enough for all: 'Give us this day our daily bread.' Not bread for tomorrow, just for today. In accepting the presence of Christ in the highs and lows of one's daily life there is completeness, sufficiency, no superfluity and a joy and peace that are beyond understanding.

Chapters 17 – 18: The Problem of the Amalekites

The Israelites had gone hardly any distance before they were at it again, complaining. For a couple of days there had been no water so once more they rounded on Moses and told him it was his fault. It looked as if some of them were about to stone him when Moses called on God for help. Again God came to the rescue. He told Moses to walk ahead and strike the rock at Horeb with his rod. Moses struck the rock as he was bid, and water gushed from the stone. This story is told differently in a later part of the Torah; and in that version it has fatal consequences for Moses.

When the Israelites resumed the march, a desert people, the Amalekites, fell upon the strugglers at the back, mostly women, children and older men. Moses sent a detachment to their rescue under the leadership of Joshua – the first mention of Joshua. While Moses watched the action from a nearby hill with his hands extended over his people, they gained the upper hand, but when through exhaustion he allowed his arms to drop, the Israelites began to lose. Aaron and Hur found a rock for him to sit on, and stood on either side of Moses holding up his arms. The Israelites won. Now comes another of those difficult verses, verse 14 in chapter seventeen. Here it is from the King James: And the Lord said unto Moses, 'Write this (again suggesting that it was Moses who wrote the account) for a memorial in a book, and rehearse it in the ears of Joshua: for I will utterly put out the remembrance of Amalek from under heaven.'

What's with the Amalek? What is immediately clear is that God did not want them to be forgotten; on the contrary, he insisted that the fight against the Amalekites be written down and remembered for ever, as indeed it has been. That leaves the bit about God utterly blocking out the remembrance of Amalek from 'under heaven.' Nobody can know precisely what that means but it suggests that as a people the Amalekites would never be under the control of the Kingdom of God. They would never be under heaven. The Amalek, or the Amalekites as they are more often called, are mentioned in many Old Testament books and are always described as the inveterate enemies of God and the Israelites.

There's something else about the Amalekites, for which one needs to go right back to Genesis. In the 12th verse of the 15th chapter of Genesis, Abram was given a vision in which God showed that his descendants would be enslaved for 400 years, but that in the fourth generation they would return to the Promised Land *'for the sin of the Amorites has not yet reached its full measure.'* (The Amorites and the Amalekites are often spoken of together or as one people in the Bible.) God who stands outside time and space, could see that the Amorites and the Amalekites would be godless and violent. In the fullness of time he would use the Israelites to punish and defeat them. In the same way, as the centuries went by, God would allow Gentile nations to rise up against the Israelites and defeat and enslave them because of their own wrongdoing.

Moses reunited with his Family and Jethro contributes to the Ten Commandments

The news that the Israelites were approaching reached Jethro, father-in-law of Moses. In Chapter 18 one reads that he set out with Zipporah, his daughter (wife of Moses) and his two grandsons, Gershom and Eliezer, for Mount Horeb where Moses had seen the burning bush, and to which he was leading the Israelites. Informed that his family were coming, Moses went out to meet them, and was delighted to be re-united with his wife, his children and Jethro, clearly a man whom he loved and revered. He told Jethro everything that had happened and Jethro was enormously pleased to hear how God had acted to save His people. The two men offered sacrifices to God.

Jethro! He's a significant figure and somewhat shrouded in mystery. In the Book of Judges in the King James Bible (chapter 4, verse 11) the father in law of Moses is called Hobab, while in Numbers in the King James it says (chapter 10:29) Hobab, the son of Raguel (Reuel) the Midianite. The NIV study-note compilers, going back to Hebrew Texts, clear up the mystery somewhat: Ancient Hebrew did not distinguish between in-law relatives, just used a generic term, *chathan,* translated as Hobab, for all in-laws. Reuel-Jethro, then, was the Midianite father-in-law of Moses. Throughout their history, the Israelites came across god-fearing men and women who were not of their own people but who had a profound influence upon them and who often became involved in their blood lines. Such a one was Jethro. In Genesis 25 it said that Midian was one of the sons of Abraham, through his second wife, Keturah. Jethro who was descended from the Midianites turned out to be not only a priest but also a superb organiser and in a strange way one has Jethro to thank for the Ten Commandments. When he saw Moses trying to judge a myriad of disputes among the Israelites, he said that would not do at all because Moses would wear himself out. He persuaded Moses to draw up a list of God's commandments, teach them to the people, appoint deputies to act as local magistrates, have a system of higher judges to hear more difficult cases and appeals, and to confine his own role to that of appeal judge. Once Moses had this all in place, Jethro, satisfied, returned to his own home.

Chapters 19 – 24: The Ten Commandments

Nobody knows exactly where biblical Mount Sinai is. There is a Mount Sinai near the southern end of the Sinai Peninsula and many authorities think that this is where Moses received the commandments. But other scholars think it is elsewhere, in Saudi Arabia or on the border between Egypt and Canaan. There's another controversy about Mount Sinai. Is it Mount Horeb under another name? Nobody knows; some scholars believe one thing and some another. Wherever it is, when they reached biblical Mount Sinai, the Israelites stopped and prepared for an indefinite stay.

God called Moses up the mountain and told him that if the Israelites kept his covenant, they would be his 'treasured possession, a kingdom of priests and a holy nation.' Moses told the people that what was about to happen was of utmost importance. They had to prepare for it carefully by washing themselves and their clothes, outward cleanliness to symbolize inward consecration. They were to keep away from the mountain itself in the same way that they would not be allowed into the holy of holies in the tabernacle or the temple. The preparations took two days during which time they were to have no sexual relations, a clear break with the sexual orgies that characterised many of the surrounding religions.

On the third day God appeared to the Israelites at the top of the mountain. It sounds as if there was a volcanic eruption, thunder and lightning, clouds of smoke, the ground trembling, fire, and a 'very loud trumpet blast.' The people were terrified. Moses and Aaron, obeying a call from God, went up the mountain. Before God gave the commandments to Moses, he identified himself. 'I am the Lord your God, who brought you out of Egypt, out of the land of slavery.'

And then He gave Moses those definitive laws:

1. You shall have no other gods but me.
2. You shall not make yourselves idols.
3. You shall not misuse the name of God.
4. You shall keep the Sabbath Day holy.
5. You shall honour your father and mother.
6. You shall not murder.
7. You shall not commit adultery.
8. You shall not steal.
9. You shall not tell lies about other people.
10. You shall not covet other people's possessions.

The Ten Commandments – the Decalogue! The fifth one is difficult. There are parents who have shamefully abused their children, either with neglect or with physical or emotional harm. How could their offspring possibly honour them? Is it even possible for the children of abusive parents to have a concept of God as a loving father? There's another problem with the Ten Commandments. Rape and paedophilia are not mentioned. However, the seventh commandment not to commit adultery covers both these crimes. Any sexual activity outside marriage was considered adultery for which the punishment was death. This is spelled out in Leviticus and Deuteronomy, the third and fifth books of the Torah, where rape is listed as a crime.

When Moses read the commandments to the Israelites, they cowered in terror. Moses told them God had come to test them and said they were to build an altar to God and offer burnt sacrifices to Him. Moses went backwards and forwards between God and the Israelites. It took days – and days – and days. Moses was not given only the Ten Commandments but many other instructions as well. Interestingly, after the Decalogue the very first laws concerned servants and their rights. In biblical times there was little difference between servants and slaves, so the laws that pertained to the care of servants applied to slaves. Then came instructions on how to deal justly with those who had suffered personal injury or loss, were involved in fighting, had killed or assaulted others or damaged their property, or had indulged in sorcery, bestiality or blasphemy. The punishments were harsh, mostly capital. Many of the instructions seem arbitrary today and those about women particularly so, but one needs to remember that the Bronze Age was a fraught, horrendously difficult time when only the strictest control by the defenders of the tribe, the men, ensured survival. Inevitably, it produced a patriarchal structure.

Yet the very first mention of 'eye for eye, tooth for tooth' verses 22 to 25 of the 21st chapter, concerns women. If a man hurt a pregnant woman, causing her to miscarry, and there was serious injury to the mother or child, or both, 'you are to take life for life, eye for eye, tooth for tooth, hand for hand, foot for foot, burn for burn, wound for wound, and bruise for bruise.' A woman may have been a man's possession but it was in the same way that he possessed his body, part of his bone and flesh. In addition to the many 'Don'ts' the Israelites were encouraged to be socially responsible, to be kind to the poor and to aliens, to care for animals, to let the land lie fallow and have its rest and to celebrate the three annual festivals - Passover, Unleavened Bread and Harvest.

It is true that the Ten Commandments are not the oldest known code of laws from the Near East. Hammurabi's famous code dates from about 1772 B.C. and it already contains elements that influence the Jewish idea of 'eye for eye, tooth for tooth.' There were several other codes as well, particularly the Sumerian Code of King Ur-Nammu from about 2100 – 2050 B.C. Since the Israelites lived in all the areas in which prototypes or knowledge of their laws have been found it would be difficult to say which code influenced which, but at some time in their early history the Israelites received a code of laws that were centred on God, which prohibited infanticide and human sacrifice and which contained all the positives that to this day underpin the social order of most civilized societies.

Having ordered them to lead godly, law-abiding and caring lives, God promised the people that he would send an angel to accompany them to the Promised Land, urging them with powerful language to have courage. He said he would send 'hornets' ahead to terrify the other nations into fleeing. 'Hornets' is obviously a metaphor for weakening the Canaanites in some way. It may have been disease or perhaps it is a reference to the Egyptians who invaded Canaan at about this time and seriously undermined the power of the Hittites and their allies. God was purposefully intervening to keep the nation of Israel intact and was ensuring that nothing stood in the way of his purpose. It is unclear why this bothers people so much; every person on earth has physically to die, and God determines when and how. Atheists should not bother about it at all. They do not believe in God and it is therefore incomprehensible to me why some of them should write so much about what somebody (who they say does not exist) says or does. Unless of course they are determined to rid others of their belief, in which case they are not scientists or philosophers but merely proselytisers.

The fourth verse of chapter 24 says: 'Moses then wrote down everything the Lord had said.' The chapter ends with Moses going up the mountain for the final laws. In his mid eighties by now, he was perhaps beginning to feel his age because he took Joshua as an aide.

Chapters 25 – 30: The Ark

At the beginning of Chapter twenty five God told Moses to build a chest of acacia wood covered in gold. This is the beginning of the story of the Ark, a state-of-the-art wooden chest with a special gold lid called the 'Atonement Seat' (in some English translations the 'mercy seat') adorned with engravings of two golden cherubim. The Ark would be kept in the holiest place in the Tabernacle. It had rings through which two long poles could be inserted to carry it on the long marches. All the Tabernacle objects were fitted with rings and carrying poles, typical of the objects carried in Egyptian ritual processions, indicating that the Israelites learned much from the other Bronze Age cultures among which they lived.

The fact that the cover was called 'atonement' has enormous significance for both Judaism and Christianity. Atonement means reconciliation, and therefore Grace, since it is only by grace that sinful humans can be reconciled with God. On the cover the shed blood of sacrificial offerings would be sprinkled. However, the ultimate at-one-ment with God would be achieved not by the spilling of animal blood but by that of Jesus, the Christ. Another object in the Tabernacle that has significance for Christians is the golden lamp-stand representing Christ as the Light of the World. The seven candles represent God in the centre of his creation. Seven is a mystical number used often in the Bible to show perfection. There were four other objects in the Tabernacle, all likewise pointing towards Christ, the basin for ritual washing, the incense altar, the bronze altar of burnt offering and the table for the bread of the presence.

The Ark, the physical symbol of God's presence among them, was cherished and cared for by the Israelites for centuries until, during the horror of the Babylonian defeat, it disappeared. The stories, myths and legends of where it could possibly have been hidden or taken, have never stopped. Even in our own day there is the Indiana Jones film, 'Raiders of the Lost Ark.' A fundamentalist Christian group claims to have found the Ark directly under where Christ was crucified. A chapel in Ethiopia professes to have it, claiming that it was taken to Ethiopia for safety by Menelik, son of Solomon and the Queen of Sheba. The truth is that the Ark has not been found, or if it has it is kept secret, but it continues to haunt the popular imagination, testifying to its huge role in the story of the Israelites, and to its abiding interest to the Judaeo-based religions.

Special Clothing for the Priests and Painted Toes

After the Ark the next thing demanded of the Israelites was that the Priests be dressed in special raiment. Dog collars are not a new idea. Among the items of clothing was the 'breast-piece of judgement' which was magnificently adorned with jewels. Nobody knows exactly what Urim and Thummim mean (Exodus 28:30) but because they were placed in a pocket of the breast-piece of judgement (or decision) and also because the Jewish words probably mean curses and perfections, it could be that they were a type of dice, or lots, representing good and evil. These would be cast if a difficult decision had to be made.

What comes next causes hysterical derision among Biblical critics, the injunction that priests had to paint their toes with the blood of sacrificed animals. Before one considers it, why sacrifice animals in the first place? Is it because the association of blood with life is more obviously symbolic than breath which is invisible? Christians do not perform sacrifices. (Jesus was not a sacrificial victim. He chose to lay down his life as a supreme demonstration of love.) Jews no longer perform sacrifices. Muslims and Hindus sacrifice animals. Buddhists don't. Many ancient religions offered animal or human sacrifices from a belief that the spiritual world had to be appeased to prevent dreadful things happening on earth. Christ put an end to sacrifice by instituting the bread and wine as symbols of his body and blood.

But it remains a truth that to live one has to kill. By vesting the act of killing with religious significance, God showed the Israelites never to take lightly the killing of a creature, whether it was for physical or spiritual survival. In the latter case priests had to have their hands on the head of the animal to be killed. It had to be done in front of everybody. In Europe and North America too many children think that burgers and sausages come from punnets in supermarkets. They are deprived of understanding the sanctity of life, and the sacrifice that humanity demands from the animal kingdom. The King James Bible (Gen.22:8) points towards Christ's becoming the end of sacrifice. When Abraham was prepared to sacrifice Isaac, it reads: 'God will provide Himself a lamb,' which points towards God giving Himself as the ultimate lamb. Other versions have changed the word order; God Himself will provide a lamb, or even inserted a preposition, God will provide a lamb for himself. I think the King James translators have got it right.

Back to the original question: Why when the Israelite priests performed the animal sacrifices, did they have to put blood on their ears, thumbs and toes? When one thinks about it, there could have been no more dramatic reminder of how the people had disobeyed God. Instead of using their ears to listen to the good, they had, as many still do, listened to the lewd, the false witness, the malicious gossip, the call to wrongdoing, the evil suggestion, the blasphemous, and the voice of family, friends and false prophets urging wrong. As the priest put the blood on his ear, the people could undertake anew to *hear God's word and* to *listen to the voice of the Holy Spirit*. Then came the blood placed on the thumb of the right hand. This time it was not what they had heard, but what they had done. The blood on the most important finger of the right hand – the opposable thumb – dramatically drew their attention to their sinful actions, their selfish or ruthless work, their inaction (negligence), their mischief, cruelty, violence, gluttony and greed. In the same way the blood applied to the priest's right toe, the front of his leading foot, enabled him to repent on behalf of himself and the community for all the places to which he and they had travelled to do wrong, or where they had moved away from God, instead of towards him. It is the same today. People go to shops, or sports, or other recreational activities, instead of to church. They go to shows that are pornographic or blasphemous, or that raise the secular above the spiritual. Like the Israelites, people still allow their feet to lead them away from God.

Yom Kippur

In Chapter 30 is the first mention of the Day of Atonement, Yom Kippur, one of the most important of the Jewish festivals. In the emphasis that the festival places on the need to be at one with God, is another pointer towards Christ, the only being who will achieve for mankind complete at-one-ment. The significance of Yom Kippur and the rituals associated with it are more fully developed in the next book, Leviticus. Only on the Day of Atonement could the Chief Priest enter the Holy of Holies to sprinkle blood from the sin sacrifice on the cover of the Ark, the Atonement Cover.

The consecrating of the tabernacle and its appurtenances with spices and perfumes 'that they may be most holy' and that 'whatever touches them will become holy' foreshadows the incident in Mark 14:3 when Jesus was in the home of Simon the Leper in Bethany and 'A woman came with an alabaster jar of very expensive perfume made of nard.' She broke the jar and poured the perfume on Jesus. He did not need the perfume to become holy, but the woman with the alabaster jar needed to make this gesture as a deep and personal act of thanksgiving. Jesus is intrinsically holy and whoever touches him or is touched by him becomes holy. That gives those who have been subject to the laying on of hands in a tradition that goes back to the apostles and to Jesus himself, a very special feeling. The touch has come down through the ages.

Chapters 31 - 34: Rebellion and The Broken Tablets

God bestowed His Holy Spirit upon Bezalel of the tribe of Judah, and on Oholiab of the tribe of Dan so that they could design and construct the tabernacle and all its sacred objects. That they were the first two people outside the priesthood to receive the Holy Spirit shows the very special link that God instituted between himself and all those in the creative arts, whom he had made in His own creator image. It says something too about iconoclasts who destroy works of art because of the commandment not to make idols. Idols and works of art are not the same thing; one has to worship something to make it an idol. The idols of today are rarely works of art; they are the things that have pre-eminence in our lives and that we put above God, things like addictions, money, celebrity, social media, computer games, marriage, sport, politics or religion.

After he had given and explained all his instructions to Moses, God 'gave him the two tablets of the Testimony.' It's odd that 'tablet' is the name of mini-computer that many children and adults possess today, and sad that tablets are often distractions that pull people away from both God and from what was inscribed on those first two tablets.

THE GOLDEN CALF

Israel got it wrong almost immediately and made themselves an idol. The juxtaposition of these two stories shows that Exodus is making a very clear distinction between a work of art and an idol. Even if one accepts that Moses, accompanied by Joshua, spent weeks, perhaps even months, in communion with God at the top of Mount Sinai, it still seems an alarmingly short time for the Israelites to have lost their faith in God, and to have resorted to building idols. But so it was. The story is well-known. When the people began to wonder if Moses was ever going to return, or whether perhaps he had died up on the mountain, they decided that they needed new gods, and demanded that Aaron make them some. The fact that Aaron acquiesced so quickly is even more alarming. It shows why God made Moses the leader of the Israelites rather than his elder brother who was the better speaker. It also shows that the Israelites were still affected by the practices of the people around them and were finding it difficult to strike out on their own and follow the one true but invisible God, even after all the miracles they had witnessed.

The Golden calf that they constructed was probably in honour of the Egyptian Bull God Apis. When one considers how often and how easily throughout their history, as recounted by themselves, the Israelites were drawn back into the worship of natural and fertility gods, one understands God's relentless efforts to keep them separate. Aaron tried to hedge his bets and said, 'Tomorrow shall be a feast to the Lord' implying that they could do what they liked today! They did make offerings to God the next day but afterwards 'they sat down to eat and drink and got up to indulge in revelry,' just like those Sunday worshippers who think that they can do what they like the rest of the week.

God told Moses the Israelites were a stiff-necked people who had become corrupt and he had done with them. He would make a new covenant with Moses and his descendants. But Moses pleaded with God to relent. God responded to his love-based pleading, as God always does respond to love. Moses and Joshua rushed down the mountain towards the Israel encampment carrying the precious tablets. In Exodus 32:15 one reads that the tablets 'were the work of God; the writing was the writing of God, engraved on the tablets.' That might be poetic licence. It is more likely that Moses wrote out the commandments. He would never have damaged the tablets if God had personally inscribed them. So the fact that the distraught Moses when he saw what the Israelites were up to hurled the precious tablets to the ground shattering them, proves that he had written them himself. He grabbed the golden calf and threw that into the fire where it melted, then he ground the melted bits into powder, threw the powder into water, and made the Israelites drink it. Nothing in the Bible is simplistic. There are those who do not distinguish between idol and art and regard Moses as the first iconoclast.

Moses was clearly trying to prove how ridiculous it was to worship a metal object that one had fashioned oneself. Furiously he turned on Aaron and asked him why he had led the people into such great sin. Aaron tried to wriggle out of it. He said that when the people gave him all their gold jewellery he threw it into the fire 'and out came this calf' by magic, as it were. Moses summoned to his side those who were for the Lord and when the Levites rallied to him, he ordered them to kill the pagan revellers. Perhaps the Levites did execute people or perhaps it was the plague that swept through the camp just then. Whatever it was, many died. Moses made it clear that it was because of their apostasy. He informed the survivors that because of their disobedience God would not stay with them as he had until now and would destroy them if they persisted in evil. Mourning and grieving, deprived of God's presence, the Israelites stripped themselves of all their jewellery and almost in sackcloth and ashes, repented of their sin.

Moses pitched his tent outside the camp, there to commune with God. The people noticed a pillar of cloud at the entrance of the tent when Moses went inside it. 'The Lord would speak with Moses face to face, as a man speaks with his friend.' When Moses left the tent at night, Joshua stayed behind to guard it. Moses pleaded for the Israelites and God agreed to stay with them. A grateful Moses prepared two new stone tablets and pleaded with God to appear to him. God agreed, so Moses went alone to the top of Mount Sinai where God placed him in a cleft and covered him with His hand so that he would be safe when God allowed the Spiritual Realm briefly to intrude upon the physical. *'Then the Lord came down in the cloud and stood there with him.'* It seems that on all those other occasions when Moses encountered God face to face, He was in fact coming face to face either with Christ, the incarnation of God, or with an angel. But on this particular occasion, he caught a glimpse of the magnificence of God in the spiritual realm. There is only one other occasion in the Bible in which such an encounter with God occurred, and that was in the Transfiguration of Jesus, when he went up a mountain with Peter, John and James, met His father, and became transfigured, his face and his clothing radiant with light.

When Moses went down the mountain with the new tablets, having encountered God in that mystical, spiritual realm, his face was so alight with radiance that Aaron and the Israelites were afraid to go near him, but Moses called out to them to come near and to hear what God wanted them to do. This is the moment at which that greatest of sculptors, Michelangelo, sought to portray him. The statue is in the Church of San Pietro in Vincoli in Rome. Michelangelo has Moses seated with the newly inscribed stone tablets under his right arm. He has summoned the people to come towards him, and he is about to give them the commandments.

There have been many wrong interpretations of this statue over the years. Many think that Moses is holding the original tablets and is about to break them, or that the new tablets have not yet been inscribed. Neither is true. The moment in which Michelangelo portrays Moses in what must be one of the greatest religious sculptures in the world, is when Moses, having re-written the commandments on the new tablets (Exodus 34:28) and holding them protectively under his right arm, sits himself down and summons the Israelites to draw near, his face radiant. Only a genius of Michelangelo's calibre could have hewn a block of marble to achieve the awed expression on the face of Moses. How we know that this is the moment that Michelangelo sought to capture, is not only because of the radiance of the expression, the awed tension of the posture and the way in which Moses has caught up the strands of his beard as if he does not know how best to express his deep delight of being, but also because of the infamous horns!

There are two horns on the top of Moses's head – the same horns that appear in many stained-glass, painted, sculptured and engraved portrayals of Moses in medieval times. They were to mystify generations of worshippers as horns are traditionally associated with the devil. Why on earth did Michelangelo and so many other artists give Moses horns? They are directly attributable to the Latin Vulgate of St Jerome, the Bible of the Middle Ages, as influential in its own time as the King James was to become in later times. The horns are because of the following verse in the Vulgate: 'And when Moses came down from Mount Sinai, he held the two tables of the Testimony and he knew not that his face was horned from the conversation of the Lord.' Jerome had difficulty with the Hebraic word *keren* which means 'like a horn'. He probably realized it was a simile for something, but was not sure what, because when he translated Ezekiel he said that the face of Moses 'had become glorified or as it says in the Hebrew, horned.' So that's where the church picked up its erroneous idea that Moses had horns, from a text in an ancient language that did not have a word for radiant or rays and sought to express the idea as having horns coming from the face.

Chapter 35 – 40
Final Instructions

Having reminded them to keep the Sabbath Day holy, Moses proceeded to give the Israelites their final instructions. In addition to the temple tax, the people were asked to bring precious metals and jewellery to the priests, and also fine linens, yarns and skins. (Linen weaving was known in both Mesopotamia and Egypt.) Beautiful acacia wood was also demanded, as was olive oil. All these would be used to make the tabernacle and its furnishings and drapes. The people responded magnificently and Bezalel, Oholiab and their apprentices set to work. The tabernacle, the ark, the table, the lampstand, the altar of incense, the altar for the burnt offering and the basin for washing were all completed exactly as the Lord had decreed. The last items to be made were the priestly garments. Finally it was all done, and in chapter thirty nine, verse thirty two, Moses inspected all the work, and blessed the people.

In the last chapter of Exodus, the tabernacle was finally erected, and Moses set the various furnishings in their right places. 'Then the cloud covered the Tent of Meeting, and the glory of the Lord filled the tabernacle - in all the travels of the Israelites whenever the cloud lifted from above the tabernacle, they would set out; but if the cloud did not lift, they did not set out.' And so ends Exodus.

Exit from Exodus

So what does one make of it, this second book of the Old Testament? Probably its greatest gift is a moral code that nobody could deny would make the world a better place if everybody upheld it. Even the first four commandments that concern man's relationship with God rather than with his neighbours, and would not appeal to atheists, are worth keeping. They restrain one's worst desires and compulsions because the sad truth is that people today are as stiff-necked as ever. If one is not making an idol of a religion, political correctness, post-modernism or science, one is making an idol of something. Whatever it is, it inevitably lands one in a horrific mess.

And Moses? One learns things about him that are seldom mentioned in books that describe him as prophet, law-giver and leader, and yet these other facts are the endearing ones. He must have had a charismatic and magnetic presence, someone who would light up a place and to whom others instantly gravitated. Coupled with his dynamic charisma was a quiet and genuine humility. He had no idea how he appeared to others; God had constantly to remind him. He appears not to have been an avid talker, or orally adept in any way, which was why God suggested he use Aaron as his mouthpiece. But the reason for this could have been that he had been brought up in the Egyptian court and Hebrew was his second language, little practised. As the years in the desert went by, he became more proficient in its use and towards the end of his life he addressed the vast Hebrew crowd with confidence. Clearly he could commune with God for days and weeks on end, and he could write.

He was brave and would not hold back if he perceived an injustice. This led to his having to flee from Egypt when he killed an Egyptian slaver that was abusing an Israelite. Soon afterwards he intervened when a group of bullying shepherds prevented some women from watering their flocks. This time it led him into the presence of Jethro, who would have such a positive influence on his life, and into his marrying one of Jethro's daughters. He was naturally curious and this together with his bravery caused him to approach the burning bush. Rather than run away from what appeared weird and supernatural, he went nearer to try to find out what was happening. On the negative side, he could lose his temper. His fury with the Israelites led him to fling to the ground and shatter the original stone tablets containing the law. A worse result of his temper happened earlier at the Rock of Meribah. Exodus does not develop this but it is repeated in the Book of Numbers where one reads what serious consequences it had for him.

Above all in Exodus one learns more about God. One learns that he is a jealous God. Sceptics and mockers love this one. A jealous God! Jealousy is a nasty trait, suggesting possessiveness and resentment. If, however, one looks up its origins, one sees that it comes from a root meaning intense feeling or *zeal.* In fact, jealousy and zealousness, have the same root, and some translations have zealous god rather than jealous god. By calling himself jealous or zealous, God sought to convey to the Israelites not only his intensely protective love, but also his longing for their trust, which of course they all too often placed elsewhere. That brings one to the end of Exodus. Moses, Aaron, Joshua and the other leaders have begun to regulate the unruly host that set out from Egypt and get them into some sort of order, but God has called them a stiff-necked people, and one senses trouble ahead.

Part Four
LIVING LEVITICUS

Love your neighbour as Yourself

Introduction

Three hundred years before the birth of Christ the scribes of Alexandria who produced the Septuagint called the third book of the Torah Leviticus in the realization that it was of more concern to the Levitical priests than to the Israelites in general. Since the *raison d'etre* for the Levitical priesthood was wiped out when the Romans destroyed the temple in 70 A.D. and the priesthood in effect ceased to exist, the book would appear to have little or no relevance today. Rabbis are different from Levitical priests. Rabbis can be descendants of any of the tribes. Jesus, of the tribe of Judah, was a rabbi, one who had religious authority and could interpret the scriptures. He was not a Levite and could not have become a priest of Israel.

Leviticus is the most fraught and difficult book in the Old Testament. Homosexuals revile it; atheists despise and mock it; even Christians are embarrassed by it. But the truth is that if one reads it in context and explores its deepest themes, which were to instil in those early Israelites an understanding of the holiness of God and the need for people to try to become holy too, then it becomes a meaningful book.

Chapters 1 – 4: Sacrifices

Even with that in mind as soon as one starts reading it, it becomes obvious that very little in the first few chapters applies to any reader today since they concern animal sacrifice. This should warn one that there might be other instructions in Leviticus that people today will not be able to obey. Those who believe in the utter inerrancy of the Bible, and that every word was written by God himself and has to be obeyed, will land themselves in a decided muddle. God operated through humans of every type and description, and they sometimes made mistakes, or, at best, did not see far enough ahead. So with Leviticus. It was written in a certain place at a certain time, and although in broad outline the problems faced by the ancient Israelites were similar to those of today, in detail they differed, and it remains true that it is in the detail that the devil often is. God is unchanging but humans change from generation to generation. The way to read Leviticus is to follow its leads towards inclusiveness and compassion and to resist anything that suggests judgmentalism, exclusiveness or legalism, all of which Christ abhorred.

The Tabernacle was completed by the end of Exodus. Now in Leviticus are instructions on how the Israelite priests were to carry out their duties and perform the tabernacle rituals. God's holiness is a major theme of the book, as is physical perfection. To the ancient Israelites, physical beauty or perfection were regarded as an indication of inner purity and goodness. Disease and physical imperfection were despised. The Israelites were still centuries away from the realisation that spiritual and moral goodness have nothing to do with appearance but reside in attitude, action and character.

The book's opening is significant in the light of the insistence of much Biblical scholarship that it was not written by Moses but by priests during the Babylonian exile or afterwards. Leviticus points to Moses as the author: 'The Lord said to Moses.' Similar words occur some 50 times in Leviticus. The third person style, using Moses or 'he' instead of 'I' is simply that, a matter of style.

Chapter 5: Whistle-blowing, Clean, Unclean and Taking Oaths

From the beginning of Chapter 5, Leviticus begins to be relevant for the twenty first century. Four sins are listed. The NIV study notes say that these first four are all unintentional but that's not quite right. The first one is about failing to testify or to speak up when one has learned of wrongdoing. That can never be unintentional. If one perceives something wrong, one makes a deliberate decision either to ignore it or to do something about it, which in the twenty first century probably means whistle-blowing of some sort. It isn't easy. When is it mean tale-bearing and when is it sincerely done for the common good? Also, reporting something can adversely affect the wellbeing not only of the one exposed but also of oneself, or even of one's community or country. Apart from that, Christ introduced many grey areas, above all, his injunction not to judge others. The fact remains that when one sees wrongdoing and decides either to report or ignore it one makes a deliberate decision;

it is not unintentional. Leviticus insists that one *should* speak up. Not to do so is the sin. Transparency and revealing the truth are not new ideas!

The second sin has little application today since it involves contact with unclean animals. One is reminded of God saying to Peter: 'Do not call anything impure that God has made clean.' This would apply to the next 'sin' as well, the inadvertent touching of a person regarded as unclean, and that would include a menstruating woman! Christ makes it possible for us not to despise anything that he has made. So 5:3 is turned on its head.

Before one judges ancient Israel too harshly, one needs to remind oneself how vulnerable they were. Plagues often swept through communities bringing near annihilation. Even today, health officials increasingly warn that dirty hands are the source of many infectious diseases. There is no way Christians can keep their hands from becoming involved in the dirty business of suffering life. Christ ordered his followers to serve, to help, to clean, to heal and to restore. But people could possibly be more conscientious about washing their hands more often! Back in that far-off Bronze Age when germs and viruses were unknown, God impressed upon his chosen people the need to use fire and water for cleansing and making holy. These are accepted means even today of keeping microbes at bay.

By the time of Jesus, the Pharisees, scribes and lawyers were abusing the strictures against uncleanness as a means of distancing themselves from the poor and emphasising their positions of superiority. They made a public display of washing their hands when they had been in contact with others, to show that the rest of mankind was unclean, and only they, the chosen ones, were clean. Jesus paid no heed to these rituals and when the Pharisees challenged him about it, he responded, Mark 7: 5-19, that they had abandoned the commands of God and were holding on to the traditions of men. He said that nothing that entered a man from the outside could make him 'unclean.' It was what was in his heart that could do so, 'evil thoughts, sexual immorality, theft, murder, adultery, greed, malice, deceit, lewdness, envy, slander, arrogance and folly all these evils came from inside and made a man unclean,' Jesus said.

The last sin in this Leviticus group is the casual promise or the careless taking of an oath. Now this one Jesus was severe about. He said there was no room for thoughtlessness in the hearts of his followers, and warned his disciples against any kind of oath taking or exaggerated language; a plain yes or no was all that was required, which shows that the British legal practice of making witnesses swear an oath on the Bible is against one of the laws in the very Bible upon which they are swearing!

Two of the fundamental themes of Judaism and Christianity, confession (When anyone is guilty in any of these ways he must confess in what way he has sinned) and penance (as a penalty for the sin he has committed he must bring to the Lord a female lamb or goat as an offering) are given increasing prominence in Leviticus. Conditions are being established that will culminate in the incarnation, ministry and crucifixion of Christ. The very first words attributed to Christ in the New Testament are: 'The time has come. The Kingdom of God is near. *Repent* and believe the good news!'

Chapters 6 - 9: Dealing With Sin in The Millennium Before Christ

In these chapters are described sins that were deliberately committed, where the perpetrator had stolen something, or had lost or damaged something entrusted to him. In such cases a guilt offering had to be made, and the stolen property returned, together with an additional fifth of the value of the stolen property as indemnity. Western law does not deal adequately with the problem of restitution. Fines are exacted by the state, but not enough compensation granted to victims, unless a victim institutes a civil action, often beyond his means or ability. So concerning this issue, the laws of the Israelites were superior.

It was Moses himself who ordained Aaron and his sons as the first Israelite priests. The instructions for the ordination were given in the 29th chapter of Exodus. Here in Leviticus one reads how they were carried out. After a ceremonial washing, the priests were robed in their new vestments, and Moses consecrated Aaron as chief priest by anointing his head with oil. Animals were sacrificed and Moses put some of the blood of the ordination offering on the ears, thumbs and right toes of the new priests, signifying that they would have to obey God's commands, do as he commanded them to do, and go where he ordered them to go.

What has often mystified readers is why Moses ordered part of the sacrifice to be 'waved before the Lord.' It was the fellowship or peace offering (in this case the ordination offering) that was waved towards the Lord because it was part of this offering that the priest was allowed to keep for himself. He waved it towards the altar and then back towards himself. (The priest was not allowed to partake of guilt or sin offerings.) The fellowship offering often formed part of a ceremonial meal that the priest and the worshipper shared after the worshipper had been forgiven and reconciled with God.

The ordination festival lasted a week. Chapter nine ends with: 'Fire came out from the presence of the Lord and consumed the burnt offering and the fat portions on the altar. And when all the people saw it, they shouted for joy and fell facedown.'

Chapter 10:
Sudden Disaster

It seems that a violent thunder storm struck the area in which the sacrifices were being performed. Although the Israelites shouted for joy and fell facedown, when they arose, they saw that two of the young priests had been struck dead. Moses felt that it was because the two priests, Nadab and Abihu, sons of Aaron, 'had offered unauthorized fire before the Lord, contrary to his command.' It seems a dreadfully harsh punishment, and makes sense only if one remembers how often in the Bible there are similar incidents at the start of new stages in the history of Israel or Christianity. There is, for instance, a similar story in the fifth chapter of 'Acts' where Ananias and Sapphira died instantly after it was revealed that they had withheld part of the money that they had promised, and had lied about it. Moses felt that Nadab and Abihu had been more concerned with their authority and power as priests and leaders of Israel than with God's authority. Their deaths remind us of how very nearly Moses himself died at the beginning of his mission to free Israel. He and Zipporah had disobeyed God, and only when they decided to obey did God relent and was Moses able to continue his journey.

Chapters 11 – 15:
How to be Holy and How to be Safe

Although the first part of Leviticus deals mostly with worship and sacrifices, much of the rest is about walking with God in every aspect of life. Food and how they should prepare it were among the most important considerations for the Israelites. As they came closer to the land they had been promised, God gave them strict instructions about what they could and could not eat, and so-doing made sure of their physical wellbeing and spiritual safety. They could eat only animals that had cloven hooves and that chewed the cud, not animals that had one or the other. Pigs have cloven hooves but do not chew the cud, rabbits have a similar digestive process to chewing the cud but do not have cloven hooves. The issue here was to confine the Israelites' meat sources to animals that were less prone to disease and rapid decay. Goat meat and mutton were among the safest. For the same reason they were forbidden the flesh of raptors, predators, fish without scales, shellfish and reptiles. Interestingly, there is actually no such thing as kosher or non-kosher food. Kosher means food. What is not kosher is not food. This was the physical side of it. On the spiritual side, it is difficult to share a meal with people who eat what you have been forbidden to eat, so these laws helped to keep the Israelites separate from the practices of their pagan neighbours.

Also in this chapter one reads for the first time (verse 44) God saying to the Israelites: 'I am the Lord your God; consecrate yourselves and be holy, because I am holy.' How does one be holy? The Israelite word for 'holy' is *qadosh.* The Septuagint scholars translated that into *hagios.* Both words mean separated or set apart from. Food restrictions were among the ways in which God separated the Israelites from the pagans that surrounded them. The restrictions were to remain in place until Jesus appeared on earth. By commanding Peter not to regard as unclean anything that God had made, and by washing the disciples' feet, Jesus showed that his followers had to be ever present and ever helpful to everybody they encountered on life's long, muddy road, including their enemies. Where separation came into it was that they had to refrain from doing what was culturally relevant and to do what was God reverent and relevant.

It is one's living in Christ that protects from evil, makes one holy and enables one to serve one's fellows and draw them towards goodness and peace. That means of course that one has to define evil, and that is one of the things that makes the Torah so relevant for the twenty first century: It teaches that both evil and good reside in each human heart. Evil is that which demeans God and abuses creation and one's fellows. Good is that which proclaims and glorifies God and serves creation and one's fellows. For a Christian, choosing good means identifying with Christ in every thought, word and deed even if it means being mocked or persecuted. The Bible shows that being holy does not mean dressing piously or behaving with demonstrable and often sadly hypocritical morality. On the contrary, it insists that more than being moral one needs to be holy, and the best way to be holy is to be wholly for God and of God and in God in everything one does, making one of far greater use and benefit to society than any other kind of behaviour one could practise. As one progresses through Leviticus, one sees that many of the laws have this purpose, encouraging the Israelites to lead holy lives not only by separating themselves from the harmful practices of the people around them, but also by devoting themselves to the well-being of all including the care and protection of the alien and vulnerable.

There are of course those who say that one can be a caring, generous and loving person without being a follower of Christ or a believer in God. True. But it is also true that those who love God are the ones that go far beyond the expected to render help, care and love wherever it is needed.

The strictures about women may seem harsh and discriminatory but in fact they were protective. This is almost certainly an instance in which a poor and limited vocabulary led to an unfortunate choice of words. To be pronounced 'unclean' during menstruation or after giving birth was almost certainly not what was meant. What was really intended in those pre-tampon, pre-sanitary-towel days, was that women, who in the days of the patriarchs had only limited hygiene resources, be absolved from embarrassing social and marital demands while they were bleeding. As usual, Jesus speaks the last word on the subject. In the midst of a crowd he sensed the need of a woman suffering from menorrhagia, prolonged and heavy bleeding, who had dared to venture out and to touch his clothes. He spoke no word of this to her, in spite of realizing that both he and the men pressed around him, had been made 'unclean' by the woman as she physically forced herself through the crowd of men to touch his cloak. Instead he said to her (Luke 8: 48) 'Daughter, be of good comfort: thy faith hath made thee whole; go in peace.' I wonder what all the surrounding men would have said if they had known what was wrong with her! Jesus must have told his disciples afterwards, that being how the story came out. Or perhaps the woman herself in the joy of being healed is the source of the story.

Leprosy and Other Diseases

At first glance there seems an irrational emphasis in chapters 13 – 15 on skin conditions like leprosy, and on bodily discharges, but of course this is not so. Rashes, eruptions or colour changes of the skin, and discharges from body orifices can reveal instantly that a person is ill and something about the nature of the illness. So these chapters draw attention to vital diagnostic symptoms. One needs to remember how disease could decimate, if not wipe out, the small population groups of those days. There were few cures or remedies and it was obvious that when someone became ill it could spread through the whole tribe, so some form of quarantine was essential. As the only authority figures, the priests were in charge of diagnosis and quarantine.

Chapter 16:
The Engraved Cherubim

In this chapter in Leviticus Yom Kippur (Day of Atonement) is instituted, although it is first mentioned in the 30th chapter of Exodus. Through Moses God informed Aaron, Israel's first high priest, that he was never to enter the Holy of Holies except on the Day of Atonement or he would die. On the Day of Atonement he could enter it after ritually cleansing himself and bearing an incense burner whose smoke would partly conceal the atonement cover while he sprinkled the blood of the sin offering on it.

One needs to take a closer look at the engraved figures of the Cherubim on the atonement cover. They seem in direct violation of one of the laws they were guarding: 'You shall not make for yourself an idol in the form of anything in heaven above or on the earth beneath or in the waters below.' Arguably, the cherubim were in the form of heavenly beings. Since, however, only the High Priest could enter the Holy of Holies nobody else was ever going to see the Cherubim. The High Priest himself would have to do so in a cloud of incense so even he would never see anything very clearly. When the Israelites prepared to continue the march, a cloth would be draped over the Ark in a set procedure that enabled little to be seen, and similarly when the Ark was replaced. So the statues of the Cherubim were not idols. They were completely different from the golden calf that was publicly displayed and which they all worshipped.

Significantly, the angels that prevented the exiled Adam and Eve from returning to the Garden of Eden were Cherubim. They ensured that sin-ridden humanity could not return to where God had dwelt in at-one-ment with sinless man. In the same way the golden statues stood on guard above the place where the holy laws prevailed. The cover separated man from goodness. It was the blood on it that achieved atonement and reconciliation.

In the other great Yom Kippur ritual, Aaron placed his hands on a goat and confessed the sins of the people. The goat was led into the desert and released it to a lonely death. This was the scapegoat, who, like Christ, experienced isolation and death for the sins of all the people. The scapegoat is movingly portrayed in two paintings by Holman Hunt executed from sketches that he made on the shores of the Dead Sea. One is in the Manchester Art Gallery and the other in the Lady Lever Art Gallery in Port Sunlight. It is easy to Google up images of both paintings.

To this day the Israelites observe the annual ritual of Yom Kippur, although for the past two thousand years it has of course been confined to readings, traditions and prayers. No sacrifices are involved. Strange, isn't it, that within only a very few years of Christ's offering himself for the sins of the whole world, the Romans all unknowingly broke down the temple and destroyed the means by which the Israelites could perform sacrifices. They were never able to perform them again, and still can't. The ultimate sacrifice had been made.

Chapters 17 – 18: The Sexual Taboos

Now comes one of the most fraught chapters in the book, chapter 18, in which all the sexual taboos are listed including bestiality, incest, adultery and homosexuality, which were all practised by the peoples of the Middle East at that time. Leviticus does not denounce people who are gender-ambivalent or who have sexual feelings for members of their own sex. What it does demand is celibacy from all whose desires are among the taboos, and that includes homosexuality and much heterosexuality.

In the Late Bronze and Early Classical Ages homosexuality was involved in two aspects of society: The military and the religious. Powerful groups of warriors and huntsmen established intimate bonds with younger cadets in a system known as *Paederestia.* An older man called either *eispnelas* or *philetor,* took possession of a young, often beautiful, young man called *aitas* or *kleinos*. Until the young man had endured together with his training the sexual demands of his mentor he could not be admitted into adult society. The rights or wishes of the young were not considered and abduction was often practised. Homosexual gang rape was not an unheard of occurrence. So there were evils connected with the practice. Then there were the highly attractive cults of Baal and Asherah that involved sexual activities with both male and female prostitutes, and child sacrifice. Perverted forms of sex descended into masochism, sadism, cruelty, brutality and bestiality. All of this is outlawed in Leviticus.

Does Jesus say anything about homosexuality? No. He does not. But he has a lot to say about lust. In the Sermon on the Mount he makes it clear that sex belongs in marriage. He does not define marriage. He was speaking to people who were familiar with Leviticus, and instead of telling them that the Leviticus sex laws did not matter, he told them that they needed to go further, that even to *look* on a person for whom they were not permitted to have sexual feelings, could cause them to have stirrings of lust and to commit adultery in their hearts. Here are his actual words: Mat 5: 27-30 'You have heard it was said, 'You shall not commit adultery.' But I say to you that everyone who looks at a woman with lustful intent has already committed adultery with her in his heart. If your right eye causes you to sin, tear it out and throw it away. For it is better that you lose *one of your members* than that your whole body be thrown into hell. And if your right hand causes you to sin, cut it off and throw it away. For it is better that you lose one of your members than that your whole body go into hell.'

There are those who would argue that Jesus says nothing about looking on a *man* with lustful intent and that that absolves all gays (but not lesbians of course.) This fact alone, that it would absolve gay men but not gay women, makes the argument specious. Jesus is clearly talking of any kind of sexual attraction outside marriage, which is how adultery was defined in those days: Any sex outside marriage. Jesus says nothing about gay marriage.

It becomes clear as one goes through the rest of the Torah that adultery is increasingly used as a metaphor for breaking faith with God and destroying one's relationship with him. The point Jesus makes is that what one looks on and desires with one's heart is what one will pursue when the opportunity presents itself, and any kind of lust puts someone or something ahead of God, which is why he said that if one's eye caused one to offend, it was better to blind oneself. He's pretty severe about divorce as well. If people took to heart what Jesus said about divorce they would be very careful; no, not about divorce, but about marriage. They would never contemplate marriage as anything but a commitment for life, easy if for better, exceedingly difficult if for worse. Of course there are injured parties in divorces, those who were forced into separation. One thing is certain. Jesus who loved the injured, the hurt, the abused and the victimised, opens his arms to them.

Chapter 19:
The Second Greatest Commandment

Leviticus Chapter 19 is one of the most sublime chapters in the Bible. It is wonderful and rarely noticed that immediately after the sexual strictures and constraints come the greatest commandments about love and inclusiveness in all literature. The chapter continues the theme of holiness, pointing out that it is not achieved by being pious or ritually clean but by treating those who are poor or different with respect, love and care.

It begins in verse nine where the Israelites were forbidden to reap to the edges of their fields, or to pick up the gleanings (the bits that fell during the main harvest.) They were not allowed to harvest their vineyards more than once, or to avail themselves of the windfalls. No. All the bits at the edges, the bits that fell, or were blown off, or were missed on a first picking had to be left for the 'poor and the alien.'

Stealing, lying and deception were all forbidden by the next few laws, as were swearing and taking God's name in vain. The Israelites were not allowed to defraud or rob one another, or to hold back wages, or to make things difficult for the disabled. They were not allowed to be unfair, to pervert justice or to spread slander. They were to do nothing that would endanger another person and were not to feel hatred for others. If somebody did wrong, that person had to be fairly rebuked by the person who discovered it, or the discoverer would share in the guilt. However, revenge was blacklisted, and even bearing a grudge was punishable.

Then comes one of the central messages of the Bible, one that Jesus quoted as the second most important commandment and on which, together with the first, he proclaimed that all the law and the prophets were based. It is in verse 18 of chapter 19:

'Thou shalt love thy neighbour as thyself.'

Neighbours included aliens, foreigners and immigrants, all of whom had to be treated with love and respect. From verse 33 one reads, 'And if a stranger sojourn with thee in your land, ye shall not vex him. But the stranger that dwelleth with you shall be unto you as one born among you, and thou shalt love him as thyself; for ye were strangers in the land of Egypt: I am the Lord your God.' Those who condemn the Bible as a book that preaches exclusivity, racism and dislike of immigrants rarely remember, or have never read, the nineteenth chapter of Leviticus.

The chapter goes on to forbid mating different animal species or mixing seed or weaving cloth from two kinds of material. (This last one is not as odd as one might think. In an age when re-cycling has become imperative it would be difficult to re-cycle clothing containing different kinds of material.) One of the odd strictures was that men could not trim their beards or the hair on the sides of their heads! One can think only that God, through Moses, was trying to get the Israelites to separate themselves from the pagan practices of the surrounding tribes. Other don't-do-as-the-pagans-do commandments were not to cut themselves as a sign of mourning and not to wear tattoos. There were health considerations involved with these; cuts and burns can become infected.

A frightening one is Leviticus 19:29: 'Do not degrade your daughter by making her a prostitute, or the land will turn to prostitution and be filled with wickedness.' It's not just that child-abuse is so powerfully prohibited. Equally impressive is the realization that abusing a child symptomises the absolute depth of moral degradation, an evil so iniquitous and complete that it can contaminate the entire earth with evil. The next commandment insists on Sabbath observation and respect for the tabernacle, and warns the Israelites not to dabble in any kind of spiritualism other than that associated with the tabernacle. The aged had to be shown respect and Moses insisted that the Israelites behave with scrupulous honesty in all their dealings with one another. Throughout the giving of these laws, Moses has God repeatedly telling the Israelites, 'I am the Lord.' He is warning them that others will try to persuade them to do things differently, but that the way of life he is demanding is the way of the Lord, the only right way.

Chapters 20 - 23: The Punishments and the Perfect Priest

The punishments were horrendous – the death penalty for almost all the listed crimes. The first and most heinous crime was child sacrifice but the death penalty was also incurred for spiritism, bestiality, incest, adultery and homosexuality (not gender ambivalence but sexual activity.) Even cursing one's parents was criminal. Moses repeatedly informed the Israelites of the danger of doing the abhorrent things that the Canaaanites were guilty of, and urged them to be holy because the Lord was holy and had set them apart to be his own.

In chapter 21 God seems to demand something virtually impossible from the Levites: A perfect priest, a man with no blemishes. The High Priest had to be permanently 'clean,' could never go near a corpse, could not shave his hair or his beard, could not marry a widow or a divorced woman, and could not be blind, lame, disfigured, deformed, crippled, maimed, hunch-backed or have any defect whatsoever. But this is a fallen world and no human is perfect; all have defects in varying degrees. The Israelites would never have been able to find a perfect candidate and would have had to make do with as good a candidate as they could get. So why did God insert this bit when it was impossible to meet all the criteria? The only reason that makes sense is that God was pointing the Israelites towards the one and only sinless being, the God-man, Jesus Christ, who in the fullness of time would be both perfect High Priest and unblemished Sacrifice, the one who would finally bring humanity into atonement with God. From the beginning God prepared the Israelites to recognise Christ, but sadly, when He came, there were but few who did. It's strange how again and again, as one travels through the Old Testament, these wondrous old writings are not fully comprehensible until one reaches forward into the New Testament, there to discover what they really mean. The ritual sacrifices and ceremonies of the tabernacle and later of the temple, and the character, status, dress and behaviour of those appointed to minister there, were all leading towards that blazing moment when Christ the Holy, Christ the Perfect, in the last days of his incarnation, entered the temple to begin his triumphant and final work of cleansing and restoration. It was not until Christ carried the sins of the entire world into destruction that the huge, heavy curtain separating the Holy of Holies in the Jewish Temple was torn from top to bottom (not by humans in other words) and God became accessible to all who chose to follow Christ.

Chapter 24 – 27: Coming to the End

The chapter begins with clear instructions on how the holy table in the Tabernacle was to be provided with bread and how the sacred lamps had to be filled with oil. This outward demonstration of physical holiness was contrasted with the dire consequences of inner, spiritual uncleanness in the grim story of the blasphemer, the son of an Israelite mother and an Egyptian father, who got into a fight with an Israelite and began to blaspheme the name of God. He was taken before Moses, who prayed and then ordered that the blasphemer be stoned to death.

All the laws about caring for the poor, for aliens, for the deprived and for servants or slaves are repeated. There was to be no ruthlessness, abuse or exploitation. Sabbath years and Years of Jubilee when all debts were wiped out and slaves freed were to be strictly observed. Everything was to be done to rehabilitate the poor and downtrodden. God also made humanity aware of the needs of the land at the very dawn of recorded history. The commands in Chapter 25 include the first ecological instructions, that the 'land itself must observe a Sabbath to the Lord. For six years sow your fields, and for six years prune your vineyards and gather your crops. But in the seventh year the land is to have a Sabbath of rest.' Not only that, but after seven cycles of seven years was to come the Jubilee Year, the fiftieth, which was to be a second fallow year.' Slaves who were permitted only from the surrounding nations, had to be treated humanely, and had to be freed in a Jubilee Year. For remaining faithful and obedient, God would grant the Israelites rain in season, and good crops, and they would live in safety in the land. However, if they persisted in disobedience, He would 'break down' their stubborn pride with dreadful afflictions and would drive them out of the land and disperse them among the nations, which is of course what happened in the end.

Leaving Leviticus

So there it is, the controversial book of Leviticus. I think the Septuagint translators got it right, calling the book Leviticus and thereby showing that it had more to say to the Levite priesthood than to the general populace. But it still has something to say to the rest of humanity, including those of the twenty first century. The stress that the book places on perfection, beauty and holiness throws into sharp relief the tawdry ugliness of western culture. Clothes are hideous; figures are obese or anorexic, behaviour is aggressive, rude, careless, unkind and dishonest; children when they lift their myopic gazes from their screens are loud, demanding, disrespectful and greedy; restraint is an unknown word; entitlement is on every lip that isn't mouthing off about the sanctity of freedom, spontaneity and impulse. Sex and celebrity are worshipped. Backs are turned on holiness, spirituality and the fine tuning of discipline, order, practice and hard work. In art, beauty has become an unacceptable word. Only the original, the outrageous, the seedy and the ugly matter. In music decibels, dissonances and discords triumph over subtlety, harmony and balance. Politically correct egalitarianism, nepotism, cronyism and bribery over-ride gift and talent.

And yet, when people seek respite and recreation, it is to God's creation that they go, to the mountains, the lakes, the seas, the night skies and the beaches, there to experience a sense of rest, peace, mystery and awe. It is then that one can perhaps find time for reflection and perhaps even the time to pick up a book like Leviticus and hear the quiet voice of God say: 'Ye shall be holy unto me: for I the Lord am holy.'

Part Five
SAFETY IN NUMBERS

The Lord Bless Thee and Keep Thee

Introduction

Suggesting, as the Septuagint title does, that the fourth book of the Bible consists of numbers, statistics and in all likelihood genealogies, makes the thought of ploughing through it wearisome. But don't be put off by the name. It's an exciting book and deep within its pages are not only one of the most fascinating short stories in all ancient literature, that of Balaam and his donkey, but also the account of the Israelites finally leaving Sinai and getting going again, and, best of all, it contains one of the most beautiful blessings in the whole Bible.

As the Israelites packed up after their long break at Mount Sinai, and got ready to set out on the second stage of their journey, it was in the knowledge that God had given them a spiritual and social infrastructure that would enable them to deal with any contingencies. All they needed were faith and trust. But the story of the Israelites is a microcosm of the story of mankind. In the same way that people today lack precisely those two commodities, so did the Israelites.

When they compiled their sacred writings and put the Torah together, the Israelites called the fourth book of the Pentateuch, *Bemidbar* 'in the desert.' Had they been obedient and trusted God, they would probably have settled in Canaan within a year or two, but they got cold feet and were too afraid to advance into the Promised

Land. One lives by one's choices. God kept the entire generation of doubters and unbelievers out of Canaan and in the desert for almost 40 years, wandering along desert paths and camping at long-forgotten oases. With the exception of Joshua and Caleb, no adult Hebrews who left Egypt, entered Canaan. (More later about why Moses didn't make it.) Their children were the ones who finally got to Canaan. The Book of Numbers tells the story of the faithless parents' wanderings in the desert.

The book has a second Hebrew name, *Wayedabber,* which translates as 'And he spoke.' The first words of *Numbers* are: 'And the Lord spoke to Moses.' Similar words occur more than 150 times in the book; in Leviticus they occur 50 times, indicating that Moses was almost certainly the recipient of the laws and revelations.

Chapters 1 – 2:
Too Many Israelites

Foreshadowing the New Testament, Numbers begins with a census and a genealogy. Whereas the purpose of the New Testament genealogy was to show that Jesus was a descendant of the House of David, the purpose of the Numbers genealogy was military, designed to discover how many able bodied men could fight for the Holy Land. The Levites were exempt; they had to look after the Tabernacle and its rituals. From each of the other tribes, a leader was appointed. Both Joseph's sons, Ephraim and Manasseh, were now tribes in their own right bringing the number of participating tribes back to twelve.

Now comes a huge problem and, not surprisingly, it's about numbers. If one counts all the able-bodied men over the age of 20, it comes to 603,550. That's an army of more than half a million men, and it presupposes a Hebrew population of more than two million. Sceptics refuse to allow that there could have been that many Israelites. This time I agree with the sceptics. Even if in the desert they could walk fifty abreast, if one allows two yards between walkers, the column would have been more than forty miles long. That's not very likely. If there were 200 000 Israelites the marching column would have been four and a half miles long. Even that is stretching it. I'll go along with the fact that there were very many Israelites, but they were probably more like 20 000 than two million. Even that would make the queue almost half a mile long.

In the second chapter one reads how the twelve tribes were organised when encamped. Always in a square, the camp would have the tabernacle in the middle with three tribes arranged on each of the four sides. The Eastern tribes were Judah, Issachar and Zebulon. They would form the vanguard when the journey recommenced. Behind them would be Levites carrying the Ark and the Tabernacle. Then would come the Southern tribes, Gad, Simeon and Reuben, followed by Levites carrying the Tabernacle furnishings, then the Western tribes, Ephraim, Manasseh and Benjamin (all descendants of the beloved Rachel) and finally the northern tribes, Napthtali, Asher and Dan.

Judah, the tribe of the fourth brother, was now leading the Israelites. It is from this tribe that Jesus would come. It is strange how God kept favouring younger sons over older ones. It was happening even before the Israelites came into the picture, in the story of the origins of man. It was through Adam's third son, Seth, that the line to the Messiah continued. Isaac was a younger son, as was Jacob. It isn't as if the younger sons were particularly honourable or morally superior either. A possible answer is that the risk that attaches to primogeniture is pride or hubris, a self-importance that leads towards defiance of authority and ultimately of God. C S Lewis calls pride the great sin. In *Mere Christianity,* he says: 'Pride leads to every other vice: it is the complete anti-God state of mind.' It seems to me that many if not all of the firstborn sons of whom we read in the Pentateuch suffered from this God-denying fault. Assured of status and wealth, they believed that they did not need God in their lives. Almost always, firstborn sons have early physical domination over their siblings and this in itself can lead to pride and stubborn refusal to submit to authority. As for Israel's own sons, the three oldest broke God's laws, so God elevated Judah above them.

    Even in this there is a prequel of Christianity. Jesus began his ministry among the Jews, the elder sons, but they, proudly believing that they alone were the sons of Abraham, rejected him; it was among the adopted younger sons, the Gentiles, that his disciples found humility, weakness, vulnerability and a preparedness to accept Him as Lord and Saviour. Never let it be forgotten, however, that the most important early Christians, the ones who carried the knowledge of Christ to the world, and most of whom paid with their lives, were Jews. And let it not be forgotten, either, that among Christians themselves the hideous sin of pride was soon to rear its ugly head.

Chapters 3 - 5:
The Mysterious Bitter Water Test

Chapters three and four list the Levite clans and gives their duties as priests. Then in chapter five comes something much beloved by sceptics and scoffers: God's instructions through Moses on how the guilt or innocence of a woman suspected of adultery had to be determined. From the perspective of the twenty first century with its drive towards gender equality, the *'Bitter Water Test'* appears laughable. But if one considers it in the light of a patriarchal and intensely male-dominated society, as still prevails in much of Asia and Africa today, then one perceives that the procedure sought to *protect* a woman who found herself trapped in a very difficult and life-threatening situation.

Adultery is almost impossible to prove since both parties are bent on secrecy. It is done behind backs and in hidden corners. Because of this it is almost impossible for a woman to prove that she hasn't done it. So it was a good thing that God devised a means to make the judgement himself, through the priests. Unlike tests for witchcraft in the Middle Ages, and for adultery in some parts of the world today, the test could not of itself harm the woman. She simply drank some fresh water with some bits of dust and carbon in it. She would not die, or become sick, or suffer any pain, but it was believed that if she were guilty she would become barren, whereas if she were innocent, she would bear healthy children.

Briefly the test, described in Numbers 5: 11-28 demanded that a suspicious husband not take the law into his own hands and administer rough and ready justice based on his jealousy or suspicion.

Neither could his or her family have any say in the matter. The husband had to take his wife to the priest and make a grain offering for the sin of his jealousy. The priest would give the wife her husband's grain offering to hold while he himself added a pinch of dust from the tabernacle floor to a jar of living water (meaning water from a stream, spring or well, and not stagnant water) that he himself was holding. Then the priest would intone the bitter water curse, that she would become barren if she had committed adultery but would bear children if she had been faithful. (The word 'thigh' was often used in Israelite times as a euphemism for genitalia, and perhaps the swollen abdomen meant a false pregnancy or a miscarriage.) The priest would pour some fresh water onto the written version of the curse, let it drain into the cup of bitter water, and tell the woman to drink some of it. Finally he would burn the jealousy offering on the altar; the woman would drink the rest of the water. And that was it.

What does one make of it in this day and age? First of all, ironic though it appears, there was protection for the woman built into these proceedings. No husband could act precipitately merely because he was suspicious or jealous. Secondly, it would take a long time before the ordeal could be proved; a woman might not conceive for years before having a child, as some of the patriarchs' wives did (Sarah and Rachel). It gives time for faith and trust to be restored between husband and wife. It encourages the woman not to be flirtatious and provocative towards other men, and the man not to be jealous and suspicious.

As always, one needs to remember the context. The Israelites were many. They were often described as a 'host.' They were nomads, on the march, needing to camp overnight. Conditions were crowded.

People were close together in the camps. There was little privacy. On moonless nights there was little light. One doesn't have to go further. The opportunities for all sorts of goings-on were legion. To preserve the safety and unity of the host demanded a highly intelligent legal and judicial system. That's what the Law of Moses provided. The Israelites managed superbly and they had no jails. Not only did the Bitter Water Test provide a wise and workable means for the people to live in peace, but it also strove to demonstrate to both the early Israelites and to readers of the Bible today that the sanctity of marriage, which is at the heart of the Bitter Water Test, was being used by God as an earthly demonstration of heavenly love.

The Bible makes this clear in many passages in both the Old and New Testaments: Marriage is an institution designed by God to demonstrate the relationship between himself and humanity. Revelation speaks several times of the church as the bride of Christ. Adultery means infidelity, breaking faith. It's not the embracing of an unlawful partner so much as that this severs a relationship. Anything that destroys the mysterious relationship between God and man, is called adultery in the Bible. That means that whenever one follows false doctrines or allows any idol to come between God and oneself, one commits adultery, and that is why Jesus, speaking to the crowd that had surrounded him, talks of 'this adulterous and sinful generation' (Mark 8:38.) If that's what he said about that generation, I wonder what he would say about ours! In the King James it says that adultery is to 'break wedlock.' That's the problem with adultery. It destroys marriage. In the third chapter of Jeremiah, the prophet says that God asked him, 'Have you seen what faithless Israel has done?

She has gone up on every high hill and under every spreading tree (sites of pagan worship) and has committed adultery there.'

It is true that in Numbers 5 one hears of only a woman suspected of adultery being put to death, but the law applied to men too. In Leviticus 20:10 both adulterer and adulteress had to be executed, and in Deuteronomy, the last book of the Torah, one comes across the same warning: if a man sleeps with another man's wife, both must die. What Numbers 5 is concerned with however is not the proven crime, but the suspicion of it.

One cannot read this Numbers 5 account of suspected adultery without recalling one of the best known New Testament passages on the subject: That of the Pharisees bringing to Jesus a woman taken in adultery. The story is between the seventh and eighth chapters of John: 7:53 – 8:11. Christians have worried about this story for centuries. Sometimes it has been left out of the gospel and sometimes it has been put back. In its comment the NIV states: 'The earliest manuscripts and many other ancient witnesses do not have John 7:53 – John 8:11' but then it includes it. It's been omitted from my copy of The New English Bible.

There are good reasons for Bible scholars omitting this story. It's not only that it doesn't appear in the earliest manuscripts. It's also a very uncomfortable story. Most people love it unquestioningly, believing that it demonstrates how Jesus embarrassed the Pharisees by forcing them to acknowledge their own sin, and that it shows his mercy towards the woman who was taken in adultery. But it creates a difficult situation for any earthly system of justice based on Christian principles. Jesus said to the Pharisees, 'If any one of you is without sin, let him be the first to throw a stone at her.'

Nobody is without sin. There has only ever been one sinless person. Judges, jurors and magistrates are all sinful but they are essential elements of our judicial system. Without them the system could not function. However, as the reader will see, the context of this story is important. It significantly alters what at first appears to be the meaning of the words.

According to St John, some Pharisees and lawyers brought to Jesus a woman who had been caught in adultery. The Torah required that if adultery was suspected, the husband had to take his wife to the priest and that there had to be at least two witnesses who would be required to throw the first stones of execution. However, there were no witnesses in the group that approached Jesus. If they had been there, they would have stepped forwards when Jesus asked for those who were without sin to throw the first stone, because the sin that Jesus was talking about was the sin of bearing false witness, for which the penalty was death.

The Pharisees who brought the woman to Jesus were simply using her as bait to trap their inveterate enemy, Jesus, into making a false move. They told Jesus that she had been 'caught in adultery' and that the Torah demanded that she be stoned to death. Knowing that Jesus had gained an enormous following with his acts of mercy and love, they thought that they'd got him, because there was no way he could show mercy to this woman without contradicting the Torah, but if he upheld it and agreed that she be stoned to death, the people would lose faith in him. The Pharisees must have found it hard not to gloat when they asked Jesus, 'Rabbi, What do you say?' They were going to get their own back at last. This Jesus had accused them, in this very place, of being hypocrites, blind guides, death dealers (whitewashed tombs), unclean and wicked! With expectant faces they watched him. What they failed to recognise was that they were dealing with God. He knew exactly what they were thinking and what they were trying to do. His response to their question and the very few words that he uttered sent every one of them away, humiliated and probably more than a little afraid. How could a humble nobody who had grown up in a carpenter's shop have had the knowledge and wisdom so summarily to defeat what were supposed to be the best minds of the day?

He did it in a way they least expected, not only by upholding the Torah but also by acting it out before them, this fifth act of Numbers to be precise. In a very few minutes the men slid ignominiously away, the woman walked off free, and I am sure the crowd looked on with open-mouthed astonishment before cheering to high heaven. The Pharisees and teachers of the law did not realize, or did not want to realize, that Jesus was the Christ. But reading the account two thousand years later, and accepting that Jesus is who he said he was, a reader can enjoy an awesome moment of revelation.

One needs to look at what happened from two perspectives, that of the Jews who crowded around Jesus that day, and that of Christians today who know that Jesus is God, and that he is the source of living water. All that the clamouring crowd would have been aware of was that two witnesses were needed to throw the first stones, and that there did not seem to be any witnesses. It is only Christians who can see that Jesus acted out the Bitter Water Test on that memorable occasion. Here's how he did it.

- The woman had to be taken to the *temple* to stand before the High Priest and God; Jesus, who *is* both God and our High Priest, was preaching in the temple when this incident occurred.
- There had to be living water, and Jesus is the source of living water (he told the woman at the well in Samaria that if she asked him he would give her 'living water' and she would never thirst again - John 4: 10 and 13)
- The holy water had to be mixed with the dust of the temple floor, and the *written* name of God (which would have made the original curse valid) would have to have been washed into it. Jesus is living water, the source of our being. By bending down and writing in the dust, he brought the dust into contact with the living water. He wrote in the dust, as the priest had to write the curse for the water ordeal.
- It is God who is the final judge. Jesus is God.

If there were no witnesses to accuse the woman, anyone throwing a stone at her would be guilty of murder and liable to execution. When Jesus invited one who was without sin to throw the first stone, they were caught. Not one of those present had been a witness. If there had been, he would have stepped forward when Jesus spoke. *The sin Jesus was talking about was the sin of lying and bearing false witness for which the punishment was death.* The men were hoist by their own petard. It is a brilliant piece of courtroom drama and would not have been lost on the crowd. They understood well the Law of Witnesses and The Bitter Water Test, which was still being used at the time of Jesus. It was done away with by

Rabbi Yochanon Ben Zakkai just before the Romans destroyed the Temple in 70 A.D.

At the end when the Pharisees had all slunk away, Jesus asked the woman if anyone had condemned her (only a witness could) and she replied: 'No-one.' He told her to go and to leave her life of sin. (This indicates that she almost certainly had committed adultery.) As always one senses his deep love and compassion for her and any reader must feel that she was saved in more ways than one. (A wonderful website 'Toraclass Podcasts' was a great help with this interpretation.)

Chapter 6:
Total Commitment and the Great Blessing

To be a Nazirite means to make a vow to God that one will lead a life of abstinence and discipline. It was open to both men and women and meant not partaking of any alcohol, not even grapes, not cutting one's hair and above all remaining ritually absolutely clean. One could not therefore go anywhere near a corpse. The temple rituals and sacrifices involving the taking of the vow and ritual cleansing after inadvertently breaking it (such as the death in one's abode of a family member) are all spelled out in chapter six. The most important thing about being a Nazirite was consecration to God. This is reiterated in verse eight: 'Throughout the period of his isolation he is consecrated to the Lord,' and in verse twelve: 'He must dedicate himself to the Lord for the period of his separation.' Some made the commitment for a limited period only, but others made a lifelong commitment to remain completely consecrated to God. Jesus lived his entire life consecrated to the Godhead but there were times, like the fast in the desert, when he intensified his commitment and embarked on a period of utmost abstinence and self-discipline.

Possibly the most famous Nazirite in the Old Testament was Samson, who was duped by Delilah into revealing the source of his inordinate strength, his vow not to cut his hair. The story of Samson is in the Book of Judges.

At the end of chapter six, after all this talk of total commitment to God, come some of the most beautiful words in the Bible, the reward for commitment. If one links this to what Jesus told his followers, to be in the world but not of it, one can see that all those who take it upon themselves to walk with God in the course of their daily lives are open to this blessing. Here it is:

The Lord bless thee and keep thee,
The Lord make His face to shine upon thee
And be gracious unto thee;
The Lord lift up His countenance upon thee
And give thee peace.

John Rutter has set those words to exquisite music. There are many recordings of it on YouTube. It was sung by our church choir one Sunday morning. In the choir were my four grand-children, my younger daughter and my daughter-in-law. (It is the church in which John Newton was vicar when he wrote the words of 'Amazing Grace.)

Play any version of the John Rutter setting and you will understand why I had tears in my eyes that Sunday morning.

Chapters 7 – 11:
The Tabernacle Dedicated and on their Way at Last

The tabernacle was completed, furnished and dedicated, and the leaders of the twelve tribes provided the Levites with oxen and carts to convey the tabernacle and all its appurtenances. The holiest things were going to be carried on the shoulders of the Kohathites, one of the Levite tribes. No longer a disorderly, frightened rabble but an orderly and disciplined people focussed on God with a powerful system of law and order, the Israelites finally resumed the march. They woke one morning to find the sign they had been waiting for; the cloud had lifted from the Tabernacle. The excitement must have been immense. Even as they packed the last-minute things, rounded up the children and got themselves to their assemblage points, the purpose-built silver trumpets sounded, and Nahshon, son of Amminadab of the tribe of Judah, led them away, with the Ark of the Covenant borne before him and the standard of Judah flying above. As the family of Moses took their places near the front of the march, Moses asked his brother-in-law, Hobab, son of Jethro, to go with them because of his great knowledge of the desert. Although it does not say so in Numbers, it seems that Hobab acquiesced. (Judges 1:16)

It is difficult to credit, but after only three days on the move, the people were at it again, complaining bitterly about the terrible hardships they were enduring. They were sick and tired of bland, tasteless manna; also, a fire had broken out in the camp. Moses heard all the wailing and gnashing of teeth and told God the burden of leadership was too much. God told Moses to appoint 70 elders as assistants and said he would supply the people with meat, so much meat they would get sick of it.

Poisonous Quail

The meat came! On the wind! Quail! Thousands of the birds descended on the camp, and the Israelites caught, killed and spread them all around and ate their fill. But God was still angry with them and they did indeed get sick; a dreadful plague struck the camp. I was intrigued with this and wondered if it was possible to become sick from eating quail (members of the pheasant family.) I found that indeed it is. Quail can be poisonous when they are migrating. Usually the spring migration is much farther west but there have been accounts of spring migrants travelling across the Sinai, particularly if they have been blown off course, and one reads in the Bible: 'Now a wind went out from the Lord and drove quail in from the sea.' The condition that develops in people who have eaten poisonous quail is Coturnism. It is presumed to be caused by a poisonous berry or insect consumed by the birds as they store energy for the long migration flight. The complaining Israelites may have eaten such contaminated quail or perhaps some of the meat went bad when they tried to preserve it by sun-drying dead birds, 'they spread them all around the camp.' (11:32) In whatever way it happened, many Israelites died.

Chapter 12: Aaron and Miriam's Disloyalty

As if the death-by-quail story wasn't enough it's instantly followed by another sad story, at the beginning of chapter 12, this one caused by the pride and jealousy of Aaron and Miriam. They criticised Moses for marrying a Cushite woman. Whether Zipporah, a Midianite, was being contemptuously labelled Cushite by Miriam and Aaron, or whether Zipporah had died and Moses had married a Cushite, is not clear. What is is that Moses's wife was not the real problem. It was the pride and jealousy of Miriam and Aaron who no longer wanted to accept that God spoke only to Moses. Weren't they as good as he was? The next verse (12:3) is clearly an insertion by a later editor. There's no way Moses would have called himself the most humble man on the face of the earth. It's hardly a humble remark.

God summoned all three of them to the Tabernacle, and ordered Aaron and Miriam to step forward. He spoke these remarkable words to them: 'When a prophet of the Lord is among you, I reveal myself to him in visions; I speak to him in dreams. But this is not true of my servant Moses; he is faithful in all my house. With him I speak face to face, clearly, and not in riddles; he sees the form of the Lord. Why then were you not afraid to speak against my servant Moses?' Those are amazing words, not only because Miriam and Aaron were in fact hearing God, as they had wanted, but also because of the revelation that God was not communicating with Moses in dreams and visions, but in direct talk when Moses could see 'the form of the Lord.' It means Jesus. God the Father revealed himself to Moses only once, at the top of Mount Sinai, when God protected Moses from seeing him completely because such an appearance is not possible for physical life. Moses emerged from that meeting ablaze with the radiance of God and had to pull a scarf around himself to prevent his people from running away. The incident is recounted in Exodus.

After God's appearance in a cloud to Moses, Aaron and Miriam, Miriam discovered that she was leprous. Aaron, realizing it was jealousy and pride that had brought this on them, brokenly acknowledged to Moses that they had sinned, and begged Moses not to hold it against their sister. Moses instantly cried to God to heal her. God replied that she would have to remain outside the camp for seven days but could be brought back, healed, after that. The Israelites were unable to resume their journey for the week of Miriam's banishment. As soon as she returned they set off again, their next stop Kadesh in the Desert of Paran. The long march was nearly over – or was it!

Chapters 13 - 15: The Fatal Sin of the Spies

God told Moses to send a man from each of the tribes on a reconnaissance trip to Canaan. Two of the spies have earned their places if not in history then certainly in legend. These were Hoshea (Joshua) son of Nun from the tribe of Ephraim, and Caleb from the tribe of Judah. It was Moses who changed Hoshea's name to Yeshua, Joshua, which means 'God is generous' or 'God saves.' It is of course that other Joshua, Jesus, in whom one finds the ultimate demonstration of the generosity of God and his determination to save his people from sin and death. In Hebrew the name Joshua is *Yeshua*, which becomes *Iēsous* in Greek, and in English 'Jesus.'

Moses ordered the spies to find out as much as they could about Canaan and its people. What sort of resistance would the Israelites encounter? Were the towns strongly fortified? Could they bring back some fruit? The spies who were actually more like journalists than secret agents duly explored the Promised Land. The first city that they came to was Hebron and they were amazed at its size and the strength of its fortifications. The surrounding fields looked fertile and lush. They explored most of the country and on the return journey slung some pomegranates and figs over a pole and carried it back to the Israelites camp where they made their report.

Yes, they announced at the tops of their voices, it was indeed a land flowing with milk and honey. Then came the 'but.' The inhabitants were too powerful, they cried. 'We even saw descendants of Anak there!' (The Anak were giants.) The cities were too strongly fortified. There was no way they would be able to occupy the land promised to Abraham. The two pro-government journalists, Joshua and Caleb, protested loudly. 'We should go up and take possession of the land,' Caleb called out, 'for we can certainly do it!' But the opposition press howled them down. 'We can't attack these people! They are huge! We even saw Nephilim giants. We seemed like grasshoppers in our own eyes and we're sure we looked the same to them.'

The inevitable happened. It never did take long for the Israelites to become thoroughly demoralised, and like their twenty first century counterparts, they allowed the media to shape their fears and emotions. If only they had died in Egypt, they sobbed, or in the desert. Why had they been brought to Canaan to be hacked to death by enemy swords? What would happen to the women and children? It was too ghastly to contemplate. There was only one thing to do. Back to Egypt! They would choose a decent leader and follow him back to dear old Egypt. Why had they ever left it?

Moses, Aaron, Joshua and Caleb, remonstrated, pleaded and tore their clothes in frustration. Desperately they tried to convince the Israelites that God had removed his protection from the Canaanites; 'The Lord is with *us*. Do not be afraid of *them*.' The Israelites refused to listen. In spite of all the miracles, they had lost faith in God. Things became nasty. The people picked up stones and prepared to rid themselves permanently of Moses and his assistants.

Then God appeared. It must have been a dramatic appearance. The ten negative spies were struck down and died instantly. The Israelites were turned from a death-dealing mob into a pack of terrified cowards. Dropping their stones they prayed for forgiveness. 'We have sinned,' they cried. 'We will go up to the place God promised us.' But it was too late. God told Moses that he would no longer tolerate the contempt of the people and would make a new covenant with Moses and his family. Moses begged God to reconsider. 'By your power,' he pleaded, 'you brought these people up from among them (the Egyptians).' He said God would lose his reputation among the other nations if he allowed the people to perish in the desert.

As always in his dealings with people, God responded to the love and goodness of Moses. He agreed not to put the people to death but neither would he allow them to enter the Promised Land. Only their children would. The 'grumbling Israelites' (God's words) would die in the desert. One can't help but respond to a history in which the teller or writer denounces his own people as cowardly, weak, contemptible and negative. It is much easier to believe such a story than one in which the writer everlastingly tells us how wonderful, brave and true his people were. When Moses informed the Israelites of God's decision, instead of accepting what they had brought upon themselves, a large group said that they would go up towards the high country anyway and take possession of it. Moses tried desperately to explain to them that they would be going without God's protection and would be in mortal danger. But 'in their presumption' they went, and were slaughtered by the Canaanites. There will of course be some who read this to mean that when the Israelites made their first attempt to conquer Canaan they were beaten back and it was only after several more attempts that they managed to overcome the indigenous peoples and take possession of the land. Perhaps. There is no way anybody can prove exactly how Israel was established. In fact there is a serious school of thought that there was no military conquest at all but that the Israelites drifted in from the desert over a period of time, gradually claiming the land by force of numbers.

Because they would never live in the land promised to their ancestors, it must have been like coals of fire on the heads of the Israelites to have to listen to God's instructions on how to behave in 'the land I am giving you as a home.' However, their children would live there, so they had to learn the instructions and pass them on. Moses probably devoted much of the ensuing forty years to his writing and to making sure that Joshua learned to write so that he could take control of the documents when Moses died.

Two verses worthy of note are 15: 15-16: 'The community is to have the same rules for you and for the alien living among you;

this is a lasting ordinance for the generations to come. You and the alien shall be the same before the Lord: The same laws and regulations will apply both to you and to the alien living among you.' If God was making provision for aliens so early in the story, it seems unlikely that he would condone, or even order, the slaughter of every man, woman and child among the opposition tribes, in which case those very worrying verses in which God appears to command such slaughter need to be read with circumspection. This is why it is so necessary to read the Bible in its entirety. Only then can its abiding message be understood and its anomalies and errors be assigned their proper place, as the outpourings of a vulnerable and often desperate people who sometimes allowed their fears and lack of faith to compromise the great revelations they were being given.

I find the story about the man stoned to death for gathering wood on the Sabbath difficult and uncomfortable because of the pietism of the holier-than-thou accusers who hauled him before Moses. It was Jesus of course who finally made people see the danger of judging others; until then judgmentalism and tale-bearing seemed to have been the norm. Possibly, though, this story is included to show that the Israelites were indulging in flagrant Sabbath-breaking. The next law is strange, Numbers 15: 37-41, but delightful: Each man had to wear tassels at the four corners of his outer garment. Tassels! The bits of corded fringe would swing with each movement. I like the Hebrew word for the fringe, the onomatopoeic tzitzit. I can just hear those tassels going tzitzit tzitzit as the wearer walked, reminding him to obey God's law.

Chapter 16:
The Korah Rebellion

No sooner were the tassels instituted than some Israelites were committing the very crimes that the tassels warned against, 'going after the lusts of their own hearts and eyes.' This time it was the lust for power. Korah, a Kohathite Levite who already enjoyed a prestigious position caring for and conveying the Ark and other Tabernacle furnishings, decided that he was just as good as Moses and Aaron, so why wasn't he a priest, or better still, overall leader of Israel? Like all who lust for power, he needed accomplices. He couldn't find any among his fellow Levites, so he went to the tribe next door, the Reubenites, and among them found Dathan and Abiram. These three managed to get another 250 Israelite leaders to join them. As a body they approached Moses and Aaron and demanded why they had set themselves above the rest of the Israelites because the 'whole community was holy.' It is always the way of revolutionary power-seekers to pretend that they want power for the entire body politic when in fact they want power for only themselves.

A distraught Moses fell on his face, perceiving that the presumption of Korah, Dathan and Abiram would end in tragedy. Finally, he stood up and announced that in the morning God would decide who was 'holy.' He commanded that the rebels appear on the morrow carrying censers charged with live coals and incense. This must have delighted them because normally only the priests could bear censers before the Lord. Moses then took Korah and the Levites who were supporting him aside and asked why they were not content with the role God had assigned them. God had distinguished them by separating them from the rest of the community to work in the Tabernacle and look after it. Now they wanted Aaron's priestly role as well. He was unable to convince them so he dismissed them and summoned Dathan and Abiram to appear before him. Those two refused even to appear! 'We will not come,' they said. 'Isn't it enough that you have brought us up out of a land flowing with milk and honey to kill us in the desert?' How short are men's memories! The land flowing with milk and honey was Egypt, where they had been slaves.

The next morning all the rebels appeared before the Tent of Meeting, defiantly carrying their censers. God told Moses and Aaron to stand aside so that he could obliterate the ungrateful, ever-complaining Israelites, but both Moses and Aaron fell on their faces before the Lord, begging him not kill all for the sins of a few. As always, God responded to their love and concern and told them to order the rest of the Israelites to stand away from the conspirators. Moses got up and warned the people to get away from the tents of Korah, Dathan and Abiram, telling them that they would realise that if the ground opened up and swallowed the tents, it was not the doing of Moses, but of God.

And that is what happened. A major earthquake erupted under the encampment, swallowing the tents and families of all the conspirators. At the same time fire, possibly lightning, struck the 250 leaders who were standing with their censers before the assemblage, and killed them all. Instead of accepting that their leaders had acted irreverently and rebelliously, the Israelites accused Moses and Aaron of killing them. God became angry but Moses tried desperately to save the Israelites, telling Aaron to run among them offering incense and making atonement for them. By their love and efforts, Moses and Aaron managed to save many from the wrath of God but thousands died in the plague that God allowed to sweep through the camp.

Chapters 17 – 19: Aaron's staff blooms and the Red Heifer Sacrifice

After the horrendous happenings of the previous chapter, God made it clear in Chapter 17 that Aaron and his descendants were priests of Israel, and nobody else. God told Moses to order the leader of each of the tribes to bring his staff inscribed with the tribal name to the Tent of Meeting. One staff would sprout, and that one would belong to the man chosen to be His priest. The next morning the Levite staff, Aaron's, had not only sprouted but had budded, blossomed and produced almonds. When the Israelites saw this they were terrified, and, for a while desisted from complaining.

That the red heifer sacrifice is introduced at this point in the story is significant because a plague had swept through the camp (at the end of chapter 16) leaving thousands dead. The sacrifice is concerned with purification after death but much about it remains mysterious. Part of the answer probably lies in that God, through Moses, found it necessary to separate these Egyptianised Israelites from the embalming, funereal and entombing practices of their former overlords, and to ensure that the Israelites dealt speedily with thousands of rotting corpses. Unlike all the other sacrifices, this animal had to be a cow, not a bull; It had to be completely red, meaning rare or one of its kind; it had to be three years old, unblemished and never yoked; the sacrifice had to be performed outside the camp, not in front of the Tabernacle; the animal had to be slaughtered and burned with all its blood (all the other animal sacrifices had to have had their blood drained away); It ritually contaminated the priest who performed the sacrifice and any assistant who helped him; items used to cleanse leprosy (cedar wood, hyssop and scarlet wool) had to be burned with the heifer; unlike all the other sacrifices, the ash of this animal had to be preserved and used in water to give it cleansing properties, making it the 'water of separation;' it, and the similar heifer sacrifice described in Deut. 21: 2 – 9, were the only sacrifices that led to the cleansing of a person or persons who had been in presence of death or the dead, and the only sacrifices performed away from the Tabernacle; the priest sprinkled an unclean person with the water of separation, but the act of cleansing made the priest himself temporarily unclean.

According to the records of the Rabbis, the Israelites have only ever had nine red heifers, whose ashes must have been kept for generations. The Jews do not expect to have a tenth red heifer until the coming of the Messiah. Christians see the red heifer as yet another extraordinary symbol of Christ. Like the red heifer, Christ is unique, had a three-year ministry, and was sacrificed outside the city. From the crown of thorns and the scourging by the Roman soldiers, he was red from his own blood. The cedar wood symbolises the cross, the hyssop symbolises purity, and it was of course a stalk of hyssop on which a sponge was raised to the lips of Jesus when he hung on the cross. The scarlet wool represents the blood of Christ. The sacrifice of Jesus purifies and sanctifies all who acknowledge him, but to achieve that, just as the priest who performed the red heifer sacrifice became unclean, so did Jesus become unclean as he took the sins of the world upon his shoulders, separating himself from God. Just as the water of separation containing the ash of the red heifer brought cleansing from death, so did the risen Christ, the source of living water, defeat death and bring eternal life. It is another breathtaking prequel to Christ, and within a few years of Christ's ascension, the temple was destroyed and the Jews could no longer perform either the Red Heifer or any other sacrifice.

Chapter 20:
Moses not allowed to lead the Israelites into Canaan; Deaths of Miriam and Aaron

Isn't it extraordinary how Miriam's death is brushed off in just a few words at the beginning of this chapter? She played such an important role in the story of Moses. It is true that Miriam joined Aaron in a conspiracy against Moses but it seems to me that she paid her dues, and to have her death dismissed so summarily is very sad, but symptomatic I suppose of the patriarchal times in which she lived.

Now follows another version of the water-from-a-rock story: Just as in Exodus, this version tells how the desperately thirsty Israelites were trudging across the Desert of Sin, although it is called Zin this time. The NIV notes say that after wandering around the desert for forty years, the Israelites finally came to the same place from which they'd started their wanderings and had exactly the same quarrel with Moses and Aaron as they had had on the previous occasion. That sounds a bit far-fetched to me. Having said that, though, there is a significant difference between the two accounts. In the Exodus version God ordered Moses to strike the rock with his staff, after the Israelites had been almost ready to stone the brothers for leading them away from Egypt and bringing them to a place where they were convinced they were going to die of thirst. Moses struck the rock as he was bid and water gushed forth. This time, in the Numbers story, God told Moses not to strike the rock but to speak to it. But Moses was desperately angry with the rebellious Israelites. It seems as if he had finally lost patience with them. Instead of doing as God ordered, he yelled at them, demanding to know whether they thought he and Aaron couldn't bring water out of a rock if they so wanted. Then he struck the rock twice, instead of speaking to it. Water ran but God told Moses that because he had not trusted him and had not honoured him, Moses would not lead the Israelites into the land he was giving them. It seems that no matter who you are if you enjoy power for any length of time, it corrupts you. So with Moses. I don't think Moses was a bad man but I think that for a moment he forgot who was really in charge.

One is not told what Moses felt about his punishment. But he writes in conclusion to this incident: 'These were the waters of Meribah, where the Israelites quarrelled with the Lord and where he showed himself holy among them.' Moses perceived instantly that by claiming the miracle for himself and Aaron he had lied to the people. The miracle was from God. The holiness was God's. Having by now learned much about Moses, one imagines that he would have been deeply repentant, and accepting of his punishment. In any event he must have been getting very tired by now; he was 120 years old. I suspect he wanted nothing so much as to surrender his charge and to be gathered to where his ancestors dwelt in eternal communion with God. Although he knew now that he was not himself going to be allowed into the Promised Land, he set out doggedly to lead the Israelites along the last stretch, fulfilling his duty to the end.

It seems that most of the adults who had listened to the cowardly spies must have died by now, and the next generation of Israelites was ready to make the final advance. When the Edomites refused to allow them to cross their land, Moses led them towards Mount Hor, where Aaron died. Moses appointed Aaron's son, Eleazar, as the new high priest. So ends Aaron's story. He had been a good, powerful and loyal man, most of the time. It is not easy to accept the leadership of a younger sibling but except for two occasions, Aaron accepted his secondary role and supported Moses through all the years of opposing Pharaoh and leading the Israelites towards the Promised Land.

Chapter 21: The Brazen Snake

As they continued their journey, the King of Arad sent an army against the Israelites. They asked God for help. It is interesting that it was not Moses who made this plea to God, but the Israelites themselves. It seems that Moses's own health was beginning to fail. God granted the Israelites a victory and they felt that God was helping them at last to fight for their homeland. Afterwards Moses directed them towards the Red Sea, so that they could go around Edom, but the Israelites were furious. Forgetting that it was God who had enabled them to win, they brandished their weapons, keen to take on Edom. They told Moses they were not going to listen to him, and added that he had better know too that they were sick to death of manna. 'We detest this miserable food.' It was tantamount to rejecting God's mercy and grace.

As a result, God sent a plague of snakes among them. Terrified, dying in agony and acknowledging their guilt, the survivors begged Moses to ask God for help. God told Moses to make a bronze image of a snake, put it on a pole and hoist it up. The afflicted who looked at the engraved snake would be cured. Now this is a really strange incident. It seems in almost total violation of the second commandment not to make and worship any graven image. It is difficult to come up with an answer to the mystery of it but there are some verses in the Gospel of John that throw light on it. St John quotes Jesus saying: 'Just as Moses lifted up the snake in the desert, so the Son of Man must be lifted up, that everyone who believes in him may have eternal life.'

In Judao-Christianity the serpent or snake is associated with evil. The Israelites, dying of snakebite in that far off time, looked up at the bronze snake, acknowledged that the venom of evil was within them, and sought God's mercy and forgiveness. They were saved. In the same way Jesus calls on those who trust him to look up at him on the cross, acknowledge their guilt and repent, and he will carry their evil into extinction and grant them eternal life. The bronze-serpent story is yet another incident that makes little sense without the fulfilment of the New Testament. That the Israelites were unable to see it as a prophecy becomes clear when one reads in the eighteenth chapter of the second book of Kings that Hezekiah breaks into pieces the bronze snake of Moses because the Israelites had begun worshiping it as an idol called Nehushtan, which is simply the Hebrew word for bronze snake.

After the snake incident, Israel abandoned its attempt to take on Edom and waited at Kadesh Barnea, the place from which Moses had sent the spies into Canaan long years before. From here Moses led them to the north east so that they could come into Canaan from that direction. Two powerful countries had to be crossed or overcome: Moab and the land of the Amorites. When Sihon, the King of the Amorites, refused to allow them to pass through his territory, the Israelites defeated him, conquering most of the Amorite cities, including Heshbon. Next they defeated Og, the giant king of Bashan, and all his army.

Chapters 22 – 24
Balaam and his Donkey

Now, camped on the eastern bank of the Jordan, opposite Jericho, the Israelites had Canaan in their sights at last. But they were encamped right next to the Moabites, and Balak, the king of Moab, was unconvinced that Israel had no designs on his country. He had heard what had happened to the Amorites and King Og and he thought Moab was next in line. Terrified, he decided the only way to get rid of the menace was to employ powerful magic. So he sent for Balaam, son of Beor, a magician with an international cursing reputation.

The Story of the Torah

There is archaeological support for this Bible story. Stone fragments inscribed with visions that appeared to the 'cursing prophet, Balaam, son of Beor' were found in 1967 at Deir Alla in Jordan. The fragments were from the wall of a building that was destroyed somewhere between 840 and 760 B.C. Alan Millard describes the Deir Alla Inscription as 'the oldest example of a book in a West Semitic language written with the alphabet and the oldest piece of Aramaic literature.'[38] It is this that strikes me as significant about the Deir Alla Inscription, not only that it suggests that a seer called Balaam once lived, but that centuries before the Israelites were enslaved in Babylon, a corroboration of a Bible story was already written in stone in an area where they had been.

It's a strange story, the biblical story of Balaam, with subtle nuances that are difficult to unravel. Having re-read it now, I think it is possibly one of the first bits of real literature in the Bible. I think that the Story of Balaam may be based on a seer who actually lived but the version in the Bible is fictionalised with a very clear purpose: To encourage the Israelites to overcome their fears and move into the Promised Land. That a Moabite king, or another of the Israelites' enemies, would have sought help from a magician to get rid of the invaders is quite possible. However, what the Israelite story-tellers did with the facts was to create a version as imaginative as Shakespeare's *Henry V*, their intention being to get the Israelites to wave their swords on high and, crying 'For God and Israel,' charge

---

[38] Millard, Alan: *Authors, Books, and Readers in the Ancient World* in *The Oxford Handbook of Biblical Studies,* Edited by Rogerson, J. W. and Lieu, J. M, Oxford University Press, 2006

into the Promised Land. The story appears in chapters 22 to 24 in Numbers. This is what it says:

When the Moabite king, Balak, saw the hosts of Israel camped on the bank of the Jordan, he made a hasty alliance with the Midianites, at the same time sending a delegation of princes to request the help of the magician, Balaam, who lived in Pethor. The Moabite princes told Balaam that a huge tribe had come from Egypt and were encamped right next to them. King Balak wanted Balaam to curse these people so that they could be defeated and driven out of the country. The princes handed over the divination fee, and Balaam invited them to spend the night, promising to tell them in the morning what his god had revealed to him. This is perhaps an opportune moment to remember that these events were occurring during the Bronze Age collapse. It would not have been difficult for a cursing 'prophet' to build a reputation by predicting downfalls.

The Israelite story-teller says God appeared to Balaam during the night and told him the Israelites were blessed and could not be cursed, so Balaam sent the princes home. When they told Balak what Balaam had said, Balak sent another delegation to Balaam, this one with more wealth carried by more powerful princes, but with the same request: Come and curse the Israelites. God was angry when Balaam invited the princes to stay instead of instantly sending them away. He said Balaam could go to Moab but was to do only what God told him.

The next morning Balaam set off on his donkey with two servants and the princes. This is where the story becomes humorous. Balaam was hugely proud of the fact that he could 'see' what the gods wanted and was the most famous 'seer' in the entire country, but when he set out for Moab, he was unable to see the angel barring his way with a drawn sword. (The princes and servants must have gone on ahead.) The donkey took one look at the angel and scampered off the road. An irate Balaam flogged the poor creature until it turned back. The angel had disappeared. Farther along, in a narrow, walled passage, it reappeared. Desperately the donkey tried to squeeze between the frightful apparition and the wall, scraping Balaam's foot. This time Balaam's fury knew no limits. He beat the donkey worse than before until badly hurt and frightened the poor animal got going again. Ahead, the road entered an even narrower defile where there was no room to turn. In this impossible place, the angel of the Lord appeared again. Bruised and battered, the donkey took one look at the dreadful being and collapsed in a heap. Furious, Balaam leaped off and proceeded to bludgeon it with his staff. This was the moment in which God granted the power of speech to the donkey.

'What have I done to you to make you beat me these three times?' the donkey asked. Instead of being amazed at the donkey's sudden ability to talk, Balaam proceeded to argue with it. Every word that he uttered revealed his pride, insensitivity and complete inability to see beyond his nose. He told the donkey it had embarrassed him and he added that if he had had a sword he would have killed it there and then. The donkey reminded Balaam that he had always dutifully carried him and had always obeyed him, implying that something really untoward must have happened. Balaam acknowledged that the animal had always been obedient, and at that moment God opened his eyes and he was able to see the angel. Balaam fell face down on the ground. If he had been embarrassed before, he was now utterly humiliated. He, the great seer of Pethor, had been unable to see the Angel. His donkey had. He was worse than an ass. The angel commanded Balaam to continue to Moab but to say only what God instructed him to say.

Balak heard that Balaam was finally coming and went as far as the border to meet him. Irate that Balaam had taken so long, he marched the seer to the Heights of Baal from where they could see the entire Israelite host. After they had offered sacrifices to the Canaanite gods, Balaam made his first prophecy: The people of Israel lived apart and did not consider themselves one of the surrounding nations; there were many of them and he hoped when he was judged he would be considered as righteous as the people of Israel. Clearly this was written for the Israelites. They would hear this blessing not pronounced by one of Israel's own prophets, but by a seer of a foreign people, worshiping a cult of man-made gods. In other words, the Israelites were being told how they were being seen by their enemies – as a vast, orderly nation, living apart, under the protection of an all-powerful God.

Not unnaturally Balak was rampantly mad when he heard Balaam's oracle. Had he not sent for the man to curse the horde of interlopers and now Balaam goes and blesses them! One can imagine the hapless Balaam, profusely apologetic, trying to explain that there was nothing he, Balaam, could do about it; he was merely speaking the words 'that the Lord puts in my mouth.' It wasn't his fault. It was the Lord's. Balak decided it was the size of the Israelite army that had terrified Balaam into blessing them so he altered his strategy. He took Balaam to where he could see only part of the Israelite camp. Balaam drew aside, listened to God, returned to where Balak and the princes of Moab were offering sacrifices and made his second prophecy. He said neither misfortune nor misery was observed in Israel; the Lord their God was with them and they had the strength of a lion.

This was clearly a battle cry for the Israelites, a strengthening of the heart and stiffening of the sinew, a before-Agincourt type of speech, crescendoing to the mighty, 'The Lord their God is with them!'

Balak seems momentarily to have got the message. He accepted that Balaam could not curse the Israelites but begged Balaam at least not to bless them! He took Balaam to a place overlooking the desert where Balaam pronounced his third oracle, a song of praise to Israel and their God, Numbers 24: 5-9. The song linked the Israelites' wandering, nomadic, tent-based existence, to the settled conditions they would experience in Canaan where they would have gardens of beauty with aloes and cedars, wells with abundant water and where their kings would be greater than all the neighbouring monarchs. This is another Messianic prophecy; 'their king will be greater than Agag.' Agag was an enemy of the future king Saul, but it was a common name of Amalekite kings, Amalekites being one of the traditional enemies of the Israelites; it is therefore a metaphor for those who oppose the Messiah and a prediction that he will be greater than and will ultimately defeat the enemies of goodness.

When Balak heard this hymn of praise, his fury knew no bounds. He beat his hands together and told Balaam to get out of his sight and not for one minute to think he would receive any divination fee. Getting his own back, he told Balaam that it was not him refusing to pay, it was the Lord. Balaam agreed that yes, from the beginning, he had been able to pronounce only what the Lord told him to say. In Numbers 24: 15-19 he produced his last oracle: A star would come out of Jacob and a sceptre from Israel (both Messianic prophecies.) Edom and Seir would fall but Israel would grow strong. Assyria would defeat the Kenites but Assyria itself would fall to people that came in ships from Kittim. In the end all these races would fall.

There can be little doubt that Balaam's Messianic prophecies were written centuries before Christ, and only Jesus of Nazareth makes sense of the words. He is indeed a star (author of light) that came out of Jacob, and a sceptre (royal) that arose from Israel. He crushed evil and defeated death. Significantly, the lesser prophecies in the last few lines have also come true and they apply to events that happened *after* the Babylonian Diaspora which is when the critics say these writings were produced, so they remain predictive. Asshur (Assyria) fell to people who came from the shores of Kittim (Cyprus) the Greeks. Jerusalem fell to Alexander the Great long after the Babylonian Diaspora. 'But they too will come to ruin' says the prophecy. The Hellenistic Empire was defeated by the Romans and of course the Roman Empire came to ruin too. The Balaam prophecies are in the Septuagint which was written three hundred years before the birth of Christ and before Rome conquered the Middle East. So these are awesome revelations and predictions. The chapter ends with the simple fact that after he had uttered his last oracles, Balaam returned home, but not before he had given Balak a sure fire way of getting rid of the Israelites, and it nearly succeeded. But for Moses's love for his people it would have.

Chapter 25:
Worshiping Baal and Sexual Orgies

What Balaam told Balak to do was to drive a wedge between the Israelites and God by getting the Israelites involved with Canaanite women. It nearly succeeded. When the Israelites began 'to indulge in sexual immorality' they were living in a place with an appropriately sounding expletive as a name – in English anyway – Shittim. That's where the men of Israel fell for the fatal charm of Moabite women, and indulged in the women's Baal-worshiping sexual orgies, fertility rites and sacrifices. Human sacrifices were still being practised at that time so one shudders to think just how far the people fell. The result was that 'The Lord's anger burned against them.' Moses sentenced the ringleaders to death and a devastating plague swept through the camp. Thousands died. Penitent and bereaved, the survivors gathered before the tent of meeting, but even as they did so, a defiant Israelite, Zimri, marched past the assembly with his pagan mistress, Cozbi, in tow and took her into the family tent. It was a fraught moment. Would all the rest of the assembly follow suit and return to their sexual shenanigans, or would they remain penitent and continue to seek forgiveness? Before they could decide, Phinehas, a grandson of Aaron, took the law into his own hands. He grabbed a spear and rushing into the tent where Zimri and Cozbi were copulating, drove a spear through both of them.

It's one of the most horrific tales in the Old Testament. Even today the violence of it stuns one rigid. It must have had the same effect on the Israelites. Subdued, they obeyed God, separated themselves from the Midianites, who had led them into depravity, and attacked them. It's dreadful and difficult to understand. Perhaps it is a parable loosely based on a plague that swept through the camp prior to the attack on the Midianites. Perhaps the leaders and priests were trying to find a reason for the disaster, at the same time seeking a just cause for attacking the Midianites. There's no way one can know. The only thing one can take from the story, the only moral, is that when people turn away from God, life disintegrates into meaninglessness and horror.

Chapter 26 – 27: Another Census and Zelophehad's daughters

A census was held to re-organise the Israelites after the long desert exile both for military purposes and to work out a fair distribution of land in Canaan. It is an appropriate moment for the story of Zelophehad's five daughters (Chapter 27.) They walked with God, did those women, and when they encountered a problem not covered by the laws of Israel, they went to the Tent of Meeting and informed Moses and Eleazar. Their father, Zelophehad, had had no sons, so his name would disappear from the clan records. It would not be listed among those who were apportioned parts of the Promised Land. They felt this was unfair, particularly as Zelophehad had not been part of the Korah rebellion.

Moses prayed to God and was informed that indeed it was not fair. The law had to be changed so that they could inherit a property among their father's relatives, in their father's name. In future this was always to happen. If a man had no sons, the property was to become his daughter's. If there were no daughters, the father's brothers should inherit, and failing that, his nearest relatives. So, because of the sisters' gumption and determination, a new law was added to the Torah, safeguarding women's rights. It shows too how step by step God was enabling Moses to construct a just and equitable code of law.

The chapter ends with God telling Moses to go up a mountain in the Abarim Range from where he would be able to see the Promised Land. Some commentators feel that this was cruel. Having just made provision for Zelophehad's daughters, God was showing Moses the Promised Land in which he would have no inheritance. However, Moses was very old and very frail by this time. Leading his stiff-necked, recalcitrant and difficult people all these miles and all these years had taken their toll. He must have stood up there in the Abarim Mountains looking across at the Promised Land with a heart grateful that his people were at last within sight of their destiny, but at the same time acknowledging that his own longing was for a different country.

To the end he showed his concern for his rebellious, complaining brethren. He asked God to appoint a successor who could take over the leadership, so that the people would not be like sheep without a shepherd. God chose Joshua, son of Nun, filling him with the Holy Spirit. In front of the Tent of Meeting, Moses laid his hands on Joshua, delegating some of his authority to him so that the transition could begin smoothly and be thoroughly in place by the time he died.

Chapters 28 – 30: Oath-taking

The huge emphasis on sacrifices and offerings that Moses commanded the people make on a daily, weekly, monthly and annual basis was to prepare them for orderly worship under the leadership of Joshua. He followed this with explanations of some of the laws, first, in Chapter 30, about the sanctity of a vow, which could not be broken under any circumstances whether it were made to God or man. As usual, the whole problem of vows and oaths was sorted out once and for all by Jesus. In the Sermon on the Mount, he told the crowds that had come to listen to him, (Matthew 5: 33 – 37): 'Again, you have heard that it was said to the people long ago (He's referring to these particular verses in Numbers) 'Do not break your oath, but keep the oaths you have made to the Lord. But I tell you, do not swear at all: either by heaven, for it is God's throne; or by the earth, for it is his footstool; or by Jerusalem for it is the city of the Great King. And do not swear by your head, for you cannot make even one hair white or black. Simply let your 'yes' be 'yes' and your 'no,' 'no.' Anything beyond this comes from the evil one.'

Chapter 31 – Battle against the Midianites

The battle fought by the Israelites against the Midianites resulted from the way in which the Midianite women had tempted the Israelites into abhorrent acts of pagan worship, child sacrifice and sexual depravity (chapter 25). Moses ordered the Israelites to kill everybody, except the virgins, who had obviously not been involved in the depraved behaviour. It remains a horrible, difficult story, but it won't do for one to sit back and be pietistic and holier-than-thou. It is not so long ago that the men, women and children of Dresden, Coventry and Hiroshima were bombed into mayhem, horror and oblivion. Can one say that that was righteous?

Among those who fell when Israel attacked Midian was Balaam son of Beor who had told the Israelite enemies how to use women and sex to weaken the Israelites. The chapter ends with the division of spoils after the battle. It is all uncomfortable reading, and not the sort of thing one hears in the Sunday-by-Sunday readings from the lectionary. Which is another of my grumbles. I feel one ought to hear the whole Bible, in its entirety, and not bits and pieces chosen by church leaders as appropriate readings for the day. Often it is the difficult bits that sharpen one's thinking, deepen one's understanding, develop one's empathy and love, and ultimately align one with God's purpose for the whole of creation.

Chapters 32 – 33: The Journey

The earlier chapters showed that the Israelites had marched in a north easterly direction so that they could turn and come into Canaan from that direction. This would place them on the far side of the Jordan. It was while they were there that the Reubenites and Gadites realized that the trans-Jordan lands were highly suitable for grazing. They asked Moses if they could stay there, assuring him that although they would build pens for the livestock and places for the women, they themselves would accompany the rest of Israel and help to bring them safely into their inheritance. Moses granted their request, and the trans-Jordan lands were apportioned to Reuben and Gad. The descendants of Manasseh, son of Joseph, decided to settle in Gilead after they had helped to drive out the Amorites.

In chapter 33 is a summary of the entire journey that the Israelites made from Egypt to Canaan, including the 40 years of wandering in the desert. Place after place is named but they are mostly forgotten desert oases that have never been identified. The only significance is to see the journey as an allegory of the human pilgrimage that all have to make and that often involves struggling along twisting, turning, difficult, desert tracks, hungry for understanding and thirsting for meaning, with danger and failure dogging one's footsteps. As with the Israelites so with today; those who walk with God find the pilgrimage a quest and an adventure.

Chapters 34 – 36: Final Instructions

Moses decreed that the leaders of nine and a half of the tribes be allotted land in Canaan. (The lands were apportioned by lot.) Reuben, Gad and the half tribe of Manasseh, would hold their lands on the east side of the Jordan. For the Levites, 48 towns were established, with adequate pasture and grazing around them. Six of the Levite towns were to be 'cities of refuge' to which a person could flee if he had killed somebody. This was necessary to prevent revenge and retaliation, and to give the community time to arrange a proper trial. Although perpetrators of manslaughter or accidental killing could make use of the cities of refuge, the penalty for premeditated murder was death. It was made plain to the Israelites that to shed the blood of another was to defile the land.

Moses decreed that in order for Zelophehad's land not to pass out of the possession of his descendants, his daughters should marry men from only their own tribe and this was always to apply if there was no male inheritor. There was to be no passing of bits of land from one tribe to another. Numbers ends, with the words: 'These are the commands and regulations the Lord gave through Moses to the Israelites on the plains of Moab, by the Jordan, across from Jericho.'

Conclusion: The Son Rises Higher

Faced with humanity's everlasting cowardice and treachery, ever-loving God develops His plan to save humans from themselves. From the blinding moment when He created the universe until mankind rose to its feet millions of aeons passed. The years of human babyhood and childhood are but as yesterday. Out of the human dawn came the Israelites, and now in this twenty first century humanity stands at the noon-time, rebellious prodigal sons, suspicious, selfish and treacherous. It is a dangerous moment. All migrants, one way or another, humans need a guide, someone they can trust, or there's no way they'll reach any Promised Land. Like the Israelite rebels and traitors they will end as numberless specks of dust driven by the desert winds, infinitesimal atoms in a swirling chaos of matter and energy. This book of Numbers shows that the first part of the answer could be in searching deep within ourselves for that still, small, voice.

Part Six
DUE TO DEUTERONOMY

Love the Lord thy God

Introduction

The name, Deuteronomy, comes from two Greek words, *deuteron,* meaning 'second' and *nomos* meaning 'law'. It is the title given to the book by the Septuagint translators in 300 B.C. Hence the word 'second' and its serendipitous association with Israel's second chance. Because of course it wasn't a new, or second, set of laws, merely a re-telling of the first lot. Deuteronomy consists largely of the last sermons that Moses made to the young Israelites before he died.

Chapter 1: No Progress

He began by reminding them that they were only eleven days' journey from where they had set out forty years earlier – that's all the progress they had made. Their rootless drifting backwards and forwards across the desert was because their parents had allowed themselves to be misled by the treachery and perversity of the spies. It seems that the new generation of Israelites had had enough of their aimless existence and were prepared to commit themselves to the adventure in a do-or-die mode, and Moses was right behind them, or, perhaps more accurately, right in front of them.

With only a few of their dithering parents still alive, the young people listened avidly as the frail and aged Moses whose love for God had never wavered, told them that it was indeed the moment to proceed and to take possession of the land. He reminded them what God had said: 'See, I have set the land before you,' urging them to go in and occupy what the Lord had promised their ancestors. However, Moses made it clear that if they marched forward under the banner of God, they would be successful, but that if they tried to do things their own way they would fail. He pointed out that there were enough of them to achieve their goal and that they were an orderly, well-governed people, with a hierarchical system of leadership. Their leaders were 'wise, understanding and experienced men,' and they had a good judicial system with judges hearing cases and judging righteously 'between a man and his brother, or the alien who is with him.' And he added: 'You shall not be partial in judgement. You shall hear the small and the great alike. You shall not be intimidated by anyone for the judgement is God's.' The words demand an impartial, un-corrupt, un-intimidated judiciary. They are among the reasons the Bible is so hated by tyrants and despots.

Before getting to the law itself, Moses reminded the young people before him of how grievously their parents had erred when they listened to the treacherous spies rather than to God who had loved and sustained them with many miracles on their long journey. He reminded the young people too of what he had said to their parents 40 years before, that it would be their children 'who today have no knowledge of good or evil' who would enter Canaan.

The bit about them having no knowledge of good and evil is interesting. It gives a reason for Moses's using this opportunity to repeat the laws, suggesting that during the dreary trudging through the desert, the Israelites had forgotten many of the commandments. But the exile was over and a new generation stood ready to hear the law and to advance into the land.

Chapter 2 - 3: The Lands they could not possess – and Og's Bed!

Chapter two begins with Moses reminding his people that God had not allowed them, when they came stomping out of the desert, to possess any territory on Mount Seir because that land God had given to the descendants of Esau. The Israelites had to pay for every bit of food and water that they consumed while they were travelling across Seir. They had built up their flocks and herds in the desert and become wealthy so they could afford to pay for what they needed. They were given similar instructions about Moab; under no circumstances were they to harass or fight the Moabites to whom God had given the land they occupied.

As they advanced across Seir and Moab, the last adults involved in the spy-led rebellion died. It was then that God, through Moses, gave the Israelites the go-ahead to cross the border at Ar, and enter the land of the Ammonites. But just as with Seir and Moab, they were strictly forbidden to settle on any of the land belonging to the people of Ammon. Deuteronomy says that the inhabitants of Seir, Moab and the Land of the Ammonites had all ousted giant predecessors before taking possession of their countries. God is telling the Israelites that since he had allowed weaker and smaller people to overthrow powerful, giant-like original inhabitants in other countries, he would certainly do the same for the Israelites.

In Chapter Three is a re-telling of the battle that the Israelites fought against the Bashan and of their conquest of Gilead. Now, in the first of his final addresses, Moses sought to encourage the young Israelites by reminding them that King Og of Bashan was the last member of the Rephaim giants. He said Og's huge iron-studded bed, with dimensions for a man twice the height of a normal man, was in Rabah and that many people went there to wonder at it. The Israelites needed to take courage from the fact that they had defeated a man this size. (Was the house in Rabah with its iron bed one of the first museums ever?)

Chapter 4: Tampering with the Law

The first commandment in the re-telling of the law was: 'You shall not add to the word that I command you, nor take from it.' It seems that even in the short space of time since Moses had first issued the commandments, the Israelites had begun to alter the laws, striking out some and adding others. People still do it, trying to make the laws relevant, arguing that what was all right for the Bronze Age is certainly not all right for today. It's a dangerous practice leading to cultural and political correctness. One needs an ultimate authority, which is what the Bible gives.

Having warned the Israelites not to tamper with the law, Moses reminded them how their parents, in an orgy of wine, women and song, had been drawn into the cult of Baal and of the dreadful punishment that had ensued. He urged the young people to keep the law and keep their faith in God. The first law Moses reminded them about after warning them not to tamper with them, was the one forbidding the worship of idols. No created object, whether made by God or by man, could be worshipped. It was the Creator whom they had to love, not the created.

Moses pointed out too that they were not to think that because they were the race to whom God had made Himself known, the chosen race, they could trade on that. They couldn't. If they did not keep the commandments they would be thrown out of the Promised Land and scattered among the nations (Numbers 4: 25-27.) After this dire warning, Moses spoke what are among the most beautiful and encouraging words in the Bible, especially for those who through grief or despair feel separated from God: Here they are: (Deuteronomy 4: 29-31) 'But from there you will seek the Lord your God and *you will find him,* if you search after him with all your heart and with all your soul. When you are in tribulation, and all these things come upon you in the latter days, you will return to the Lord your God and obey his voice. For the Lord your God is a merciful God. He will not leave you or destroy you or forget the covenant with your fathers that he swore to them.'

This is of course one of those passages that critics of Mosaic authorship revel in because if it is genuine, it contains predictive prophecy, and as I've now pointed out several times, in the eyes of many critics, such prophecy does not exist. The words must have been written when Israel was in captivity in Babylon, they say, because that was when they needed comfort and support. Perhaps. There's no way one can tell. I believe in predictive prophecy, and I believe that anyone can seek God from any depths of degradation, guilt or despair. Whatever else, the words were written before the Romans sent the Israelites into their worst ever Diaspora and nobody even tries to pretend that these words were written after 70 A.D.

Chapter 5: The Second Sermon

Summoning all Israel for the second sermon, Moses reminded them how God had spoken directly to them from Mount Horeb when he had given them the Ten Commandments. Then he repeated them. There is little difference between the commandments in Deuteronomy and Exodus. Honouring one's parents, the fifth commandment, remains a difficult one for the thousands who have been neglected, abused or cruelly treated by parents. It is noticeable, however, that this law does not command one to love one's parents but to honour them, and the distinction is important. Whatever they do that they shouldn't, or don't do that they should, one owes one's existence to one's parents. Without them, one would not have life. It is this that God is calling one to honour, those who contributed to one's existence.

Chapters 6 – 9: The Central Belief of Judaeo-Christianity

Pleading with the Israelites to be obedient, Moses then made the unique summary of the law that Christ was to quote with such telling effect when he began his own ministry: *Hear, O Israel: The*

Lord our God, the Lord is one. Love the Lord your God with all your heart and with all your soul and with all your strength. (Deut. 6: 9) It is noteworthy that one is not asked to honour or worship God, but to love him.

How well Moses knew his fellows! Faced with their ongoing sinfulness, he realized that it wasn't good enough for them merely to hear the law. Imperative was the need for them to *remember* the laws, to *live* by them, to write them in their hearts, to tell their children about them, and to discuss them, 'When you sit at home and when you walk along the road, when you lie down and when you get up. Tie them as symbols on your hands and bind them on your foreheads. Write them on the doorframes of your houses and on your gates.' In other words, live every moment of your lives under the protection of the laws of God. When they settled in the Promised Land, said Moses, they would find cities that they had not built themselves and vineyards and olive groves that they had not themselves planted. Then they had to remember and be grateful to the Lord who had brought them out of slavery and had procured such bounty for them.

In chapter 7 comes one of those nasty bits; to occupy the Promised Land the Israelites were going to have to drive out the original inhabitants, the Hittites, Girgashites, Amorites, Canaanites, Perizzites, Hivites and Jebusites. They were to show no mercy and were not to allow their sons and daughters to inter-marry with them. I've already discussed these difficult instructions. To many, they suggest a tribal and warlike God, not the great God of the universe. This is where one needs to remember that although reading and understanding the Bible have grown and developed over the centuries, the original writing was an attempt to understand God by a Bronze Age people who, from the confines of a narrow and tribal world, were trying to hear and interpret what they believed the Holy Spirit was revealing to them. In the consciousness of Israel, the perception that God loved the entire world and all its peoples was still in its infancy, but the first seed had been planted. As early as Genesis one reads that God told Abraham, the founder of the Israelite nation: 'All the peoples on earth will be blessed through you.' (Genesis 12:3.) All that Moses could hope for as the Israelites began their conquest of Canaan was that they would remain true to God and not have their faith and belief contaminated by the sexual orgies and human sacrifices that prevailed among the surrounding peoples. Nobody can deny that humans have an awful tendency to drop to the lowest morality around and to follow what appears to be an easier, more fun-filled, less strict regime than to adhere to a more difficult way controlled by seemingly harsh, inviolate laws. This is why most people today have turned away from God and from a theistic rule of life. A recent panel of speakers on the Radio 4 programme, 'The Moral Maze' tried to determine how to teach morals to today's children. (They could not agree on how best to do it but they all agreed that there was increasing immorality and lack of concern for others among the young.) The question would never have arisen had the children been taught about God, *said one of the panellists*. The current kindness campaign in Britain reinforces the realization that the world is less kind.

So Moses was not wrong when he told his people that the inhabitants of Canaan would 'turn your sons away from following me to serve other gods, and the Lord's anger will burn against you and will quickly destroy you;' which is why God, through Moses, ordered the Israelites to break down and destroy the altars, sacred stones, idols and Asherah poles of these other nations. It was imperative that they remain God's 'treasured possession.' However, this would happen only if they remained committed to God and loved the *neighbours* and the *aliens* in their midst! (Exodus 23:9, Leviticus 24:22 and Psalm 146: 9.)

WILD ANIMALS

In the seventh chapter God told the Israelites not to expect the conquest to be achieved quickly because if they wiped out the Canaanites they would be threatened by the wild animals that abounded in Canaan at that time. This sounds outrageous and is in direct contradiction of God's supposed instruction to wipe out all the Canaanites. It helps one to realize that the Israelites were allowing their fears and anxieties almost to drown out the voice of God which nevertheless comes through, quietly and insistently, encouraging them to treat aliens as they would themselves, provided they did not follow their religion and customs.

It was when he was reminding them, in Chapter eight, how God had provided their forebears with manna while they traversed the parched wastes of the desert, that Moses spoke another sentence that Jesus was to repeat when he himself was starving in the desert and was tempted to use his miraculous powers to turn stones into bread: ' *man does not live on bread alone but on every word that comes from the mouth of the Lord.*' (Deut. 8: 3) That should give one a two-fold confidence, not only in Jesus, the Word of God, but also in the word of scripture that preceded him.

Springs Flowing in the Valleys

There's a lovely description of the promised land in Deut. 8: 7-9 'For the Lord your God is bringing you into a good land – a land with streams and pools of water, with springs flowing in the valleys and hills; a land with wheat and barley, vines and fig trees, pomegranates, olive oil and honey; a land where bread will not be scarce and you will lack nothing; a land where the rocks are iron and you can dig copper out of the hills.' The words suggest that this was a period between the Bronze Age (copper and tin) and the Iron Age, and they give some understanding of why there has been such an interminable fight throughout the millennia for the land of Israel; in all those barren desert countries of the Middle East, many of which are admittedly rich in oil, that small land in the eastern Mediterranean was part of the lush and bountiful Fertile Crescent.

Moses impressed on the Israelites the need to be grateful to God and never to feel that they deserved the Promised Land because 'then your heart will become proud and you will forget the Lord your God, who brought you out of Egypt, out of the land of slavery.' A salutary message for the countless millions today who think they are entitled to anything!

Hear, O Israel

One of the themes of Deuteronomy, and a reminder of the enormous importance of the oral tradition, is found at the start of the ninth chapter, the call to Israel to listen to the word of God: 'Hear, O Israel.' Again Moses warned them against entitlement. The reason they were going to be able to drive out the powerful Anakites was not because the Israelites were in any way righteous; they were not, he said but because the Anakites were so unbelievably wicked. 'Do not say to yourself, 'The Lord has brought me here to take possession of this land because of my righteousness.' No, it is on account of the wickedness of these nations, for you are a stiff-necked people.' He reminded them of how quickly they had turned away from God and built a golden calf and all the other occasions on which they had turned away from him and angered him.

Chapters 10 – 14: Circumcise your Hearts!

Recalling how Aaron had died and been buried at Moserah, Moses spoke about how his and Aaron's tribe, the Levites, had been instructed to carry the Ark and to provide the priests who would minister to the people. The function of the rest of the people, he said, was to fear God, to walk in His ways and to love and serve Him with all their heart. It was not enough for them to be circumcised as a physical and demonstrable way of showing their allegiance to God. Far more important was to: 'Circumcise your hearts, therefore, and do not be stiff-necked any longer.' (Deuteronomy 10: 16) He reiterated that God showed no partiality and accepted no bribes: 'He defends the cause of the fatherless and the widow, *and loves the alien*, giving him food and clothing. And you are to love those who are aliens, for you yourselves were aliens in Egypt. Fear the Lord your God and serve him.' (Deuteronomy 10: 19-20)

This emphasis on God's *love for the alien* is often overlooked by those who condemn the entire Bible because, they say, it is about a tribal deity who ordered the Israelites to destroy the original inhabitants of Canaan. The ideas are contradictory. As one reads the Bible in its entirety, making allowance for human fallibility and incomprehension, it becomes abundantly clear which of these two perceptions of God is ultimately correct. The bit about circumcising one's heart is one much loved by Christians. Jesus was to draw attention to this: the need to have the law in one's heart.

Because they were only children, and some of them not even born, when the Israelites escaped from Egypt, Moses reminded them of their history. It emphasises the importance of the oral tradition with Moses re-telling the story and insisting that they tell their children and their children's children how God had enabled them to escape and how he had sustained them with miracles of manna and quail during their long sojourn in the desert.

The Third Sermon

One can safely say that the third sermon begins in Chapter twelve. What it says is often called the Deuteronomic Code. Re-iterating that the Israelites were to destroy all the altars and places of pagan worship that they found in Canaan, Moses pointed out that this was in order that they not be tempted into following the idolatrous practices of the Canaanites. It is of course a warning that can be taken to heart today, that it is safer to keep away from temptation than to contemplate idols and then try to deal with them. Jesus himself insisted that one's eyes and ears, in fact all one's senses, could lead one astray and that it was safer not to look on temptation than to try to resist it.

The only place where they could worship God, said Moses, was the tabernacle. During their nomadic existence they had not always been able to worship God as they ought but when they were settled in Canaan they had to remember and carry out correctly the rituals and ceremonies that he, Moses, had relayed to them. The thirteenth chapter begins with yet another warning about false gods, and about those who prophesy and perform miracles in the names of unknown gods. The Israelites were not to fall for this, said Moses. Just as Abraham had resisted temptation and had not put his son, Isaac, before God, so were the Israelites to show that there was nothing that they would put above God. 'If your very own brother, or your son or daughter, or the wife you love, or your close friend secretly entices you, saying, Let us go and worship other gods (gods that neither you nor your fathers have known, gods of the people around you, whether near or far, from one end of the land to the other) do not yield to him or listen to him.'

Then comes another of those difficult ones. Moses insisted that those who tempted the Israelites away from God had to be stoned to death. It is again to Jesus that one must turn for a way out of this dilemma. He frees one from it when he tells one not to judge. Certainly Christians should not listen to those who would tempt them away from God, but Jesus removes the right to judge the tempters. Since He came and showed people how to live life to the full, he made it clear that the right to judge belonged to God and to nobody else. (This obviously applies on a personal level only; on a societal level there has to be judgement.) An interesting sidelight to this is that Moses, knowing how easily people were corrupted, warned his fellows that if they executed someone for apostasy, they could not help themselves to that person's property. Instead they had to burn all his goods and livestock. Moses could see that one of the mortal dangers of judgement was to allow oneself to be affected by greed, covetousness, prejudice or any other kind of personal agenda.

Chapters 15 – 18:
The Implementation of the Rule of Law for the First Time in History

The cancellation of debts, already mentioned in Exodus and Leviticus, was the next subject tackled by Moses. He made it clear that loans to fellow Israelites had to be cancelled after seven years. They did not need to absolve foreigners from their debts. Interestingly, Moses told the Israelites that as a nation they could lend to other nations but could not borrow from them; if they obeyed this injunction they would rule over other nations but none would rule over them, an understanding of the power that a lender has over a borrower, and a warning to those who think borrowing is the cornerstone of a good economy. It provides another reason for the age-old hatred of Jews: Jealousy. Because God would not allow them to borrow from aliens, only to lend to them, Jews have invariably become the wealthy elements in any society.

Moses made clear that the law made special provision for the poor; the Israelites were not to be, 'hard hearted or tight fisted toward your poor brother. Rather be open-handed and freely lend him whatever he needs. Be careful not to harbour the wicked thought: The seventh year, the year for cancelling debts is near, so that (afraid of not being able to have the debt repaid) you show ill will towards your needy brother and give him nothing. There will always be poor people in the land. Therefore I command you to be open-handed toward your brothers and toward the poor and needy in your land.' If everybody obeyed this law, there would be no need for a welfare state!

Laws governing the treatment of servants came next. The poor could sometimes become servants to work off debts. If this happened, said Moses, not only were the debts to be cancelled after seven years, but the servants would have to be rewarded for the service that they had performed. 'When you release him do not send him away empty-handed. Supply him liberally from your flock, your threshing floor and your winepress. Give to him as the Lord your God has blessed you.' The law made provision even for a servant who had become a loving family member and did not want to leave. He would have to have his ear pierced – and presumably have a metal ring placed in it – as a sign that he had become a family member. Servants were little different from slaves so these laws concern the treatment of slaves as much as servants. Whatever one thinks of slavery, this type of enforced labour was practised in the Middle East and it is significant that the Law of Moses provided for the fair treatment of slaves/servants and their enforced release after a certain number of years. The twenty first century falls far short of Israel in terms of fair wages: Everything was done in Moses's time to ensure that the poorest members of society received a living wage, or help if they were impoverished. Many working men today are not paid a living wage. If they were, their wives could choose to stay at home and rear their children if that is what they desired. Few of them have the choice; they *have* to go to work if the mortgage is to be paid and the children's needs are to be met.

The next chapter is devoted to the keeping of the Passover and all the other festivals, all of which were covered in Exodus, Leviticus and Numbers. At the end of Chapter Sixteen is the law governing judges. Each tribe had to appoint both judges and officials. Whether this was done democratically or whether power groups held sway is not made clear, but the behaviour of judges is. 'They shall judge the people fairly,' was the decree. 'Do not pervert justice or show partiality. Do not accept a bribe, for a bribe blinds the eyes of the wise and twists the words of the righteous. Follow justice, and justice alone, so that you may live and possess the land the Lord your God is giving you.' No more need be said.

That no imperfect or blemished animal could be sacrificed to God is stressed again at the beginning of the seventeenth chapter, which then goes on to make yet another denouncement of apostasy. But now there is a proviso. No single person could accuse another of worshiping false gods and expect to be believed. The Law of the Witnesses, first promulgated in Numbers 35:30 had to be applied. In no case could the evidence of just one witness be accepted. Always there had to be the testimony of two or more witnesses, and it was these witnesses who had to throw the first stones of execution. Although judges would normally be able to decide issues, the Levites and a senior judge would act as a court of appeal (Deut.17: 8–13.) All appeal court decisions had to be obeyed and contempt of court was a capital offense.

The Rule of Law

Capital punishment for contempt of court is a difficult one but one needs to remember that Moses and the priests, who were both the government and the judicial system of Israel, were trying to implement what was a completely new concept, the Rule of Law. It is in the Torah that one first comes across the idea. Among the Greek philosophers, Plato felt kings were above the law. It was Aristotle (384-322B.C.) who felt that nobody, not even a king, or any kind of ruler, could be above the law. Even if one accepts the documentary hypothesis that the Torah was written during the Babylonian exile, that still puts the Israelites several centuries before Aristotle. So it is in the Torah that one first encounters the concept that the law is paramount and even a king or government cannot be above it (Deut. 17: 18-20.) It bears repeating that Stephen Langton, 13th Century Archbishop of Canterbury realized that the insistence that Deuteronomy paces on the sanctity of the Mosaic Law enshrined human rights and had to be built into any government daring to call itself Christian. Hence the relevant chapters in Magna Carta. Here are the Deuteronomy verses: 'When he takes the throne of his kingdom, he is to write for himself on a scroll a copy of this law, taken from that of the priests, who are Levites. It is to be with him, and he is to read it all the days of his life so that he may learn to revere the Lord his God and follow carefully all the words of this law and these decrees and not consider himself better than his brothers and turn from the law to the right or to the left. Then he and his descendants will reign a long time over his kingdom in Israel.' Needless to say the kings thought they knew better, with appalling consequences.

An obvious question is why one reads about kings at all this early in the Bible. Israel did not have a king; it was a theocracy, ruled by God through Moses and the priests. However, aware that all the surrounding nations had kings, Moses knew that in time the Israelites would want one too. He urged them to choose as king one who was approved by God and who was committed to the sanctity of the law. He had seen at first hand the tyranny of the Bronze Age kings and he tried to warn the Israelites. If only they had listened. That he was speaking here about the written law (the scroll) supports the contention that somebody was writing it, almost certainly Moses himself, perhaps assisted by Joshua and the priests.

Chapter Eighteen begins with an explanation of how the tithing law was to be used to provide for the Levites and priests who were never to be given any land. His continued insistence that 'other' religions were evil shows how aware Moses was of the evil that was, and is, inherent in any kind of religion that removes its focus from God. A religion is often the worst of idols. From the time that Christ dwelt in our midst one cannot claim that it depends on how one interprets God's laws. Christ interpreted them all and said categorically that if anything led one to judge, demean, harm, deceive or hurt any other person one had become an idol-worshiper.

The chapter concludes with Moses promising that in the years ahead God would raise from among the people another prophet: 'I will put my words in his mouth, and he will tell them everything I command him. If anyone does not listen to my words that the prophet speaks in my name, I myself will call him to account. But a prophet who presumes to speak in my name anything I have not commanded him to say, or a prophet who speaks in the name of other gods, must be put to death.' He added that the people would know if a prophet were not speaking in God's name because such prophecies would not come true. Almost certainly Moses spoke about 'another prophet' to prepare the people for his death and to help them to accept Joshua as their new leader. But I think it goes further than that. I think he wanted them to realize that future generations would have their own prophets and they had to develop the ability to discern who were true prophets of God and who were not. Ultimately of course it points to Christ.

Chapters 19 – 22: The Law of Retaliation; How to Get out of Conscription; Care of Animals; Difficult Laws about Women

The cities of refuge were first mentioned in the Book of Numbers. There are some Biblical scholars, including those who contributed to the NIV Study Bible, who think the establishment of refuge cities was because Israel was just emerging from a nomadic, pastoral life in which vigilantiism, retributive justice and vengeance had been practised, into a society ruled by law. By providing safe places for those who had, perhaps unwittingly and without 'malice aforethought', committed capital crimes, they were providing them with a temporary haven and giving the law time to work. The cities of refuge were the means to bring revenge killings to an end and to prevent family and tribal feuds.

At the end of this section in Deuteronomy is the prohibition not to move a boundary stone to make one's piece of land bigger, no land-grabbing in other words. There are those who will point out that Israel has been land-grabbing in recent years, and encouraging settlers to live in disputed lands. The trouble is that those lands were originally part of Israel, and, sadly, it is from Palestine and parts of Gaza that most attacks are launched against Israel by those who believe that it has no right to exist.

In all the crimes listed in Deuteronomy, the evidence of one witness was not enough. There had to be two or more. If perjury (lying when giving testimony) was suspected, the judge would have to investigate the matter carefully and if a person was proved to have given false evidence, the punishment that he desired for the accused, would be inflicted upon him instead. That's neat. Chapter 20 begins with instructions about going to war. Before they advanced into any battle they were to be addressed by the High Priest who would remind them that God was with them.

How Did They Ever Raise an Army?

How on earth Israel ever managed to raise an army to fight for the Promised Land is a mystery to me because it seems that a man could be excused national service for almost anything. In fact, if countries in Western Europe had accepted these Deuteronomic objections to enforced conscription in 1914 and 1939 I wonder if either of the two world wars would ever have been fought. In Ancient Israel a man would be exempt from military service if:

- he had built a house and not yet dedicated it
- he had planted a vineyard and not yet begun to enjoy it
- he had become pledged to a woman and not yet married her
- he felt afraid or faint-hearted

Surely the last one alone would have accounted for the vast majority, or maybe I feel that way because I'm a woman, and a pacifist one at that. Still… Contrary to the earlier directive that every member of the enemy, be it man, woman or child, had to be wiped out, listen to what comes next. 'When you march up to attack a city, make its people an offer of peace. If they accept and open their gates, all the people in it shall be subject to forced labour and shall work for you. If they refuse to make peace and they engage you in battle, lay siege to that city. When the Lord your God delivers it into your hand, put to the sword all the men in it. As for the women, the children, the livestock and everything else in the city, you may take these as plunder for yourselves.' That's not the same as being ordered to kill every man, woman and child. But I'm not out of the woods. This last proviso did not to apply to the Hittites, Amorites, Canaanites, Perizzies, Hivites and Jebusites who had to be wiped out in their entirety 'otherwise they will teach you to follow all the detestable things they do in worshiping their gods and you will sin against the Lord your God.' Deuteronomy has pointed out several times that among the heinous practices of these tribes was child sacrifice. But to kill men, women *and children* because the adults were practising child sacrifice is an obscene nonsense and exposes the inability of some early scribe or editor to understand the will of God. The same issue has reared its ugly head today; Islamic State and Boko Haram give themselves the right to put to death entire communities including children. Jesus showed categorically that such brutality was anathema to God. That is why reading the whole Bible and not just portions is so important because it enables one to discover its central message, an understanding of the loving and merciful nature of God, and an understanding of the purpose of every individual life. Chapter 20 ends with a bit of military pragmatism; don't cut down the fruit trees growing outside a city that you are besieging. Use non-fruit-bearing trees for your siege works. That one gave me a chuckle.

At the beginning of Chapter 21 is a second instance of a heifer, cow, being sacrificed, this time to make atonement for a killing where the perpetrator was unknown and there was no way of establishing who had committed the murder. The elders of the town nearest to where the body was discovered were ordered to make this sacrifice to absolve the innocent.Provision was next made for marrying a captive woman. She had to be taken to the home of her captor and have her hair shaved and her nails trimmed. It seems the Israelites did not think much of the hygiene standards of the surrounding tribes. Either that or it was a traditional act of mourning because before she could be taken as a wife she had to be left alone for a month to mourn for her parents. If the marital relationship proved unsatisfactory, the woman was to be allowed to go to wherever she wanted. She could not be sold or treated as a slave.

Dealing with Teenagers

The next section, Deuteronomy 21:15-18, is horrendous. The parents of a rebellious, drunk, disobedient or profligate son had to take him before the elders, who would order the men of the community to stone him to death. I'm sure that few if any parents would have resorted to such means to secure obedience, and equally sure that few sons would have pushed the boundaries to where they risked being publicly executed. But the threat was real, so amicable familial existence was probably assured, even if it was not for the best of reasons. Love had not yet supplanted fear. That would come with Jesus. The chapter ends with instructions to the Israelites not to leave the body of an executed person hanging on a tree for more than a day; he had to be buried the day he was killed because such a person was 'under God's curse' and 'would desecrate the land.' This was the reason Jesus had to be taken down from 'hanging on a tree' by the end of the day. Bearer of all our sins he became desecrated, taking upon himself the curse intended for all humanity.

Social conscience and community responsibility are the themes of Chapter 22. In addition to caring for strayed or distressed animals, the Israelites had to care for one another's property and return lost items when they found them. I like the instruction about building a parapet around one's roof so that nobody could roll off it. That's cool, as my grandchildren would say, pun intended. No accidental falling from the roof on those hot nights when one slept under the stars.

Proof of a bride's virginity was the subject of verses 13 – 21. A bride had to be careful to produce a bloody sheet on her wedding night, and then to store that sheet away carefully in case her husband decided at some future time to accuse her of pre-marital sex. If she couldn't prove her virginity she would be stoned to death. The only thing that would happen to the man if he accused her falsely would be to pay a fee to the woman's father. How shockingly unfair to the woman! And how on earth would the elders be able to decide between genuine proof and a fabricated version? A man and a woman guilty of adultery would both be stoned to death, not just the woman.

The law about rape is interesting. If it happened in town and the woman did not scream for help both the rapist and his victim had to be stoned to death. However, if a woman were raped in the country, where her screams could not be heard, only the man would be executed. Again, there are too many loopholes. A woman in the city under dire threat or with her loved ones threatened would not scream, and even in the country a woman could be engaged in pre-marital or adulterous sex by choice, so why should she be spared? Israel would need wise judges, without bias, without prejudice, disinterested, impartial. Finally the law stipulated that if a man raped an unpledged virgin, he had to marry her. A man could not marry any of his father's wives.

It seems to me that when the law was originally described in Leviticus there was more compassion for women than now in the re-iteration in Deuteronomy. Perhaps Moses had been affected by the devastation caused when his people indulged in apostasy and sexual orgies with the temple prostitutes and priestesses of Baal.

When Jesus spoke about sex, it was mostly to men, and mostly to warn them about lust. In no uncertain terms he told his fellows it would be better for them to lose their eyes than to let them to look in the wrong direction, and to lose their limbs rather than to allow them to indulge in forbidden sexual activity. (Matthew 5: 27-30) To women he was always deeply compassionate, like the bleeding woman, the promiscuous Samaritan woman, the Syro-Phoenician woman, the widow of Nain and the woman 'who had led a sinful life.'

Chapters 23 – 25: More laws about Relationships

Harsh punishments of exclusion were instituted – but as one reads on through the Old Testament one sees that most of these were later moderated, another reason for reading the whole Bible and not bits here and there. Take the problem of eunuchs and foreigners, all excluded from the assembly in Chapter 23 of Deuteronomy. This was changed completely by Isaiah who in Chapter 56: 3–7 said: 'Let no foreigner who has bound himself to the Lord say, 'The Lord will surely exclude me from his people.' And let not any eunuch complain, 'I am only a dry tree.' For this is what the Lord says: 'To the eunuchs who keep my Sabbaths, who choose what pleases me and hold fast to my covenant, to them I will give within my temple and its walls a memorial and a name better than sons and daughters; I will give them an everlasting name that will not be cut off. And foreigners who bind themselves to the Lord to serve him, to love the name of the Lord, and to worship him, and who keep the Sabbath without desecrating it, and who hold fast to my covenant, these I will bring to my holy mountain and give them joy in my house of prayer.' That must surely be the last word on so-called Israelite exclusivity! I can't wait to get to Isaiah.

In Deuteronomy 23: 9–14 are sanitary rules for the Israelites' military camps. This is followed by the command to extend mercy to foreign slaves seeking refuge among them. Next the Israelites were warned not to become shrine prostitutes, not to charge one another interest (but they could charge foreigners), to keep their vows, and not to use a basket to gather grapes in a neighbour's vineyard (although they could pick some) and not to use a sickle when picking kernels in someone else's grain field. Chapter 24 allowed a man to divorce his wife for indecency but if she married someone else and was then widowed, he could not re-marry her. Here, let it be said, Jesus was harsh about divorce. In Matthew 19: 3–9 he told the Pharisees that people should not divorce: 'What God has joined together, let not man separate.' When the Pharisees argued that Moses had allowed it (in this chapter in Deuteronomy) Jesus said that Moses had allowed it because men's hearts were so hard, but that it was not what God wanted.

Among the remaining laws that Moses gave to the young Israelites was one not to force a newly-wed man to go to war, another not to take a man's millstones as security for debt because it would deprive him of his daily bread, a stern injunction not to kidnap another (the penalty was death) a reminder to them all that they had to carry out the priest's rules about leprosy, and a severe stricture never to appropriate a man's possessions as pledge for a debt but to allow the borrower to decide on a pledge. Moses emphasised that even if a man gave a cloak as a pledge, a lender was to return it to him by nightfall so that he could sleep in it; they were adjured never to hold back the daily wages of a poor man, be he Israelite or foreigner, because then he would not be able to eat, and never could a parent offer to die for the sin of a child, or a child offer to die for the sin of a parent; one could die only for one's own sin. (Jesus is the great exception. He died for everybody else's.) When harvesting they had to leave gleanings for the poor and the alien and finally they had always to remember how once they had been slaves in Egypt, and to thank God for rescuing them. Much of this was covered in Leviticus, and none of it is comfortable reading for the rich and powerful. It places upon each one of them the need to care for the poor, the alien and the vulnerable. It is easy to see why these writings have been so hated by power-grabbers and wealth-worshipers.

Chapter 25 continues with miscellaneous laws covering disputes, punishments, treatment of working animals, and the need for a brother to provide a dead brother's widow with children (the Levirate Law.) All is reasonably straightforward until one reaches verse eleven. Then come two verses much loved by Bible debunkers, the ones about a woman coming to her husband's assistance when he is involved in a fight with another man, and grabbing the other man's genitals. She has to have her hand cut off.

I've read several commentaries on this chapter and don't feel much wiser. Why such an awful punishment for the woman? All I can say is that this law seems to concern a woman who deliberately and viciously grabs the assailant's genitals intending to injure him badly. All the translations make this clear. The words they use are 'seizes', 'taketh him by', and 'catches hold of.' The Torah is making clear that human genitalia are sacrosanct. In addition to this it suggests that the woman was acting in an unseemly and shameful fashion; what she did was among the taboos and not to be tolerated, hence the dire punishment. A similar law has been found in an old Assyrian code. Shame was an important concept in the laws of the ancient Middle East, which goes some way to explaining the severity of the punishment. Another aspect is that if the woman meant business, she could have emasculated the man, and that would have meant a spiritual death for him because originally eunuchs were not allowed in the assembly. So the man would have suffered a kind of death in three ways – no sex, no children and no spiritual life. There. Not very satisfactory but one needs to accept that when these laws were first promulgated, it was a very different society from that of today, and the law itself still had to go through a long and laborious evolutionary process. The chapter ends with a reminder to use honest weights because 'God detests anyone who deals dishonestly' and I'm afraid that they are once again adjured to show no mercy to the Amalekites.

Chapters 26 – 28
Was the Altar to be built on Mount Ebal or on Mount Gerizim?

At last Moses came to what the Israelites had to do when they finally crossed into the Promised Land. As soon as they enjoyed their first harvests, he told them, they had to take the first fruits to the place that God had chosen for his dwelling, and there they had to give thanks to God for bringing them into the Promised Land. They

THE STORY OF THE TORAH

had to hand the first fruits to the priest, remembering all their history from the time of their ancestor, the 'wandering Aramean' (that's Jacob, Israel, who had travelled to Haran, then back to southern Canaan, and finally to Egypt.) They had to remember how Jacob and eleven of his sons had joined Joseph in Egypt and how they had become a great nation in Egypt. They had to remember how they had then become enslaved and how God had brought them out of Egypt with great miracles and signs until this moment when they finally stood on the border of the Promised Land.

Now, in gratitude, they had to give tithes to the priests every three years to be used for the priests' needs and for the needs of the aliens, orphans and widows in their midst. Having told them all this, Moses gave them a special prayer which they could use to show God how they had tried to keep his commandments and to express their gratitude at their deliverance and for the blessings God had showered on them: Deut:26 13-15. It's a prayer in which they tell God all the good things they have done. This is very different from most Christian prayers which always begin with an acknowledgement of sin (especially the subtle mind-sins of jealousy, *schadenfreude,* ungratefulness, self-pity and the like) and not with an appeal to God to 'Look how good I've been, please reward me.' At the end of Chapter 26 Moses reminded them once again to keep the commandments so that the Lord would regard them as his 'treasured possession.'

Chapter 27 begins with instructions to the Israelites to build an altar on Mount Ebal as soon as they crossed the Jordan into the Holy Land. And thereby hangs a problem. Mounts Ebal and Gerizim are in Palestine, on either side of the town of Nablus, which lies just west of the ancient Biblical town of Shechem. It is said that somebody shouting from Mount Ebal can be heard on Mount Gerizim, and vice versa. Although the Septuagint and the Masoretic Text both claim that Mount Ebal was where Joshua had to build the first altar in the Promised Land, the Samaritan Pentateuch claims that the altar was to be built on Mount Gerizim.

The Samaritan Pentateuch again

So far for this reading I've looked mostly at the Masoretic Text (source of the Torah in Protestant Bibles) the Septuagint (the translation of the Torah into Greek in about 300 B.C.) the Latin Vulgate and only briefly at the Samaritan Pentateuch. Now is a good time to look more closely at this third source. This is the version of the Torah that comes from the Samaritans who occupied the hilly area in the middle of the West Bank area of Palestine. It is interesting that this is the area populated by the descendants of the beloved Joseph, because although Jesus was descended from the House of Judah, it is in this area around the Sea of Galilee that he grew up and from which most of his disciples came. Other tribes associated with the area are Issachar, Zebulun and Napthali.

The immediate cause of the Samaritans breaking away from mainline Judaism and developing a separate religion and culture of their own was the dividing of Ancient Israel into two kingdoms after the death of Solomon. The northern half which contained Samaria became known as Israel while the southern half, in which was Jerusalem, became known as the Kingdom of Judah, or Judea. Both halves of Ancient Israel were defeated by other nations after

THE STORY OF THE TORAH

the split, with many thousands of Ancient Israelites carried off into captivity. It is thought that the Samaritans were among those Northern Israelites who managed to remain behind, and that they were later augmented by other Israelites and non-Israelites who drifted back over succeeding years. They kept their own scriptures, the Samaritan Pentateuch. Its main difference from the Septuagint and the Masoretic Text is that it consists of *only the Torah*, and is sometimes known as the Samaritan Torah. There are *no* psalms, prophets, writings or histories in the Samaritan Holy Writings.

Samaria has been subjected to conquests for almost its entire history. Among those who have conquered it are: Canaanites, Israelites, Babylonians, Persians, Ancient Greeks, Romans, Byzantines, Arabs, Crusaders, Ottoman Turks, Britain (after World War 1), Jordan (after the Arab-Israeli War of 1948) and Palestine after the Six-Day War of 1967, ratified by the Israeli-Jordan Peace Treaty of 1994. There still remain a small group of Samaritans in the area today, using the Samaritan Pentateuch, and believing that they alone hold the truth that was delivered to Ancient Israel by Moses. (The area is mostly Muslim.)

There are only a few significant differences between the Samaritan Pentateuch and the other sources of the Torah. (The British Library has an ancient copy of the Samaritan Pentateuch, produced in 1339, and written in Samaritan Majuscule Hebrew characters.) But there is one very significant difference. The Samaritans claim that it was *not* Mount Ebal on which Joshua was told to build the altar, but on Mount Gerizim. So firmly did the Samaritans believe that they were right (Mount Gerizim is greener and lovelier than Mount Ebal, which is hard and rocky, but, more important, Moses

285

and the elders went up Mount Ebal to pronounce the curses, and up Mount Gerizim to pronounce the blessings) that it became the centre of Samaritan worship, and they erected a temple on the mount, which was later destroyed by the Jews. Bitter was the enmity and feeling between the two peoples at the time of Christ. And what did Christ have to say about it? When the Samaritan woman told Jesus at the well in Samaria that it was clear that He was a prophet, but that 'our fathers worshipped on this mountain (Gerizim) but you Jews claim that the place where we must worship is in Jerusalem,' he told her, John 4: 21-24: 'Believe me, woman, a time is coming when you will worship the Father neither on this mountain nor in Jerusalem. You Samaritans worship what you do not know; we worship what we do know, for salvation is from the Jews. Yet a time is coming and has now come when the worshipers will worship the Father in spirit and truth, for they are the kind of worshipers the Father seeks. God is spirit, and his worshipers must worship in spirit and in truth.'

So yes, there are thin places on earth where one can feel closer to God. But they are as nothing compared to the human heart and mind where alone the Spirit of God can be encountered. One does not have to be in Jerusalem, or on Mount Gerizim, or in Rome, or in Ionia or Mecca. It does not matter if one is in the smallest hovel, or in the greyest gloom, beside a roaring waterfall, or in a quiet church, they are all immaterial for it is in one's deepest self that one is able to hear that still, small voice. So, because of what Jesus said, one will not argue with the Septuagint, the Masoretic Text or the Samaritan Pentateuch about which hill in the Promised Land Moses told Joshua to choose for an altar. It doesn't matter. What is important is that this difference of opinion led to Jesus making a revelation about where God is to be found.

Moses was clearly getting weaker by now. Supported and assisted by the elders, he told the Israelites that they had to use large stones for the altar and had to whitewash them so that they could write the laws on them. They were not to use iron tools to shape or dress the stones, but were to choose suitable rocks that were naturally formed. Having made clear how they were to worship God, Moses called for the curses to be pronounced from Mount Ebal and the blessings from Mount Gerizim. After each curse the Israelites had to say 'Amen.'

Cursed would be those who made idols, dishonoured their parents, moved a neighbour's boundary stone, led the blind astray (this probably included any abuse of the disabled), withheld justice from aliens, orphans or widows, slept with the wife of a father (polygamy was still practised), had sex with an animal, had sex with a sister, slept with a mother-in-law, killed a neighbour, accepted a bribe to kill an innocent person or did not uphold the law.

In Chapter 28 came the blessings for those who fully obeyed the law. Their children would be blessed and so would their crops, their livestock, their new-born animals, their harvests, their bread making and all their daily activities. Enemies that rose up against them would be defeated. Their barns would be full and all their endeavours blessed. They would be established as a Holy People and all the people on earth would see this. They would enjoy the seasons, with the rain and the sunshine at their appointed times. They would lend to other nations but not borrow. They would be a leading nation. All these blessings would be theirs if they continued to walk in the way of the Lord. Other nations would see that they were blessed, and that the Lord was with them in every way.

If they did not obey God's commandments there would be a blight on everything, they would be plagued with disease and fever, defeated by their enemies and become the laughing stock of the world. They would be driven from the Promised Land by a nation whose language they did not understand and would be taken to a place where they would worship gods of wood and stone, and be objects of ridicule and scorn to the other nations. They would suffer degradation and horror, famine and terror, parents would eat their own children, and finally they would be scattered among the nations where they would offer themselves as slaves but no-one would buy them.

Critics who profess that this is a description of what happened to the Israelites and Jews when they were defeated and taken into captivity by Assyria and Babylon, and was therefore written long after Moses, forget that this is equally a prophecy of what happened to the Jews when Rome defeated them and scattered them to every corner of the world. Nobody pretends that this passage was written after the Roman conquest.

Chapters 29 – 34:
The Final Chapters of both Deuteronomy and the Torah

So there they are, the commandments spelled out to the Israelites on the plains of Moab as they stood poised to enter the Promised Land. In the final weeks of his life, supported by the elders and priests, Moses gave these last instructions to the young Israelites waiting to complete the journey and enter Canaan. After the despair of chapter 29, Chapter 30 promises hope. If those Israelites who found themselves exiled from their homeland because of their disobedience and treachery, should seek God, 'when you and your children return to the Lord your God and obey him with all your heart and with all your soul according to everything I command you today, then the Lord your God will restore your fortunes and have compassion on you and gather you again from all the nations where he scattered you. Even if you have been banished to the most distant land under the heavens, from there the Lord your God will gather you and bring you back.'

It makes one wonder about the return to Israel of so many Jews in the second half of the last century from all the corners of the world. If the world survives into future centuries will some distant reader say Deuteronomy must have been written in the twentieth or twenty first centuries because there is no such thing as prophecy? It also makes one worry about the secular element among Israelites today: Are too many of them again failing to keep the covenant? With Arabs and Muslims ranged against Israel does that raise the possibility of yet another Diaspora?

Accept the Word

Above all, Moses urged the Israelites to accept the 'word.' (Deuteronomy 30: 14) The word meant life and prosperity, whereas rejection of the word meant death and destruction. It is significant that he used 'word', not law, not covenant, not commandment. 'The word is very near you; it is in your mouth and in your heart so you may obey it' That's a sublime reading for Christians, all of whom love and honour the 'Word.' It takes one forward to the beginning of John's Gospel, 'In the beginning was the Word.' It also turns one's attention to this very book, the Bible, the word of God. The Word has always had a double meaning for Christians, standing first for the Bible, but second, and more important, for Jesus. The chapter ends with: 'Now choose life, so that you may love the Lord your God, listen to his voice, and hold fast to him. For the Lord is your life, and he will give you many years in the land he swore to give to your fathers, Abraham, Isaac and Jacob.'

Moses was clearly feeling very frail now so in chapter 31 he told the Israelites that he was no longer able to lead them, but he assured them that God, who had always been their real leader, would continue to be in charge, would go before them as they crossed into the Promised Land, and would give them victory in the battles that lay ahead. Exhorting them to be strong and courageous, he summoned Joshua to stand before them, and encouraged him in the same manner, assuring him that God would be with him, and that he had to lead the tribes across the Jordan and divide the land fairly among them.

Even today these words inspire Jews and Christians. 'Be strong and courageous. The Lord himself goes before you and will be with you; he will never leave you nor forsake you. Do not be afraid; do not be discouraged.'

Verse 9 supports the contention that it was Moses who wrote down the laws. It says, 'So Moses wrote down this law and gave it to the priests, the sons of Levi who carried the Ark of the Covenant of the Lord, and to all the elders of Israel.' He went on to add that the law had to be read to the entire assemblage of the people every seven years at the Feast of Tabernacles. This could be the origin of the Bible readings that take place in synagogues and churches throughout the world to this day. The people, said Moses, had to listen 'and learn to fear the Lord your God and follow carefully all the words of this law. Their children, who do not know this law, must hear it and learn to fear the Lord your God as long as you live in the land you are crossing the Jordan to possess.'

God told Moses that the hour of his death was approaching and told him to call Joshua to the entrance of the Tabernacle. There God appeared in a cloud and told Moses that he would be going to rest with his fathers. In verse 24 Moses completed his writing and issued the following order to the Levites carrying the Ark: (Deuteronomy 31: 26-29) 'Take this Book of the Law and place it beside the Ark of the Covenant of the Lord your God. There it will remain as a witness against you. For I know how rebellious and stiff-necked you are. If you have been rebellious against the Lord while I am still alive and with you, how much more will you rebel after I die!' He added: 'For I know that after my death you are sure to become utterly corrupt and to turn from the way I have commanded you. In days to come, disaster will fall upon you because you will do evil in the sight of the Lord and provoke him to anger by what your hands have made.' If only they had listened and written the law in their hearts. And if only people today would too.

With the Song of Moses one is still battling with the problem of prophecy. The song begins with an exhortation to earth and heaven to listen to the life-giving words that Moses chants, portraying God's love as showers on new grass and abundant rain on tender plants. Then comes a hymn of praise to the Lord, which is reminiscent of the Psalms (in fact it has been set to music several times.) God is seen as faithful, just and as steady and reliable as a rock. In contrast, the people are seen as a 'warped and crooked generation.' This emphasis on the faithlessness and failure of the people is a concern to critics, who feel it is mis-placed at this point in the narrative. This new generation has not yet proved foolish and obdurate, yet Moses seems to be condemning them. But he has had long, hard years of leading their grandparents and parents, and has seen how quickly the Israelites lose faith and follow the evil desires of their own hearts. So the song goes on to remind the people of their history and of how much the Lord cared for them, and of how they consistently broke faith and turned towards idols and pagan practices. Using third-person pronouns, the song makes brilliant use of metaphor to show how God cares for Israel. NIV Bible: Deuteronomy 32: 10-11 – 'In a desert land he found him, in a barren and howling waste. He shielded him and cared for him; he guarded him as the apple of his eye, like an eagle that stirs up its nest and hovers over its young, that spreads its wings to catch them and carries them on its pinions.'

In verse 15 of chapter 32 Deuteronomy uses a poetic word for Israel, Jeshurun. Strangely, the word is derived from a Jewish root meaning upright or worthy, strange because when it is used here in Deuteronomy it has ironic overtones; it shows the Israelites abusing their new land of milk and honey to become bloated and greedy, and finally abandoning and rejecting God, the Rock, the Saviour. When that happened God would turn his face from this 'perverse generation' says the song, and allow other nations to supplant them. Horrendous volcanic-type disasters would befall them: 'It will devour the earth and its harvests and set afire the foundations of the mountains. I will heap calamities upon them and spend my arrows against them. I will send wasting famine against them, consuming pestilence and deadly plague. I will send against them the fangs of wild beasts, the venom of vipers that glide in the dust.'

Such intense suffering would be theirs that other nations would mock both them and their God. But these other nations would have their mockery cast in their teeth, says God: (King James Deuteronomy 32: 35): 'To me belongeth vengeance' (quoted later by St Paul as 'Vengeance is mine' says the Lord). Warning the nations that misled the Israelites and then mocked them, God says: 'Their foot shall slide in due time: for the day of their calamity is at hand, and the things that shall come upon them make haste. For the Lord shall judge his people, and repent himself for his servants when he seeth that their power is gone and there is none shut up (enslaved) or left.' The NIV has 'have compassion on his servants.' By saying 'repent himself,' The King James suggests that in the end God himself will pay the price.

The song goes on to ask where all those other gods are and why they do not help their subjects in their distress. It points out that they do not exist. There is only one God. 'I myself am He! There is no god besides me. I put to death, and I bring to life. I have wounded and I will heal, and no one can deliver out of my hand.' The song becomes extremely bloodthirsty as it contemplates what God will do to his enemies. The point is obvious: It is not a good idea to mock God; one could bring dreadful disasters upon oneself.

What of all the world's good, innocent and faithful people who have suffered indescribably? This is where Christians cling to the cross, the one that Jesus ordered his followers to pick up if they wished to follow him. In Christ, God gave His all for humanity, and He promised nothing but earthly suffering for those who followed him. The peace that passeth all understanding has nothing to do with the cessation of war, violence, physical or mental suffering: It abides in the heart and mind of a Christ-follower in the midst of persecution, war, violence, abuse and any kind of suffering; it is beyond human understanding.

Having finished his chanting, Moses commanded the Israelites to take heed of the song, to learn it and to teach it to their children. It meant 'life' he said. Immediately after giving the song to the people, on that very same day, Moses, obeying the prompting of God, climbed Mount Nebo. God told him that he would die there, after seeing in the distance the land that God was giving to the Israelites. He was accompanied by Joshua and all the Israelites. Having seen the Promised Land, Moses, the man of God (this is the first time that he is given this title) turned and blessed his fellow men. He began with a prayer, speaking directly to God, acknowledging his love for his people, pointing out to God that they had received the instruction God had asked him to give them, and that they were all gathered reverentially before him. The Lord would be their king, not an earthly monarch. Moses asked God to bless all the tribes. Simeon is missing from the list. It is thought that the tribe of Simeon had become part of Judah, and this is an indication that this blessing, as well as the description of the death of Moses, were much later interpolations and not part of the original document.

The blessing is not so much an actual benediction as a description of the tribes and it seems to rely heavily on Jacob's blessing in Genesis 49. Having stood on Mount Nebo in the country of Moab and having surveyed the land that God had promised to his people, Moses died. He was buried there, in Moab, but Deuteronomy tells us that 'to this day' nobody knows where his grave is. (Moses could obviously not have written any of this last chapter and equally obviously, it was written a long time after his death. The words 'to this day' suggest this.)

The writer goes on to tell us that Moses was still strong and that he could see well when he died. The Israelites mourned for him for a full month, and then Joshua took command. The last words of Deuteronomy tell us that there has never been a prophet like Moses, who spoke to God, face to face, and who performed many miracles.

Conclusion

I've come not only to the end of Deuteronomy but also to the end of the Torah whose five books contain almost the whole of the Jewish Law. Jews believe that all the knowledge in these writings was revealed by God to Moses. It begs the question: What is divine revelation, and how can one know that it is from God? I think divine revelation is when mankind is suddenly, almost out of the blue, given extraordinary knowledge or understanding, and sent along a new path.

If one looks back at notable occurrences of this, what strikes one is that almost all the recipients of such knowledge exhibited an ability to reject a current worldview and embrace an entirely new way of thinking. To transcend current thinking and reject prevailing theories, be they religious or scientific, one needs to take on one's peers, be prepared to become unpopular and make one's ideas public in the teeth of ridicule, rejection and even persecution. When in addition to all the above, revelation takes people towards not only a better understanding of the universe but also towards a better understanding of God, it becomes even more difficult. Yes God is, or no, God isn't, are equally unprovable. So how does one judge revelations about God?

Any so-called revelation that rejects or compromises truth, justice, forgiveness, mercy and, above all, love, is not from God. Quick fingers will point witheringly at Mosaic revelation with its apparent insistence that certain tribes opposed to the Israelites be wiped out, but I've mentioned several times in these notes already that the Bible has to be read in its entirety and that in the very chapters in which God appears to demand the destruction of Canaanite men, women and children, he pleads for treating aliens like one's own people. Also, within a very few chapters the people that were supposed to be wiped out appear on the scene again, stronger and more prolific than before, so no genocide or extermination ever took place. It seems clear to me that fallible scribes allowed their worldview to contaminate the writing. And it reinforces the idea that one cannot read bits and pieces of the Bible to arrive at truth. Even the devil when tempting Christ quoted scripture out of context. It is only by reading the whole of it that one can find oneself encountering God Himself – God who is merciful, forgiving and loving. Readers of these notes will have realized by now that I do not therefore believe in the complete inerrancy of the Bible. On the contrary, I believe that its wondrous truth can be discovered only by spirit-led reading, which is open to everybody; one merely has to ask. St Benedict was the one who first propounded *lectio divina,* spiritual reading, meditation and prayer in order to achieve communion with God.

Human understanding has clearly been evolving in the same way as all other aspects of life. What is amazing is the speed at which it has been doing so. The origins of the Bible lie much further back than the Middle East Bronze Age culture which prevailed about four thousand years ago. They go back about a hundred thousand years to when Homo Sapiens first appeared and who from almost the beginning perceived a spiritual dimension to existence. Even a hundred thousand years is a flash of a micro second compared with the four and a half billion years since the world began. Yet in the short space of time in which humanity has existed, the evolution of the human mind has been little short of miraculous. From being used at first as a mere survival tool, it became the means for humans to wonder about the origin and purpose of life. They have found questions and answers that are sometimes terrifying. What the Bible does is to ground one in the reality of a loving and merciful God who enables one to embark on the adventure of life with trust, hope and joy.

From where did the biblical seers including Moses derive their awesome insights? Fortunately Moses tells us how he received his own revelation, when he was going about his business, tending his father-in-law's flocks and saw a bush on fire. 'Moses saw that though the bush was on fire it did not burn up. So Moses thought, 'I will go over and see this strange sight – why the bush does not burn up.' So he went over and watched the bush. It burned and burned but remained alive. Deep into thought plunged Moses - and encountered God. Although the experience has visionary and dream-like qualities, it was not the kind of dream that could be dismissed in the cold light of day. It happened in the cold light of day. What he saw and heard changed Moses forever. He learned that God is, that because he exists outside time and space he is called 'I am', that he is holy and is deserving of respect, that people are his children whom he loves, and that he has a mission for them to accomplish.

Everything that Moses subsequently did was contingent on that encounter. Because of it he abandoned his comfortable life and undertook the hazardous and often lonely task of leading the

Israelites to a Promised Land. Something had completely changed this somewhat diffident man, and that something was a complete trust in the revelation God had given him. Indomitably determined he led the Israelites out of Egypt, taking them towards a new world with a new order of justice, mercy and the rule of law. One does not find in books or experiments the type of conviction that kept Moses on his quest. I don't even think it's something you want or search for; it comes when God reveals a truth about himself or about the universe so profound that your life and the lives of those around you are permanently changed, forever and for the better. That, I believe, is the judgement one can make about revelation. If it leads to intolerance, fear, enmity, hatred, violence or a demeaning of women, children, homosexuals, the different, the sick, the disabled, the downtrodden or the vulnerable it is not prophecy, it is not revelation and it is not of God.

How one responds to revelation is based on one's preparedness to change one's existing worldview. If that worldview causes one to oppose with ridicule, malevolence or violence another idea that in itself is either a revelation of how awesomely intricate are both the macro and micro universes, or how great and gracious God is, then it is clearly one's existing worldview that one should challenge and question, and not the revelation, which if physical will lead to a greater understanding of the universe, and if spiritual to all the qualities that Christ represents, mercy, compassion, love, empathy, tolerance, selflessness, courage, generosity, control of self, discipline, inclusiveness, and a determination not to judge others even if one abhors the sin. Simple.

That's the revelation Moses received. It enabled him to take his people towards a new world, a state in which God's rules of justice and mercy could prevail and where the Israelites could gradually come to realize that God is love. Paramount if they were to experience that love and enjoy life in all its abundance was the need to keep faith; all other roads would lead to immorality, sin, misery and perdition.

In the same way that God is not limited to religion, neither is revelation limited to religion. It couldn't be any other way. God made humans physical and spiritual beings, but too often they separate their aspects of being, or confuse spirituality with religion. Religion is merely the form and ritual of spirituality but sadly religion sometimes becomes an end in itself and distorts the spiritual. Hence the need for the word. Truth needs it. Truth wasn't made for secrecy. Insights and ideas need papyrus, parchment or paper and I don't find it particularly surprising that the most popular computer writing-software is called Word! I'm using it now. The Bible is one of the most precious pieces of writing that humanity possesses, and when one gets to the New Testament, one will see that in the gospels and the letters, is the definitive understanding of God. It will never be improved or more developed until Jesus comes again. One needs endlessly to read it if one is to become the person one was meant to be.

For Christians the supreme spiritual revelation is Christ the Incarnate. His presence on earth provided the definitive revelation of the nature of God. It can never be surpassed. The Torah begins the revelation from the moment at which a divine message was imparted to a Bronze Age personage who sought a meaning for existence and encountered God. What he or they then recorded is centred on one word, Word. The revelation was initially at the mercy of the oral tradition but almost immediately became the first purpose to which humanity put the miraculous new invention of writing. I find it deeply exciting that a wandering tribe of Semites to whom this revelation was imparted migrated from Mesopotamia where writing was invented, found themselves very shortly afterwards in Egypt where another form of writing was being developed, and who belonged to the same language group as the people who invented the alphabet. Those are just too many coincidences for me. On a lowly band of migrant Semites was bestowed not only a gift of revelation but also an invention by means of which they could record it. There were clearly purpose and method in this, God's purpose and God's method. It all makes such utter, astounding, glorious sense. Yes, of course the essential revelation became sometimes distorted by fallible, vulnerable humanity, but in spite of this, God the Holy Spirit wove in the Torah an intricate fabric of words, prophecies and revelations that in the fullness of time came to hold a newborn Israelite baby, the word made flesh.

BIBLIOGRAPHY

Ackroyd, Peter *Civil War, Vol III of The History of England,* Kindle eBook, 2014

Andrewes, Lancelot, Lively E, Harding J *et. al.: The Holy Bible containing the Old and New Testaments* translated out of the original tongues by the special command of James I, Cambridge University Press 1940 edition

Armstrong, Karen *The Bible the Biography* Atlantic Books, London, 2007

Augustine *Confessions (classical)* Kindle Edition

Barth, Karl *The Epistle to the Romans* Translated by E. C. Hoskyns, Galaxy Books, 1968

Barth, Karl *God Here and Now* Routledge Kindle eBook

Bragg, Melvyn *The Book of Books,* Hodder & Stoughton, London, 2011

Brenton, Lancelot C L, *Septuagint,* Kindle eBook, 2013

Brindle W., Diemer C., Dobson E. *et al: The NKJV Study Bible* Thomas Nelson, USA, 2008

Bright, J., *A History of Israel,* Third Edition, The Westminster Press, London; first edition published by SCM Press, London

Bullinger E W *Figures of Speech in the Bible* Kindle eBook (original in Cornell University Library)

Carlson, E. L., BArker, K. *et al: The NIV Study Bible,* Zondervan 1995

Clow, W. M. *The Bible Reader's Encyclopaedia and Concordance,* Collins, London and New York, 1962

303

Collins, C. J, Lane T. D. *et al: ESV Study Bible,* Crossway 2011

Collins, Francis S: *The Language of God* Kindle eBook edition

Collins J J *The Scepter and the Star: Messianism in light of Dead Sea Scrolls* Doubleday New York 1995

Cox, Harvey *The Market as God* Harvard University Press 2016

Finkel, Irving *The Ark before Noah* Kindle eBook edition, 2014

Fitzmyer, Joseph A. *4Q246: "The Son of God" Document from Qumran* Biblica 74 1993

Friedman, Richard Elliot *Who wrote the Bible?* Kindle eBook edition

Gardiner, Alan H, *Egypt of the Pharaohs: An Introduction,* Kindle eBook edition

Garstang, John B E, *The Story of Jericho,* Hodder and Stoughton, London, 1940

Kaufmann, Walter *Critique of Religion and Philosophy* Harper & Row 1958

Keller, Timothy *The Prodigal God,* Dutton (Penguin) 2009

Kenyon, Kathleen M, *Digging up Jericho,* Praeger, New York, 1957

Kitchen K.A., *On the Reliability of the Old Testament,* B Eerdmans, Grand Rapids, Michigan, 2003

Lambert W.G. and Millard A.R. *Atrahasis: The Babylonian Story of the Flood* Oxford Clarendon Press, 1970

Lewis C S *Mere Christianity,* HarperCollins eBook, 2015

Lewis, Mark Edward *The Flood Myths of Early China* New York State University Press (Suny paperback) 2006

Licona, Michael R, *The Resurrection of Jesus – a New Historiographical Approach* IVP Academic USA; Apollos Nottingham UK, 2010

Martinez, Florentino Garcia *Qumran and Apocalyptic Studies on the Aramaic Texts from Qumran* STD J9 Brill, New York

McHardy W.D., Dodd C.H., Mynors R *et al: The New English Bible with the Apocrypha,* Oxford and Cambridge University Presses 1970

Milik J. T. *Les modeles aramaneens du livre d'Esther dans la grotte 4 de Qumran* Rev 15 1992

Nida, E. *et al: Good News Bible* Harper Collins, London, 1994

Pawson, David *Unlocking the Bible,* Kindle eBook (Harper Collins 1999-2001)

Peterson, E H. *The Message* NavPress, Colorado Springs, 2003

Peacocke, Arthur *Paths from Science towards God* Kindle eBook Edition 2013

Peacocke, Arthur *Evolution: The Disguised Friend of Faith* Kindle eBook Edition 2009

Planck, Max: *Where is Science Going?* Norton 1932

Polkinghorne, John *Quarks, Chaos and Christianity* SPCK/Crossroads UK 2005

Polkinghorne John *Belief in God in an Age of Science* Yale University Press, USA, 2009

Polanyi, Michael *The Tacit Dimension* Chicago University Press, USA, 2009

Rawlings, Louis *The Ancient Greeks at War* Manchester University Press, Manchester, 1988

Rogerson J. W. and Lieu J. M. (editors) *The Oxford Handbook of Biblical Studies* Oxford University Press, paperback edition, 2008

Scott C and Collins Steven, *Discovering the City of Sodom* Howard Books, Simon & Shuster, April 2013

Stephany, Timothy *Enuma Elish: The Babylonian Creation Epic* Kindle Edition

Stott, John *Understanding the Bible* Revised Edition, Scripture Union, 2007

Swinburne, R. *The Resurrection of God Incarnate* Clarendon Press, Oxford, 2010

Taylor, K. N. *The Living Bible* Tyndale House Publishers, Illinois, 1971

Tyndale, William, and Miller, Theron *William Tyndale Bible in Modern English,* Kindle eBook, 2010

Vermes G *The Dead Sea Scrolls in English* The Folio Society, London, 2000 (First published by Penguin, London, 1997)

Wilson, Clifford *Ebla Tablets: Secrets of a Forgotten City* Creation Life 1979

Wise M O, Abegg M G, Cook E M, *The Dead Sea Scrolls – Revised Edition: A New Translation* Harper Collins San Francisco 2005

WEBSITES

www.torahclass.com/podcasts (2015)

www.jewishvirtuallibrary.org/source (2015)

www.gospel-herald.com/finneman/red_heifer (2015)

www.en.wikipedia.org/wiki/Deir_Alla_Inscription (2015)

www.biblehub.com/ (2015)

www.thejc.com (Jewish Chronicle On Line) (2015)

www.bensira.org (2015)

www.breakingisraelnews.com/51870/sodom-found-archaeological-evidence-proof (2015)

https://bible.org/seriespage/7-achsah-s–asking–pattern–prayer–no–2312 (17 August 2016)

Google: 7.Achsah's Asking, A Pattern of Prayer No 2312/Bible.org
(22 August 2016)
https://en.wikipedia.org.wiki/Tel_Hazor
(16 August 2016)

Lightning Source UK Ltd.
Milton Keynes UK
UKHW041332061118
331828UK00001B/28/P